DESPOTISM O

DESPOTISM ON DEMAND

How Power Operates in the
Flexible Workplace

Alex J. Wood

ILR PRESS

AN IMPRINT OF

CORNELL UNIVERSITY PRESS   **ITHACA AND LONDON**

First published 2020 by Cornell University Press

Library of Congress Cataloging-in-Publication Data

Names: Wood, Alex J., 1985–author.
Title: Despotism on demand : how power operates in the flexible
    workplace / Alex J. Wood.
Description: Ithaca : Cornell University Press, 2020. |
    Includes bibliographical references and index.
Identifiers: LCCN 2019032675 (print) | LCCN 2019032676 (ebook) |
    ISBN 9781501748875 (hardcover) | ISBN 9781501748882 (paperback) |
    ISBN 9781501748899 (epub) | ISBN 9781501748905 (pdf)
Subjects: LCSH: Flexible work arrangements—Great Britain. | Flexible work
    arrangements—United States. | Hours of labor—Great Britain. |
    Hours of labor—United States. | Precarious employment—Great Britain. |
    Precarious employment—United States. | Industrial relations—Great Britain. |
    Industrial relations—United States.
Classification: LCC HD5109.2.G7 W64 2020 (print) | LCC HD5109.2.G7 (ebook) |
    DDC 331.25/7240941—dc23
LC record available at https://lccn.loc.gov/2019032675
LC ebook record available at https://lccn.loc.gov/2019032676

In memory of William (Willy) Brown
(22 April 1945–1 August 2019)—teacher and mentor to many

Being humiliated, harassed, and abused by managers, subject to dangerous work conditions . . . such assaults on the dignity, safety, and autonomy
of workers are of concern to egalitarians over and above issues of pay and
benefits. Fundamentally, egalitarians care about eliminating oppressive social hierarchy, including relations of domination and subordination under
which subordinates can be arbitrarily subject to humiliating and oppressive conditions, and arbitrary restraints on their freedom.

—Elizabeth S. Anderson, "Where Despots Rule,"
interview in *Jacobin*, June 29, 2017

Contents

Acknowledgments   ix

Flexible Despotism: An Introduction   1

Part 1 **POWER AT WORK**

    1. Internal States in the UK   29

    2. Internal States in the U.S.   52

Part 2 **THE DESPOTISM OF TIME**

    3. Despotic Time in the UK: Overcoming Hegemonic
       Constraints   75

    4. Despotic Time in the U.S.: Undermining Worker
       Organization   90

Part 3 **THE DYNAMICS OF WORK AND SPACES OF RESISTANCE**

    5. The Dynamics of Work and Scheduling Gifts   102

    6. Limits of Control and Spaces of Resistance   120

Conclusions: Control in the Twenty-First Century   134

Methodological Appendix   147

Notes   157

Bibliography   165

Index   173

Acknowledgments

Special thanks are due to Brendan Burchell and William Brown at the University of Cambridge for four years of help, support, and constructive criticism which have hugely strengthened this book. Thanks are also due to Michael Burawoy, Judy Wajcman, Huw Beynon, and Paul Edwards for showing interest in my ideas and taking the time to discuss my research. I would also like to thank Catherine Malone, David Sutcliffe, Christabel Buchanan, Torsten Geelan, Anna Wolmuth, James Taylor, Ian Buchanan, and Richard Armstrong, all of whom have read various drafts of the chapters that make up this book and have provided me with useful feedback and encouragement and, most of all, helped me clarify and communicate my ideas. I am grateful to Vili Lehdonvirta and the Oxford Internet Institute for providing me the time to finish this work. I would like to acknowledge SAGE, which published two of my articles that parts of the Introduction and chapters 3, 4, and 5 draw and expand on. These two articles are:

> Wood, Alex J. "Powerful Times: Flexible Discipline and Schedule Gifts at Work." *Work, Employment and Society* 32, no. 6 (2018): 1061–1077.

> Wood, Alex J. "Flexible Scheduling, Degradation of Job Quality and Barriers to Collective Voice." *Human Relations* 69, no. 10 (2016): 1989–2010.

I would also like to acknowledge Wiley, which published my article that parts of chapters 2 and 6 draw and expand on. This article is:

> Wood, Alex J. "Networks of Injustice: Worker Mobilisation at Walmart." *Industrial Relations Journal* 46, no. 4 (2015): 259–274.

Finally, but most importantly, I am indebted to the workers and trade unionists who opened up their lives to me and gave me so much of their time. Without their generosity this book would consist of blank pages.

DESPOTISM ON DEMAND

FLEXIBLE DESPOTISM

An Introduction

The On-Demand Economy

The winds of change are swirling through the economies of North America and western Europe. New economic processes are taking hold in the spaces opened up by the steady decline of collective workplace regulation. No longer is working time understood as a standard, stable eight hours, five days a week. Instead, working time is flexible, on demand, and 24/7. Jobs are fragmented into tasks, or broken up into "gigs," with many workers contracted to a job on a zero-hour, "at-will" basis. Employees' schedules are adjusted in real time to match changing demand. Alternatively, self-employed workers are individually contracted via labor platforms to each specific task according to an employer's need. Consequently, many workers are increasingly employed flexibly, while others may not even have an employment contract at all, and instead be classified as self-employed—and yet have their labor controlled by a platform. As we shall see in the coming chapters, even workers with standard, full-time, permanent contracts can experience high levels of insecurity as a result of flexible scheduling within this new temporal order.

As a result, the benefits and drawbacks of flexible scheduling have been widely debated. These discussions, however, have tended to focus on issues of job quality, work-life balance, and well-being.[1] This book goes further, by drawing attention to important but under-researched issues of managerial power and workplace control. This is necessary, as it is only when we understand paid work as a power relationship that we are able to see how precarious scheduling constitutes flexible despotism—a new regime of control within the workplace. Flexible despotism represents a new domain of inequality, in which the postindustrial working class increasingly suffers a scheduling nightmare.

The Drivers of the On-Demand Economy

Across the United States and Europe, between a sixth and a fifth of employees experience precarious scheduling, that is, fluctuating working time over which they have little control.[2] The common prevalence of insecure working time exists despite hugely different institutional contexts and labor market dynamics, suggesting that the move toward an on-demand economy is a general phenomenon across advanced capitalist economies. Social scientist Susan Lambert argues that flexible scheduling has arisen as a result of employers being increasingly unwilling to pay for labor that exceeds demand, whether on an hourly or a daily basis. Typically, staffing outlay budgets are tightly linked to customer demand, and frontline managers are expected to closely enforce these budgets.[3]

The shift in employer behavior toward on-demand work has been facilitated by a number of institutional changes aimed at the creation of a 24/7 economy. These transformations include the decline of collective regulation of working time and shifts in legal and normative regulations. Additionally, there has been an explosion of data that enables employers to accurately model demand, and that therefore makes the close matching of labor supply (including real-time adjustments) to demand more profitable. For example, a *Financial Times* article on September 7, 2016, noted that it is now possible to combine weather, online traffic, and other signals with previous sales data in order to forecast future customer footfall. Meanwhile, in many countries, austerity has placed the public sector under pressure to contain labor costs through greater temporal flexibility.[4]

Temporal Firm Flexibility

It seems that the birth of the on-demand economy occurred in the early 2000s as firms increasingly experimented with a variety of mechanisms to enable greater temporal flexibility. As a consequence, precarious scheduling, in terms of workers having variable schedules that they do not control, nearly doubled in the United States between 1997 and 2004, rising from 6.6 percent to 11.5 percent.[5] By 2014, 17 percent of U.S. workers were rarely or never able to change their schedule and only knew about their schedule one week or less in advance.[6] That the on-demand economy emerged in the early 2000s is supported by the fact that in Europe precarious scheduling was already widespread by 2005 and has not, outside of the Great Recession, which began in 2007, significantly increased since.[7]

These flexible employment practices include zero hour and short hour contracts; flexible contracts that guarantee a minimum number of hours but no fixed scheduling pattern; gig economy labor platforms; and management-run labor matching reviews, whereby a firm reviews its staffing needs and as a result may shift its entire workforce's schedules. However, the temporal fragmentation of work increases exponentially the organizational complexity of workforce management. This complexity acts to limit the extent to which temporal flexibility can be adopted by firms. Previously, managers had to maintain a core of workers with stable schedules on whom they could rely to cover the central operational functions of the business. However, the connectivity provided by smartphones and other portable and wearable devices means that this barrier to flexibility is beginning to be overcome, through the algorithmic management of workers.

This trend is most apparent in the algorithms of online labor platforms such as Uber, Deliveroo, TaskRabbit, Handy, Airtasker, Fiverr, and Upwork, all of which use algorithmic rating systems to control and discipline labor, and to ensure the efficient matching of demand and supply. Workers not deemed productive enough according to an algorithm's parameters find that work quickly dries up, and in some cases they are even "deactivated" (i.e., fired) from the platform.[8]

Surveys conducted in 2017 found that 10 percent of workers in the UK received work from such labor platforms at least once a month, and across fourteen European countries this figure was 8 percent.[9] This figure is similar in the United States, where a survey in 2018 found that 6 percent of the U.S. workforce had freelanced in the past twelve months and received work from a specialized freelance website or online freelance marketplace, while 5 percent had received work from "sharing economy" apps and websites.[10] Although central to the gig economy, algorithmic management is also beginning to spread into conventional sectors of the economy, and may thus intensify the trends documented in this book.

Precarious Scheduling: The Reality of Working on Demand

Both public and academic discussions of flexible working have tended toward confusion and have been plagued by contradiction. When discussing flexible scheduling, some commentators talk of employees' ability to choose their own hours, whereas others refer to unpredictable schedules that are imposed on the worker. Thus, it is often claimed that flexible scheduling benefits both employers (by matching labor supply to demand, reducing labor costs, and enabling a more efficient service) and employees, by improving work-life balance. There is, however, an important distinction to be made between flexible scheduling that is manager-controlled and that which is worker-controlled.[11] Manager-controlled flexible scheduling is principally beneficial to employers, while worker-controlled flexible scheduling benefits employees.

In other words, whether flexibility is positive or negative for individuals' rests on their bargaining power. Research suggests that, despite employer claims to the contrary, flexible scheduling cannot be both manager-controlled and worker-controlled. For example, a study of work in the call center and software sectors found that '"flexible" working time patterns were flexible only for the employers, and actually undermined workers' own coping arrangements.[12] Other researchers have found that when employers apply strict limits to total labor hours, flexible scheduling entails a zero-sum game where more hours or scheduling control granted to one employee tends to lessen the control enjoyed by coworkers.[13] Workers with in-demand skills and knowledge will be able to use these to demand that their employer provides them with flexibility that works for them. However, those lacking these resources will find their schedules set at the whim of their employer, with little ability to provide input on their schedule.

A schedule that fluctuates at the employer's demand is not experienced by workers as flexibility, but rather as a source of precariousness. The figures from 2016 indicate that an astonishing 37 percent of U.S. workers knew their schedule only a week or less in advance, and 17 percent found out about their schedules with only one day's notice or less.[14] These scheduling practices are even more common among "early career" employees in the United States. A nationally representative survey of people born between 1980 and 1984 suggests that in 2011 around 30 percent experienced changes to their schedules that were determined solely by their employer. This was especially true for employees paid by the hour, of whom around 35 percent experienced employer-driven changes to their schedules.[15] Precarious scheduling is particularly evident in retail as highlighted by a survey of over 50,000 workers undertaken in 2016–2017. Sixty percent of workers at 80 of the largest retailers in the United States have been found to experience variable schedules of some kind with 63 percent of workers having less than two weeks' notice of changes to their schedules. Moreover, this precarious scheduling was strongly associated with poor health and well-being.[16]

A similar situation exists in Europe, with around 16 percent of workers experiencing precarious scheduling—meaning that their hours change frequently at their employer's demand and usually with little prior notice. Surprisingly, precarious scheduling is as much of a problem in Nordic countries such as Sweden (14 percent) and Denmark (16 percent), and in coordinated market economies such as those of Germany (18 percent) and France (20 percent), as it is in the liberal market economies of the United Kingdom (15 percent) and Ireland (17 percent). However, the rise of precarious scheduling is not just the result of the Great Recession. This crisis did indeed elevate levels of precarious scheduling; longitudinal data show that European countries have experienced similar levels for at least a decade. For instance, the average level of European precarious scheduling was 16 percent when measured in 2005, 19 percent when measured in 2010, and 17 percent when measured in 2015.[17]

While precarious scheduling does not of course affect all employees, it is typical of postindustrial working-class jobs. The fact that the suffering caused by precarious scheduling is confined to a particular subsection of workers should not hide the fact that it is a phenomenon that operates on an industrial scale. Indeed, economist Guy Standing claims that the growth of the on-demand economy is contributing to the creation of a new "precariat" class.[18] The available evidence suggests that around twenty million U.S. workers and forty million European workers currently experience precarious scheduling. Working time thus represents a new source of inequality in which low-end workers struggle to care for their families with jobs that provide too few hours to make ends meet, and are plagued by instability that makes planning one's life impossible. While low-end workers face a new regime of temporal suffering, those at the high end benefit from work that allows stable and plentiful hours and the potential of worker-controlled flexibility to improve their work-life balance.[19]

This book provides an original account of how this new source of inequality creates a novel regime of workplace control: flexible despotism. The following chapters highlight how this regime does not require the workplace to operate either numerical flexibility or dual labor markets, as previous researchers have assumed. Instead it demonstrates how precarious scheduling enables "flexible discipline" by providing managers with the arbitrary power to wreak havoc with workers' lives and incomes. Moreover, workers must actively seek to maintain the favor of their manager in order to ensure that they receive enough hours to make ends meet, and to avoid being scheduled at times that clash with their home life. This leads workers to work hard for their managers but also to beg them for changes to their scheduled hours. When managers accommodate a worker's request, this creates a sense of obligation to repay the manager's kindness in granting this "schedule gift." In this way, flexible despotism ensures workplace control by both securing exploitation via coercion and simultaneously obscuring that coercive exploitation through the misrecognition of schedule gifts.

By taking an approach that compares exemplars of retail workplaces in the UK and the United States, this book is able demonstrate how differences in the political and economic context lead to different forms of flexible despotism. Workers in the UK have greater statutory employment protections and rights than their U.S. counterparts, and organized labor remains stronger. As we shall see, these rights lead to a more progressive form of flexible despotism in the UK in which workers are protected from the extremes of manager tyranny and abuse. Despite the highly divergent policies that these workplaces followed, and the different political and economic contexts within which they operated, they nevertheless represented two forms, one progressive and one reactionary, of flexible despotism—that is, workplaces that achieve control through flexibility.

Workplace Regimes: Work as a Power Relationship

To understand the significance of flexible working time as a source of control, we must first recognize that paid work is not just a simple matter of market exchange but also of power relations. As the pioneering social scientists Sidney and Beatrice Webb pointed out more than a hundred years ago, "[the employer] expects his wage-earners to render him, not only obedience, but also personal deference. If the wage contract is a bargain of purchase and sale like any other, why is the workman expected to touch his hat to his employer, and to say 'sir' to him without reciprocity . . . ?"[20]

The answer to the Webbs' rhetorical question is that purchasing labor power also requires the maintaining of control over how that labor is expended in the workplace. There are two reasons for this. First, it is impossible to specify in workers' contracts the exact details of the work required of them. If we imagine a typical retail store clerk, at each moment of the day he or she will be faced by a variety of tasks to be undertaken under a wide range of unpredictable circumstances. At one point in time, those tasks might revolve around stacking shelves, at another helping customers navigate the shop or explaining a product to them, at yet another mopping up the floor, and so on. It would be impossible to write into a contract every task the clerk might be required to complete, as doing so would require an infinite amount of paper and imagination. A typical retail assistant contract, such as those used in the UK-based store I discuss later in this book, will instead state:

Your job title is: CUSTOMER ASSISTANT–REPLENISHMENT
Your job code is: xx
You will also be required to carry out other duties that may be reasonably
    required of you in any other department.

Therefore, paid work does not only entail market relations but is also a managerial relationship.[21] Labor power may be purchased for x price and y amount of time, but the exact details of the work are left vague and open-ended. This means that employers must ensure that the labor power of their workforce is expended in line with their designs. This requires workplace control in order to persuade the employee to actually work, and to determine how much work is performed and in which ways.[22]

Second, while the labor contract is indeterminate, the process of capital accumulation simultaneously generates a "structured antagonism" between capital and labor over the distribution of the surplus produced by labor and the operation of control in the realization of that surplus. In other words, structured antagonism exists at work owing to capital accumulation necessitating exploitation.[23] Sociologist Erik Olin Wright defines exploitation as a situation in which the "material welfare of one class is causally dependent upon the material deprivation of another." This causal dependence is reliant on the principle of "asymmetrical exclusion of the exploited from access to control over certain important productive resources. Typically, this exclusion is backed by force in the form of property."[24]

Therefore, in order to maintain their elevated material welfare, the owners of firms and their managerial representatives must strive to maintain control over the workplace in order to realize their profits. Capital accumulation, and by extension paid work, ultimately rests on power.[25]

Exploitation and Resistance

As exploitation entails the use of power to constrain the material welfare of others, it can lead to resistance as the exploited seek to improve their situation. There is, however, nothing inevitable about resistance. Even if the oppressed are aware of the operation of power (which they may not be), they may instead, quite rationally, seek accommodation through adaptation to the situation. Anthropologist James C. Scott explains that, even when resistance does take place, the very fact that it is undertaken by the weak against the powerful means that resistant subjects attempt to hide their resistance.

So while resistance may be expressed openly, it will more likely be disguised, for example as "rumors, gossip, folktales, songs, gestures, jokes, and theatre of the powerless."[26] However, even if they are disguised, these forms of resistance may well provide a "social and normative basis for practical forms of resistance . . . as well as the values that might, if conditions permitted, sustain more dramatic forms of rebellion."[27] In the workplace, such forms of hidden resistance include working slowly, feigned ignorance, sabotage, and pilfering, along with humor and gossip aimed at management.[28]

Sociologists Stephen Ackroyd and Paul Thompson argue that forms of resistance, as well as other forms of "organizational misbehavior," are generated out of workers' pursuit of autonomy and management's attempts to constrain it. These scholars see resistance as relating to the pursuit of autonomy in four spheres of contention, in which workers and management continually struggle to seize related material and symbolic resources. These four spheres of contention are the appropriation of time, appropriation of work, appropriation of product, and appropriation of identity. Such resistance is often not just hidden or disguised, but also supported by the informal self-organization of workers.[29] Sociologist Arlie Hochschild's famed ethnography of flight attendants showed how, in the face of constant observation via customers and supervisors, flight attendants were, nevertheless, able to undertake hidden resistance through the "accidental" spilling of a Bloody Mary over a customer and emotional work "slowdowns." For service workers such as these, slowdowns take the form of reducing their emotional labor, for example by using fake smiles or surface acting, and "rebelling against the costumes, the script and the general choreography" of their workplace.[30]

In the coming chapters I will seek not only to elucidate workplace power but also to highlight how workers continually seek out spaces of resistance. Sometimes this resistance will take manifest forms, such as strikes and demonstrations, and be supported by formal worker organizations, such as unions. However, in other spaces, it will be hidden and sustained by informal worker organizations.

Despotism and Hegemony

A central principle of this book is that patterns of power and resistance at work can be identified and understood through the concept of "workplace regimes." Workplace regimes are the political dynamics, institutional rules, and norms that workers encounter as they go about making their living. While workplace regimes are relatively autonomous to their external contexts, they are, nevertheless, influenced by the wider societal balance of power between capital and labor that exists at that precise juncture of history. A diversity of workplace regimes will therefore exist within a country, even within the same sector and at the same point in time. But, equally, within particular periods of history and specific places it is possible to identify a tendency toward discrete types of regimes. As documented in chapters 1 and 2, prior to the Second World War we can identify a clear pattern whereby workplace regimes in the UK and the United States tended to rely on coercive workplace mechanisms. These coercive mechanisms typically included the hierarchical supervision of workplace rules, enforced through fines and dismissals, and even the occasional use of violence to punish younger workers or to crush collective resistance.

However, the period after the Second World War saw the development of mechanisms that enabled workplace "hegemony." The term "hegemony" has often been used interchangeably with "ideology," but Antonio Gramsci originally used it in a quite different and more sophisticated manner. For Gramsci, hegemony was the process by which a dominant social group secures and maintains its leadership over society through legitimization. Analyzing western Europe in the 1930s, Gramsci theorized that hegemony was a process based around state and civil society institutions, in which the "dominant social group is coordinated concretely with the general interests of the subordinate groups." Meaning that a "compromise equilibrium should be formed . . . [thus] the leading group should make sacrifices . . . But there is no doubt that such sacrifices and such compromises cannot touch the essential [basis of exploitation]."[31]

Although hegemony does not actively rely on coercion, Gramsci insists that hegemony is, nonetheless, "protected by the armor of coercion."[32] Social theorist Nico Poulantzas has noted that Gramsci's analysis of hegemony requires the state to be understood as *relatively autonomous* from the dominant class. In short, if state institutions were to simply implement narrow policies for the benefit of the dominant class, they would actually undermine the compromise equilibrium on which hegemony is built. If the state were simply to follow the short-term interests of the ruling class, this would risk the reproduction of the social system that is so beneficial to them in the long term. Therefore, it is in the long-term interests of capital to provide some autonomy to state actors so as to maintain the system of stratification in which they are at the top.[33]

Gramsci's analysis of twentieth-century Europe highlighted the role of the state, civil society, and intellectuals in the construction of hegemony, but he developed an alternative explanation of hegemony in the United States. Gramsci argues that due to the United States being cut free from the residue of Europe's feudal past by the War of Independence, it lacked Europe's complex class competition, which had enabled the dominant European classes to construct hegemonic leadership. Instead, Gramsci argues that hegemony in the United States was "born in the factory" through the creation of a compromise equilibrium within the workplace. This meant that labor's interests were concretely coordinated with capital's through higher wages and benefits, and the assimilation of independent labor unions into factory-based workers' organizations (and the destruction through violence of those that resisted). Gramsci claimed that under workplace hegemony, "coercion has, therefore, to be ingeniously combined with persuasion and consent." The additional cost entailed by such compromise equilibriums could, according to Gramsci, be shouldered by U.S. employers, due to their industrial concentration and monopoly over new mass-production techniques.[34]

Workplace Regimes: The Internal State and the Internal Labor Market

Sociologist Michael Burawoy took Gramsci's investigation of hegemony as a starting point for his own studies of work in 1970s America. By applying Gramsci's work to his ethnography of a Chicago machine shop, Burawoy developed a key insight that paid work under capitalism entails not only exploitation but also the simultaneous obscuring of that exploitation. For if workers' exploitation was not obscured from their eyes, they would rationally resist it and thus threaten the reproduction of capitalism. Burawoy argued that this process of simultaneously securing and obscuring exploitation was achieved through the interaction of two *relatively autonomous* workplace mechanisms with their political and economic context: the internal state and the internal labor market.

The *internal state* refers to the internal institutions that repress and transform struggles in the workplace, principally through workers being granted both rights and obligations that are recognized in their employment contract and in the grievance process, respectively. The recognition of unions for collective bargaining also enables the concrete coordination of interests between capital and labor. The *internal labor market* refers to the shielding of labor from the external market through administrative rules and procedures—particularly the notion of seniority. Internal labor markets also provide workers with greater security and cultivate loyalty to the firm, as moving to another firm would leave a worker at the bottom of the new firm's seniority system. Workers, therefore, have an interest in the success and profitability of their firm. Despite increasing the power of workers, Burawoy demonstrates how both the internal state and the internal labor market tie the interests of employees to those of their employer, creating loyalty and transforming hierarchical conflict with management into lateral individualized competition between workers.[35]

Of course, hegemonic internal states were not introduced as part of some grand master plan to control the workplace, but rather developed gradually as a response to actual problems. For example, economist Richard Edwards argues that a major aim of this hegemonic form of control was to "limit the impact of the unions, to draw them into joint disciplining of workers."[36] Often, the development of control was the result of a struggle within the workplace. Thus, "a structure of control should be seen as the result, and a potentially unstable one, of past interactions between employers and workers, in the context of specific external influences."[37]

However, the concrete coordination of workers' and employers' interests and the maintenance of a stable compromise was not the only effect of the internal state and the internal labor market. For they also lay the basis for a third source of consent through the constitution of work as a "game." According to Burawoy, it is these work games that primarily act to obscure exploitation and thus limit resistance. By providing workers with a high level of employment security, hegemonic regimes enable workers to develop absorbing work games. These games, which involve activities such as producing certain quantities of goods so as to meet production targets according to socially sanctioned and enforced rules, were surprisingly important mechanisms of control during this period. The games not only provided workers with "relative satisfactions" that made their work bearable, but also effectively obscured exploitation. By playing work games, workers found ways to make their work more enjoyable and, in doing so, focused their attention on producing profit for their employer in order to "win" the game of increasing production.[38]

Burawoy drew comparisons between the workplace regime described by Marx in nineteenth-century Britain[39] and the ethnographic investigation of a 1940s Chicago machine shop by sociologist Donald Roy. He then contrasted this with his own ethnography of a machine shop in the same Chicago company thirty years later. Doing so enabled him to use the concepts of the internal state and the internal labor market to elucidate two Western capitalist workplace regimes: market despotic regimes—from the mid-eighteenth century to the mid-twentieth century; and hegemonic regimes—from the mid-twentieth century to the late twentieth century.[40]

Burawoy argues that this periodization should essentially be understood as workplaces having "moved along a continuum . . . That is to say, the balance of force and consent had shifted in the direction of consent."[41] Therefore, the market despotic/hegemonic typology represents stylized ideal types. In reality, workplaces make use of a varied configuration of mechanisms that elicit compliance through enforcing discipline and inducing consent. The typology should, therefore, be understood as representing tendencies toward reliance on coercion or hegemony. As industrial relations scholar Paul Edwards points out, even within a particular historical period, there was variation between workplace regimes. This was true even within economic sectors, industries, and nominally similar firms.[42] However, as I will demonstrate in the following chapters, there are identifiable tendencies toward market despotic regimes until around 1940, and toward hegemonic workplace regimes from this period until the 1980s. That is to say that there is evidence to suggest that, despite the widely differing content of workplace regimes, there was during the first period a tendency toward forms of control that relied more heavily on coercive mechanisms. And there exists an identifiable second period in which employers relied more heavily on hegemony, that is, the concrete coordination of interests.

The End of Hegemony

In the 1970s and early 1980s, improvements in systems of communication and information flows led to what geographer David Harvey refers to as a "space-time compression" and led capital to move toward "flexible accumulation."[43] The Fordist nature of space and time were being transformed to be less tangible dimensions of the social world by these new technologies, and space-time compression enabled global product markets to develop. This, in turn, increased competitive pressures on the hegemonic regimes of the Global North. Countries such as Japan were less restrictive in regulating business, while in some developing countries (such as South Africa, Brazil, and Iran) control rested on a combination of economic and extra-economic coercion. In other developing countries, export-processing zones were used to create "state planned despotism," supplying ample cheap labor outside countries that practiced hegemonic production.

The improvements in transport and communication technology of the early 1980s enabled this pool of cheap labor to be better utilized through greater capital mobility and fragmentation of labor processes. In order to increase their relative profit and maintain global competitiveness, U.S. and UK employers shifted their workplace regimes back toward despotism. Nevertheless, this undermining of hegemonic regimes should not be understood as having been driven by technological determinism, for it was only possible as hegemonic regimes had left workers unprepared for the hostile environment that employers and the state fashioned as they turned toward neoliberalism. In focusing on workplace improvements and tying workers' interests to the fortunes of their employer, working-class parties and unions had few alternatives to offer when hegemony collapsed.[44]

Burawoy maintains that this crisis for hegemonic regimes gave rise to the emergence of a new workplace regime: "hegemonic despotism." Under such workplace regimes, the priorities of capital shifted from ensuring the long-term success of firms toward maximizing short-term returns on investments: "The interests of capital and labor continue to be concretely coordinated, but where labor used to be granted concessions on the basis of the expansion of profits, it now makes concessions on the basis of the relative profitability ... No longer [is] the firm's success from one year to the next [what matters]; instead it is the rate of profit that might be earned elsewhere."[45]

Particularly susceptible were workplaces where hegemonic regimes were based on managerial philosophy rather than worker power, and thus the compromise equilibrium was quickly shifted by changes in market conditions.[46] Hegemonic despotism is best understood as the end phase of hegemonic regimes, in which the compromise equilibrium on which hegemony was based was disintegrating. This was a situation that was invariably short-lived, as the extraction of concessions from labor required the very hegemonic apparatuses that were being actively undermined and, in some cases, actively destroyed by this one-sided process in which capital was unwilling to offer real concessions to labor. Gramsci is clear that there can be no hegemony without a compromise equilibrium.

Control in the Twenty-First Century: The Electronic Panopticon and Customer Management

We have seen that hegemonic regimes existed in the UK and the United States for a relatively brief period of around forty years, between the 1940s and the 1980s. As employers sought to overcome their relative lack of profitability they transitioned toward flexible accumulation, which undermined the basis of the compromise equilibrium that underpinned hegemonic workplace regimes. However, it is not clear from the existing literature what kinds of workplace regimes followed in their wake. On the basis of research in South Africa, South Korea, and Australia, sociologists Edward Webster, Rob Lambert, and Andries Bezuidenhout argue that hegemonic despotism has given way to full-blown market despotism.[47] Yet in the Global North at least, to simply equate the workplaces of today with the satanic mills of the nineteenth and early twentieth centuries is clearly inadequate. An alternative suggestion is that contemporary control is achieved through modern electronic surveillance technology, which enables the realization of Michel Foucault's panopticon in the workplace.[48] According to accounts based on Foucault's use of the panopticon to understand the workplace, management seeks to isolate workers from each other and then subjects them to pervasive electronic surveillance and monitoring. This is argued to be a highly effective method of control: workers who never know whether their actions are being directly observed by managers end up disciplining themselves, and internalize the values of their firm, due to being in "a state of conscious and permanent visibility that assures the automatic functioning of power." Thus, the appearance of surveillance acts as an almost total mechanism of control in which the powerless are "caught up in a situation in which they themselves are the bearers" of their own domination. This means that "surveillance is permanent in its effects, even if it [is in reality] discontinuous [and ultimately] its actual exercise is unnecessary."[49] However, such arguments have been critically evaluated in what became known as the "call center debate."[50] This debate empirically demonstrated that the notion of the electronic panopticon was overly simplistic, in that it conceptually overstated the dominance of surveillance and underestimated workers' capacity for resistance.[51]

A more grounded explanation of contemporary workplace control centers on the service sector and its unique triangular relationship among managers, workers, and customers. According to this approach, customers' feedback and demands act as important mechanisms of workplace control.[52] Customer management entails positioning customers "as agents in the management circuit," so that "customers, rather than managers, are . . . the ones who must be pleased, whose orders must be followed, whose ideas, whims and desires appear to dictate how work is performed."[53] A recent extension of such customer management strategies has taken place in the on-demand economy with the rapid growth of gig economy labor platforms. These platforms use algorithms that rank workers according to factors such as customer satisfaction. Consequently, work is filtered away from workers deemed low quality or unproductive according to the algorithm's parameters, and often ultimately, as noted earlier, deactivated (i.e., dismissed). This can be a very effective form of control as workers strive to constantly maintain a high average customer rating and work accuracy scores, in order to secure more work.[54] The algorithmic management developed by gig economy labor platforms such as Uber is starting to spread into more conventional sectors of the economy such as retail.[55] But at present this algorithmic management is not yet widespread.

Flexible Despotism

An influential approach influenced by Burawoy's framework is the dual use of hegemonic despotism and market despotism in a single workplace following a core/peripheral or permanent/temporary distinction.[56] This has been argued by sociologist Jennifer Jihye Chun to constitute the emergence of *flexible despotism* as a new workplace regime.[57] Under flexible despotism the core of workers within a firm continue to experience a hegemonic workplace regime, while contingent workers face a return to the despotism of the pre–World War II world of work.

However, the conceptual importance that existing accounts of flexible despotism place on segmentation and temporary and agency work is problematic, as such employment is highly unrepresentative of many U.S. and UK workplaces.[58] Indeed, in the United States and the UK it is far more common for flexibility in low-end service sector jobs to be achieved temporally, through manager-controlled flexible scheduling rather than through the use of agency and temporary workers. Nor should the effectiveness of such control strategies be taken for granted; for example, the recruitment of temporary workers can in fact reduce managers' control.[59] Moreover, dual labor market theories have long been criticized on conceptual grounds, the most foundational being the difficulty of identifying which workers represent the core and which the periphery.[60] This problem has become exacerbated over time, as (in)security was the chief concept used to differentiate core and periphery jobs. As sociologist Arne Kalleberg, a former proponent of a dual labor market theory, states: "Precarity and insecurity were used to differentiate jobs in the primary as opposed to secondary labor market segments. Now, precarious work has spread to all sectors of the economy and has become much more pervasive and generalized."[61]

Flexible Discipline

An obvious elaboration to the dual core/peripheral model of flexible despotism, which might also apply to many more workers, is one in which both flexibility and control are achieved via precarious scheduling. This method of scheduling affords managers a high level of discretionary control over working time, even enabling real-time adjustments to schedules. This flexible scheduling affords managers significant arbitrary power over workers' work-life balance and the quality of their job.[62] This, in turn, provides managers with a potentially powerful despotic means of ensuring general workplace control. In fact, a study of a UK chemical plant provides evidence of flexible scheduling extending managerial control in just this manner.[63] Huw Beynon's classic study of Ford also demonstrates how Ford supervisors' control over the allocation of overtime led to the worker being "in the supervisors' pocket. If he doesn't behave, or if the supervisor just doesn't happen to 'like' him, he can lose his overtime for a week or forever."[64]

Similar control mechanisms have been observed more recently in the temporary help and microchip assembly industries and in the Australian retail sector.[65] In this book I will call the use of such flexible scheduling to punish and coerce workers "flexible discipline." The disciplining effect of flexible scheduling, along with the rise of the on-demand economy, clearly has the potential to liberate flexible despotism from its reliance on dual labor markets and contingent workers. In fact, it might be far more common for the despotism of flexibility to be temporal rather than numerical. However, the suggestion that workplace control can be maintained simply through the disciplining effects of precarious scheduling supposes a one-dimensional view of control. As Burawoy argues, control is maintained not only by managers actively securing it but also through the obscuring of workplace relations. In other words, control is far easier to achieve when workers do not recognize that they are being exploited and thus do not resist that exploitation.

Work Games in the Twenty-First Century

A number of researchers have emphasized the continuing importance of work games in the legitimization of workplace relations, even in the absence of hegemonic internal states and internal labor markets. For example, fast-food workers have been found to engage in sales games.[66] This is surprising given that Burawoy argues that security was important for making such games absorbing, and employment security is not something often associated with the fast-food industry. Indeed, while an "autonomous learning game" based around becoming competent at handling customer calls has been found in a call center, this game was found not to be absorbing, as the only compulsion to play it was social pressure created through interaction with customers. Most workers refused to continue playing and instead quit the work within a few weeks. This game, therefore, did little to generate commitment among the workforce.[67]

Less surprising than the existence of work games in these insecure service sector jobs are findings regarding a Japanese-style factory in France where workers were found to be engaged in a work game in which they would feign transparency and openness with regard to their work practices and skills while secretly seeking to hide their true high level of knowledge and skills from management.[68] Likewise, Las Vegas casino dealers, who have a degree of job security due to their skilled profession and plentiful labor market opportunities, have been discovered to engage in a game in which they use their discretion to help customers who provide them with tips.

Given the importance of flexible working time in contemporary workplaces, we might expect work games structured around time to play an important role in maintaining control. Time-based work games have been previously uncovered. For example, at a Chinese textile factory, workers engaged in a game centered on gaining leisure time by achieving their work tasks. Additionally, at a chemical plant in the UK, workers were found to play a game in which they made strategic use of absences in order to make gains in overtime.[69] Given these examples drawn from various contexts, it might be expected that work games continue to play a central role in workplace control in the twenty-first century. Additionally, it is possible that in firms making use of temporal flexibility these games will be structured around time. This is a proposition that will be explored empirically in chapter 5, which considers how exploitation is obscured by workplace dynamics in the contemporary flexible firm.

Normative Control

Of course, managers may attempt to dispense with work games altogether and, instead, utilize symbolic power directly through types of "normative controls."[70]

Normative control refers to control over concepts and categories of meaning, societal norms, and aesthetic and ritual practices in order to shape perceptions, cognitions, and preferences.[71] Normative controls can thus reduce conflict by causing workers to "accept their role in the existing order of things, either because they can see or imagine no alternative to it, or because they see it as natural and unchangeable, or because they value it as divinely ordained and beneficial."[72] A number of accounts have stressed the importance of direct normative controls, often via the "high performance team systems" associated with the post-Fordist paradigm that was popular among academics in the 1990s. Self-directed teamwork practices are argued to "serve powerful ideological functions, bringing workers into closer and more frequent contact with management, encouraging workers to assume proto-managerial obligations and inducing them to internalize managerial definitions of their work situations."[73]

Sociologist Steven Vallas undertook a detailed study of teamwork and normative control at four paper mills in the United States. He found only limited evidence of teamwork operating as an effective source of legitimization. In fact, by strengthening work group solidarity, teamwork can actually lead to greater levels of resistance. Relevant to the subject matter of this book is the fact that Vallas did, however, find that despite being an ineffective source of control among higher-skilled workers, teamworking was a potent source of normative control among the low-skilled workers in his study.[74]

A more recent study of normative control specifically in the low-end service sector found that call center workers were encouraged to "be themselves." Thus, they were able to practice greater freedom in terms of lifestyle, sexual, and consumer displays, while still experiencing more coercive controls over their work. However, the contradictions between the normative control mechanisms and the more coercive work controls often led to skepticism among the workforce toward the symbolic representation of their employment experience, as fun, playful, and authentic.[75] This parallels Vallas's findings from his study of paper mills that teamworking practices generate skepticism, suspicion, and distrust toward managers due to the contradiction between the claims of team participation in decision making and self-direction and the realities of high levels of detailed managerial control. This distrust combined with the inter–work team solidarity led to some significant acts of resistance, including collective mobilization despite the absence of a union. Taken together, the findings of these two studies suggest that normative controls without sufficient hegemonic supports may be unstable and ineffective among both high- and low-skilled workers. In fact, in the state socialist workplaces they studied, Burawoy and Janos Lukács found that symbolic rituals of socialist affirmation actually destabilized the regime, as they "draw attention to the discrepancy between ideology and reality."[76]

The Power of Gifts: Flexible Scheduling and Misrecognition

An alternative to both work games and direct normative controls may lie in sociologist Ashley Mears's critique of work games. She contends that understanding power in the workplace requires going beyond the "situational construction of consent" entailed by work games and instead placing greater emphasis on the relational nature of control. Mears highlights the manner in which "meanings of work are also shaped through relationships and social ties beyond the accomplishment of work activities." In particular, she draws on the seminal sociological work on gifts by Marcel Mauss in order to elucidate the power of gifts in the exploitation of "girls" in VIP nightclubs. For example, by providing a "free" expensive dinner, promoters created an obligation that "glamorous" women both attend and stay at a particular nightclub without necessitating them being paid.[77]

Mauss famously argued that there was no such thing as a free or pure gift; he showed how, in reality, all gifts come with the obligation of reciprocation and, thus, strengthen bonds of social solidarity. For Mauss, the expectations created by the exchange of gifts are largely recognized by both parties.[78] Sociologist Pierre Bourdieu developed Mauss's argument by demonstrating that the power relations underpinning gifts are, in fact, often misrecognized by both the giver and the receiver. The true power of gifts, Bourdieu argues, lies not in their reciprocation but in the inability of the less powerful party to fully reciprocate.

Bourdieu illustrates this process through the giving of gifts among Kabyle peasants in northern Algeria. He shows how the provision of gifts that cannot be reciprocated binds the receiver to the giver through an emotional debt and a sense of moral obligation, while masking the act as a gesture of generosity. Such gift-based power relations are especially prevalent when developed institutions that maintain domination in other forms are absent.[79] Not only is misrecognition the foundation on which the power of gifts rests; it is, according to Bourdieu, also central to understanding workplace relations. In a similar fashion to Burawoy, he argues that a necessary condition for the existence of labor is workers' subjective misrecognition of their objective exploitation.[80]

In the context of high levels of precarious scheduling, it is possible that managers operating within a flexible despotic regime might provide workers with what I will term "schedule gifts." Schedule gifts involve the granting of additional work hours to help workers meet their material needs by increasing their earnings. Additionally, benevolent alterations to schedules can help provide for workers' social needs by improving work-life balance. These gifts therefore ease working time insecurity. However, by accepting schedule gifts, workers might not recognize the mechanism of control operating in their workplace—namely, flexible discipline.

Support for the concept of schedule gifts can be found in a 2015 study of UK care workers, where high levels of gratitude were generated by managers' attempts to improve the workers' schedules.[81] Additionally, a survey of 325 workers at an engine gasket factory in the United States found that the more workers perceived the company's work-life balance benefits to be useful in terms of helping them and their families, the more they seemed to reciprocate. This reciprocation included submitting suggestions to management for improvements, voluntarily attending meetings on quality methods, and reporting that they assisted others in their job duties.[82]

Summary and Research Strategy

The growth of the on-demand economy in the early twenty-first century has brought with it new domains of suffering and inequality. The extent of the pernicious effects of precarious scheduling can be understood only by recognizing that paid work is a power relation. The concept of "workplace regimes" can help us identify and understand the changing patterns of control and resistance at particular historical junctures. However, it is currently unclear how control is achieved in the twenty-first century. Some contemporary accounts maintain the importance of work games, while others stress the importance of new forms of normative control. Other researchers argue for the emergence of an electronic panopticon, while still others suggest that there has been a complete return to a pre–Second World War workplace despotism.

This book will elaborate on one of the most convincing existing accounts, that of flexible despotism. But the account provided will elaborate on existing research by stressing the importance of temporal flexibility over numerical flexibility. It will demonstrate how control is experienced in the contemporary "flexible firm" by investigating the workplace regimes at two of the largest retailers in the world (referred to herein by the pseudonyms ConflictCo and PartnershipCo) in the United States and the UK, respectively.

These two in-depth case studies are particularly illuminating given that while on the face of it the two firms share similar profiles in terms of their domestic market position, they seem to have contrasting workplace regimes that are reflective of wider contextual differences between the United States and the UK. PartnershipCo appeared closer to the archetypical hegemonic regime, with a recognized union, collective bargaining, and a fairly stable and harmonious industrial relations climate. Contrastingly, ConflictCo seemed to represent a more despotic regime—being famed for its hostility toward, avoidance of, and conflict with unions, along with its low pay and poor benefits. These two firms are also representative of

TABLE 1 Comparison of labor movements in the UK, the United States, and California

TRADE UNION STRENGTH	UK	US	CA
Total union membership (millions)	6.5	14.4	2.5
Total union density	26%	11%	17%
Public union density	56%	36%	59%
Private union density	14%	7%	9%
Total collective bargaining coverage	29%	13%	18%
Public sector collective bargaining coverage	64%	40%	63%
Private sector collective bargaining coverage	16%	8%	10%
Retail and wholesale density	13%	5%	–
Retail and wholesale collective bargaining	15%	5%	–

Sources: UK: BIS, *Statistical Bulletin: Trade Union Membership 2013*; United States and California: Hirsch and Macpherson, *Union Membership and Coverage Database from the CPS*.

more general differences in the UK and U.S. employment systems. The strength of private sector unions in the UK has declined drastically over the past thirty years, but, as highlighted in Table 1, they remain significantly stronger than their U.S. counterparts. The UK also features greater statutory labor rights and protections than does the United States.

The case studies are both taken from the retail sector, as this has been identified as an exemplar of low-end service sector employment. It has been argued that "retail work is in many ways the new generic form of mass employment in the post-industrial social-economic landscape."[83] In both the UK and the United States, the largest private sector employers are retailers, and there are currently 4.7 million and 15.7 million people employed in retail in the UK and the United States, respectively.[84] In fact, Walmart (which in the UK owns ASDA) has been argued to be paradigmatic of employment in the twenty-first century, much as General Motors and Ford were during the previous century.[85]

The ethnographic method adopted included two months of working as a shelf stacker at PartnershipCo, as well as many months of participant and nonparticipant observation of union organizing at both firms in London, Los Angeles, and San Francisco. This experiential data is combined with interviews with over eighty workers and union officials as well as textual analysis of documentary material. A methodological appendix provides further details about the research, including a discussion of the extended case method and an overview of the data collection and analyses.

Analysis of this data highlights how control in the contemporary flexible firm is enabled by temporal flexibility rather than the numerical flexibility that has been stressed in previous accounts of flexible despotism. Temporal flexibility is found to be achieved at both firms through precarious scheduling across employment statuses. The consequences of flexibility for workers are shown to be severe, damaging work-life balance to the detriment of workers' family and social lives, and creating a pervasive sense of insecurity in the workforce.

What I have termed "flexible discipline" provides a powerful yet subtle means by which managers can secure exploitation within the workplace, for it provides them with the discretion to punish workers by cutting or changing workers' hours. However, flexible scheduling is demonstrated to also actively shape the workplace regime as workers attempt to win favor with managers in order to receive "schedule gifts." The granting of these schedule gifts is found to have the additional effect of obscuring the nature of exploitation in a manner reminiscent of Bourdieu's "misrecognition" of gifts. For schedule gifts are experienced as acts of kindness that cannot be reciprocated and, as such, act to bind workers to their manager through feelings of gratitude and a moral obligation to work hard.

The centrality of precarious scheduling in achieving control at both these firms reveals the existence of a previously undocumented form of flexible despotism based on temporal rather than numerical flexibility. While political and economic differences between the UK and the United States are reflected in the way in which flexible despotism manifests itself at the two firms investigated (taking a more progressive form in the UK and a more reactionary one in the United States), it is clear that despite these differences, precarious scheduling remains equally central to control at both workplaces.

The book continues as follows. Part 1 focuses on the internal states of ConflictCo and PartnershipCo, placing each within its corresponding historical and societal context. Chapter 1 investigates the workplace institutions at PartnershipCo that act to repress and transform conflict. A number of internal institutions limit the ability of managers to secure control via traditional forms of despotism in important ways. In particular, the union policed disciplinary and grievance procedures, rationalized discipline, and provided workers with employment protection. This chapter also highlights how the union at PartnershipCo operated as an ideological element of the internal state that had a normative (if unreliable) control function.

Chapter 2 moves on to investigate the internal state at ConflictCo. Here, workplace institutions were found to do little to rationalize discipline or constrain its arbitrary application by managers. The chapter demonstrates that managers at ConflictCo typically gained compliance through threats and punishments, such as termination of employment and disciplinary action. However, managers' ability to secure control in this way was identified as being challenged by a union-backed worker association. The legal and media campaign waged by the union and the worker association successfully curbed the ability of managers to impose blatant despotism. This chapter also investigates the operation of normative control at ConflictCo, showing how in this workplace a heavy emphasis was placed on propaganda and rituals to try to legitimize control. However, these normative controls were found to be dysfunctional in that they actually legitimized resistance. Part 1 concludes that control at PartnershipCo and ConflictCo could not rest solely on the traditional despotism represented by threats of job loss, nor could control be ensured via mechanisms of direct normative control.

Part 2 moves on to consider the despotism of working time, with chapter 3 documenting the historical evolution of working time and internal labor markets in the UK. This chapter goes on to investigate the temporal organization of labor at PartnershipCo. The chapter considers wage rates and pay structure, employment protections, mobility, and promotion opportunities, but finds that flexible scheduling is the most significant means of securing control. Flexible scheduling was found to be highly manager-controlled, even when institutionalized working time regulations were present. Chapter 4 provides a similar account for ConflictCo. These two chapters demonstrate how manager discretion over flexible schedules enables them to practice flexible discipline by causing significant distress to specific workers. Changes to hours are shown to cause a potential clash of work and social and family responsibilities. Moreover, increased instability and unpredictability of working time reduced workers' ability to plan their finances and social and family lives, while long-term cuts to weekly hours decreased their income. Therefore, altering working time was widely seen as a potential sanction that managers could hand out to workers.

A major strength of this mechanism of discipline was the inherent subtlety and ambiguity that it involved. It was difficult for workers to be certain as to whether they were truly being disciplined, and therefore whether the blame for their suffering lay with their manager or the omnipotent workings of "the market." Moreover, punishments such as dismissal were rigid and blunt in nature—but a decision to cut or alter a worker's schedule could easily be rescinded, making it a much more flexible means of control. This flexibility also meant that the punishment could be modulated over time, unlike the binary nature of dismissal/nondismissal.

Manager-controlled flexible scheduling was not only used as a tool by managers to punish specific workers; it also constituted an active and constant "structuration"[86] of the workplace. That is, flexible discipline provided managers with a simple, readily available, and unaccountable way to punish specific workers with worse hours and shifts, as well as requiring all workers to actively maintain their favor through being "good" and "hard-working" employees.

Part 3 focuses on the dynamics of the workplace and spaces of resistance. Chapter 5 investigates how managerial control at PartnershipCo and ConflictCo was aided through misrecognition by workers of the workplace relations. The chap-

ter begins by describing the characteristics of the work at PartnershipCo and ConflictCo, before discussing the history of work games and highlighting their absence at both ConflictCo and PartnershipCo. In the place of work games, the
chapter instead highlights the role of "schedule gifts" in aiding control through
misrecognition.

Schedule gifts are a consequence of temporal flexibility and, as noted earlier,
are reminiscent of the gift economy discussed by Bourdieu in his 1958–1962 study
of Kabyle peasants in Algeria.[87] Schedule gifts are shown to enable workers to limit
the insecurity inherent in precarious scheduling, providing them with a means
to meet their material and social needs in this unstable and capricious environment. Therefore, flexible scheduling does not merely constitute a disciplinary tool.
Flexible scheduling also creates an environment in which workers must beg
managers for schedules to be altered and more hours granted. Managers acquiescence to workers' needs, but, as workers are unable to reciprocate, this is experienced by workers as an act of kindness that requires reciprocation. Scheduling
gifts mystify workplace relations and bind workers to their manager through a
sense of gratitude, creating a moral obligation to repay a social debt to managers
through hard work.

Chapter 6 considers the limits and contradictions of control at PartnershipCo
and ConflictCo. The findings demonstrate that while flexible scheduling represents a source of managerial control, it also, paradoxically, provides fuel for resistance. At PartnershipCo, this resistance was found to be hidden as a result of
the union's individualized and integrated tendencies toward collective resistance.
At ConflictCo, however, few examples of hidden resistance were identified, owing to the high level of surveillance and fear that marked the workplace regime.
For the majority of workers, the same was also true for open resistance. However,
a relatively small number of workers managed to overcome this fear and joined
a worker association that used social media networks and the symbolic power of
direct actions to successfully challenge employer control at ConflictCo. These
findings suggest that, even when only small numbers of workers are able to carve
out spaces of resistance within the flexible workplace of the twenty-first century,
they may nevertheless be able to harness social media–based networks in order
to successfully raise labor standards through threat of reputational damage.

The concluding chapter outlines how the findings relate to previous research.
Particular emphasis is placed on the ways in which the findings depart from previous studies and the theoretical elaboration that is therefore required to understand power and control in the twenty-first-century world of work. The hegemony
of the past is unlikely to recur, as workers lack the structural-economic power to
win concessions from their employers and to enforce stable compromise equilibriums. This does not, however, mean that the securing of control at work will

be reliant on a return to the kinds of despotism that were common in the nineteenth century. Nor does control necessitate the obscuring effect of work games. Rather, flexible working time provides a powerful means of both securing and simultaneously obscuring exploitation in low-end workplaces across both standard and nonstandard employment.

This final chapter then goes on to consider how the form that flexible despotism takes is modified by the differing levels of bargaining power of workers. Specifically, it considers how the provision of greater employment rights and union protection leads to a more progressive form of flexible despotism—but one in which precarious scheduling nonetheless remains central to workplace control. This account of power at work provides a valuable insight into the experiences of control of a large number of postindustrial workers in the on-demand economy. The book ends by reflecting on the implications for the future of work in the on-demand economy and considering the forms of workplace control that are likely to achieve prominence as the century progresses.

Part 1
POWER AT WORK

The first part of this book focuses on the internal states of two workplace regimes: ConflictCo in the United States and PartnershipCo in the UK. The term "internal state" refers to the manner in which control and resistance are shaped by different institutional and ideological apparatuses within the workplace. The similarities and differences in the internal states of the two regimes will be drawn out by placing each within its corresponding historical context.

Chapter 1 investigates PartnershipCo in the UK. Workers at PartnershipCo felt highly dependent on their employer, believing there to be few alternatives available to them. However, despite their vulnerable position, the rights enshrined in their legally binding employment contracts placed restrictions on the ability of their managers to take advantage of this weakness through threats of dismissal. Workforce surveillance at PartnershipCo was also variable and often limited.

Most importantly, PartnershipCo had agreed a "partnership" collective agreement with a recognized union. This collective agreement laid out the company's highly developed grievance and disciplinary procedures and limited the use of temporary and agency workers. These policies had a hegemonic function, providing workers with important protections against traditional despotic methods of control. However, the partnership collective agreement also acted to mobilize bias against the development of collective challenges to managerial control through individualizing worker indignation and preventing the articulation of collective grievances. It also incorporated the union's representatives and officials within a narrow framework in which they came to see their role solely as ensuring that company policies (many of which were effectively decided unilaterally by

PartnershipCo) were followed. The focus on policing the company's policies, therefore, came at the expense of promoting the collective questioning of whether these policies were just in the first place.

The union thus provided a normative control function whereby company policy was legitimized, and controversial management practices, such as precarious scheduling, were justified by union reps. For example, union reps often spoke of the need to "balance the needs of the business with the needs of the worker." Moreover, the union's national campaigns did not deal with major workplace issues, and were instead limited to issues such as bullying or learning that provided mutual gains for both workers and PartnershipCo. While the union provided a source of normative control, its ideological function was uneven and unreliable due to it following its own organizational interests, which did not necessarily overlap with those of PartnershipCo. Thus, the union could not always be counted on to legitimize management practices. In particular, due to the high labor turnover at PartnershipCo, the union required its reps to achieve high levels of recruitment, which, in turn, led reps to increase discontent by stressing negative aspects of the workplace in order to convince nonmembers to join the union.

Given the importance of the collective agreement and the union to this internal state, PartnershipCo might be assumed to most closely resemble a hegemonic workplace regime. Indeed, workers' interests were concretely tied to their employers, through a profit share scheme, a relatively good defined benefit pension scheme, and pay being collectively bargained. However, during the period of fieldwork, PartnershipCo refused to award any shares due to declining profitability, while the collective agreement actually took pay negotiations out of the workplace and had resulted in declining real pay. Therefore, the internal state at PartnershipCo more closely resembled those synonymous with hegemonic despotism. The compromise equilibrium was seemingly in a state of disintegration, with the regime's remaining hegemonic apparatuses being used to extract concessions from labor in the face of growing competitive pressures resulting from the growth of e-commerce. This does not, however, mean that workers received no benefit from the continued existence of hegemonic institutions. This is a fact that can be seen particularly clearly when this internal state is contrasted with the one at ConflictCo in the United States.

While the internal state at PartnershipCo resembled that of hegemonic despotism, ConflictCo's internal state was closer to the ideal of market despotism. As at PartnershipCo, ConflictCo's workforce was also highly dependent on the firm for their livelihoods; however, here insecurity was much greater, due to the "at-will" employment status used by ConflictCo. According to this employment status workers lack an implicit or explicit legally binding employment contract.

Furthermore, ConflictCo's policies and managers made workers aware of their vulnerable positions and the ease with which they could be replaced. In fact, workers frequently complained of having been verbally abused and bullied by managers and that an atmosphere of surveillance prevailed at ConflictCo.

In contrast to PartnershipCo, ConflictCo was extremely hostile to unions. In the absence of a recognized union and collective bargaining, ConflictCo created its workplace policies and rules unilaterally without worker input. Workers even struggled to access these policies and could look them up only on the firm's intranet. That these company policies were created without their input and that they had limited access to them meant that workers perceived them as one-sided, unstable, and used by managers to catch them out. Likewise, the grievance and disciplinary procedures were underdeveloped. In fact, the disciplinary procedure did little more than provide managers with a convenient method with which to fire workers, with no burden of proof being required and workers not being allowed an independent representative or even a witness to be present at disciplinary meetings. This process was widely felt to be applied unequally and unfairly, based on favoritism or as a means to retaliate against workers who attempted resistance. The grievance procedure, which ConflictCo termed the "open door policy" (which, as one worker put it, had "been nailed shut a long time ago"), lacked the institutional oversight necessary for workers to feel that their complaints were being treated equally, and fairly investigated and dealt with.

Furthermore, even in the postwar period, ConflictCo had never fully embraced the kinds of hegemonic mechanisms, common at other U.S. companies, that tied workers' interests to their firms'. These mechanisms include employer profit sharing, health care, and defined benefit pension schemes. Even the few benefits that ConflictCo did provide had been declining in value, and, in any case, most workers felt that their wages were too low to enable them to make much use of the company's health care, profit sharing, or 401(k) retirement schemes. In fact, starting wages were declining in real terms and were close to the minimum wage. As at PartnershipCo, the declining value of wages and benefits was probably a consequence of the threat that e-commerce represented to ConflictCo's continued dominance in the U.S. retail market, and that thus created pressure to cut costs.

In the absence of mechanisms to concretely coordinate the interests of workers with those of the company, ConflictCo sought to ensure normative control and to limit resistance through directly shaping the values of workers. Such methods included an Orwellian use of language, heavy use of in-store propaganda, and compulsory collective ritual. However, these attempts at normative control were largely ineffective and in fact legitimized opposition to the current management. Much of the propaganda, along with the ritualistic "ConflictCo cheer," emphasized the supposed values embodied in the founder as pro-worker, thus the company's stressing of these values highlighted the disparity between the symbolic representation of ConflictCo and the reality of working at the company. Moreover, the stressing of the founder's support for these values also justified resistance to those currently in charge and in doing so actually destabilized the regime and undermined its control.

The failure of these normative controls was compounded by a recent curtailing of managers' ability to secure control through blatant acts of traditional despotism. Despite the hostility of ConflictCo toward unions, a union-backed worker association had provided workers with a degree of associational power. The association had been very successful at creating negative publicity around working conditions at ConflictCo, as well as filing a large number of successful legal claims against the company for unfair labor practices. These tactics proved effective at limiting obvious forms of managerial despotism.

Therefore, this first part of the book demonstrates that while internal states in the UK and the United States have generally developed along similar historical contours, PartnershipCo and ConflictCo seemingly represent somewhat divergent workplace regimes, with the former's internal state more closely resembling that of hegemonic despotism and the latter's market despotism. However, at both firms, the internal state placed limits on the ability of managers to achieve control through blatant acts of traditional despotism. It is this similarity that made flexible discipline an attractive alternative means for securing control, and it is this form of control that is elucidated in part 2.

INTERNAL STATES IN THE UK

This book's introduction outlined Michael Burawoy's influential workplace regime approach. His framework provides us with tools with which to investigate how control and resistance are shaped by institutional and ideological apparatuses within the workplace. This chapter investigates the mechanisms of control that comprised the "internal state" at PartnershipCo. These mechanisms include a union and collective partnership agreement, developed disciplinary and grievance procedures, a defined benefit pension, and bonus schemes. The chapter proceeds by considering the historical development of internal states in the UK before presenting a detailed account of the main features of the internal state at PartnershipCo.

Market Despotism

Karl Marx's depiction of early English factories provides Burawoy with the ideal type for "market despotic regimes." Marx argues that automation, such as Richard Arkwright's water-powered spinning frame in the cotton industry, significantly reduced the skill level of work in these factories. Moreover, Marx describes the organization of these early factories as being synonymous with the military, autocracy, slavery, and prisons. For example, he states that there is "barrack-like discipline . . . dividing workers into manual laborers and overseers . . . In the factory code, the capitalist formulates his autocratic power over his workers like a private legislator . . . This code is merely the capitalist caricature of the social regulation of the labor process . . . The overseer's book of penalties replace the slave-driver's lash . . . Was [the philosopher] Fourier wrong when he called factories 'mitigated jails'?"[1]

Marx also footnotes Friedrich Engels's famed study of the working class in England in which Engels states that the factory is where "ends all freedom in law and in fact . . . [The worker] must eat, drink and sleep at command . . . The despotic bell calls him from his bed, his breakfast, his dinner . . . The employer is absolute law-giver; he makes regulations at will, changes and adds to his codex at pleasure . . . the courts say to the working man: since you have entered into this contract, you must be bound to live under the sword, physically and mentally."[2]

Drawing on the work of Marx and Engels, Burawoy suggests that market despotism is characterized by four criteria:

1. Competition among firms.
2. Highly controlled labor processes.
3. Workers' dependence on their employer for a wage in return for labor power.
4. State regulation only of the external conditions of production, that is, maintaining market competition without regulating the production process.[3]

A key experience of workers under market despotism was the immense level of insecurity they experienced. There were no employer or state protections against job loss or unemployment (apart from the workhouse), and the enclosure of common land made workers highly dependent on their employment. Engels describes how "far more demoralizing than his poverty in its influence on the English working man is the insecurity of his position, the necessity of living upon wages from hand to mouth . . . Every whim of his employer may deprive [him] of bread."

In Engels's view, it was insecurity that made life worse for the English worker than for the German peasant, even though the latter was materially poorer and suffered more from want. This insecurity placed the English worker in the "most revolting, inhuman position conceivable for a human being . . . Everything that the proletarian can do to improve his position is but a drop in the ocean compared to the floods of varying chances to which he is exposed, over which he has not the slightest of control."

Engels describes the insecurity workers faced in further lucid detail: "He knows that every breeze that blows, every whim of his employer, every bad turn of trade may hurl him back into the fierce whirlpool from which he temporarily saved himself, and in which it is hard and often impossible to keep his head above water. He knows that, though he may have the means of living today, it is very uncertain whether he shall tomorrow."[4]

Other accounts endorse this dismal portrayal of life in English factories during the Industrial Revolution. In these workplaces the internal state was usually based on harsh discipline and fines meted out by overseers and managers, along with employment laws that threatened workers with imprisonment for breach of contract, but that punished employers only with fines.

In the early nineteenth century, forms of discipline similar to those practiced in the cotton mills (hierarchical supervision, rules, and fines) begun to spread to other sectors. The adoption of cotton mill–style management even affected sectors where the work remained less automated and required greater skill, for example, the new pottery factories that had sprung up.[5] Across these industries control was widely achieved through corporal punishment of apprentices and children (who made up a large percentage of the workforce), fines, threats of dismissal, and blacklists. As historian Sidney Pollard puts it, "By comparison with these commonly used examples of the 'stick,' more subtle or more finely graded deterrents were so rare as to be curious."[6] As each new technical innovation gradually extended automation in the workplace, the UK saw the systematic extension of despotism to new sectors of the economy.

Hegemonic Internal States in the UK

Karl Polanyi famously argued that the growing insecurity created by British nineteenth-century free market capitalism spurred formation of labor unions as part of a countermovement seeking to regulate the market and decommodify labor.[7] In the late nineteenth century, male craft unions were finally granted legal freedom. Consequently, these unions were able to gain a degree of control in some workplaces. Historical data suggests that, while overall union density (the percentage of employees who are members of unions) had reached only 13 percent by 1900, among mine and dock workers this was much higher, at around 60 percent by the early 1890s. The figure was around 30 percent for metal and engineering workers and printers, and around 25 percent for cotton textile workers, glass workers, construction workers, seamen, and shoemakers.[8] This led to a period of constant attack and counterattack by employers and sectional unions.[9] On average there were 932 recorded strikes every year between 1910 and 1914.[10] However, by the mid-1930s, the First World War, depression, and government policy had transformed Britain's economy into monopoly capitalism, that is, an economic system in which giant modern corporations had replaced small family-run businesses. But instead of monopoly profits enabling hegemony, employers used the relative weakness of unions during this period to "push for tighter managerial control."[11]

It was the outbreak of the Second World War that sparked the hegemonic transformation of UK internal states. Most importantly, the wartime government made it difficult for employers to sack workers and ended the victimization of union activists.[12] A unique history of shop stewards (whereby elected workers, rather than full-time union officials, represent their unionized colleagues within the workplace) and workplace bargaining that developed during the earlier sustained period of union attack and employer counterattack gave hegemonic internal states in the UK a flavor distinct from those in the United States. While the concrete coordination of interests existed, workplace-level bargaining, and its voluntary and informal nature, made the compromise equilibrium that developed in the UK far less stable than in the United States.[13]

Industrial relations scholar William Brown argues that during the postwar period before the 1980s, management could not rule through despotism, as they lacked "effective disciplinary powers," due to high employment levels and the strength unions had built up during the war. These factors meant that foremen no longer had the ability arbitrarily to discipline or sack workers. This forced them to make concessions to workers on the shop floor in order to gain their cooperation. What took place was "political activity, not in the sense of party or state politics, but as an activity in which conflicting pressure groups come to temporary accommodation through the agreement of rules."[14] Once these informal rules were agreed on, they came to be seen as "custom and practice" and were thus understood as legitimate by both workers and managers. Union shop stewards' committees came to play a central role in these hegemonic regimes by sanctioning workers who risked causing the entire system to break down. For example, shop stewards would ensure that pieceworkers did not excessively exceed the required output of a particular job or overzealously fix the job's piece rate in an attempt to increase their own earnings at the cost of making the enterprise too inefficient. Thus, the compromise equilibrium was actively maintained by the workers themselves.[15]

Paul Edwards and Hugh Scullion also documented how during this period some union shop stewards had an "impressive range of controls over effort, and the growth of these controls can be related to management's willingness to give up various aspects of managerial rights in exchange for continuous production."

While workers at another factory Edwards and Scullion studied had less control, there nevertheless existed a concrete coordination of interests and a compromise equilibrium that both managers and workers were committed to maintaining: "The company had developed a distinct 'welfarist' image, providing stable employment (together with such things as long-service pay awards) . . . Foremen in both plants were concerned to build up good working relationships . . . There was now more of an openly negotiatory stance. This reflected the development of steward organization during the late 1960s . . . Stewards were prepared to work within the system and to be, as managers often stressed, 'responsible.'"[16]

Most importantly during this period, even where workers lacked strong workplace bargaining power, hegemony often still existed, as a result of a management philosophy based on shared interests and genuine negotiation. Even workplaces that appeared more despotic were, nevertheless, usually based on the recognition of unions (whose officials were called upon by management when disputes arose) and other forms of collective regulation, job security, and relatively high wages. Accordingly, discipline was largely found to be rationalized, and if workers acted within the rules, they did not need to fear management.[17]

A study of a chemical plant by sociologists Theo Nichols and Huw Beynon is particularly illustrative of how hegemonic workplace regimes developed during this period. Management voluntarily signed a collective agreement with a union that created a closed shop (i.e., union membership was a prerequisite for and a condition of working at the factory), and union dues were deducted directly from the workers' pay. This was without the union ever having to actively run a widespread recruitment campaign. The collective agreement provided workers with relatively high pay, job security, and a profit share scheme. Shop floor relations were marked by the fact that managers did not "thrust their power in workers['] faces. They try *not* to let the iron fist behind the velvet glove show," and thus workers could use the union as an effective threat with which to sanction managers. Nichols and Beynon summarize that such workplace regimes were a "clear attempt to deal with and incorporate trade unionism . . . to the end of *subjecting the labor force to a degree of order, regulation and control*."[18] Likewise, sociologist Duncan Gallie highlighted that during this period, the formal structure of power could be legitimized by opening up key areas of decision making to negotiation, and that doing so could lead unions to help management secure workers' consent to workplace rules.[19]

Even in the midst of conflict, there could still be a tendency toward the concrete coordination of interests and development of a compromise equilibrium. Ford Motor Company is an exemplar of this trend. Henry Ford violently resisted unionization until 1941 in the United States, and only accepted unionization in the UK in 1944. Ford also continued to refuse to implement piecework (as payment by results was feared to cause upward wage drift) or to formally yield control over manning decisions and workloads to unions. In the early 1960s, there remained a great deal of insecurity and favoritism at Ford, especially with regard to the allocation of overtime, which fueled conflict over job control.

Nevertheless, Ford did sign collective agreements with the unions, and these agreements provided, among other things, a developed grievance procedure. Moreover, day-to-day acts of resistance (such as verbally abusing foremen, small acts of sabotage, and unofficial walkouts) were highly effective at undermining management control—so much so that, by the late 1960s, the union shop stewards' committee had managed to gain a degree of job control in those areas that did not seriously threaten profits. The job controls that shop stewards had wrestled from management included control of assembly line speeds, overtime, work allocation, and, in some sections, decisions over time off. This control became so extensive that shop stewards were able to decide which workers would be allocated which tasks. By the late 1960s, even at Ford, foremen were forced to make compromises with workers on a daily basis. Foremen's control relied on asking workers to do favors so that production targets were met and, in return, allowing workers to take longer breaks, and so on. In short, a compromise equilibrium developed: "For most of the time they [union shop stewards] play negotiations management's way. They learn the limits of the game and in the routine of their lives in the plant they tend not to step outside them: 'You can't fight a battle every day.'"

Therefore, even in this conflictual workplace, despite the supposed militancy of the shop stewards, they maintained "a degree of internal discipline within the workforce . . . The nature of the relationship between the union and the employer can mean the steward rather than the manager disciplines individual workers for not working properly."[20]

Another example of the operation of a hegemonic regime in the UK is provided in sociologist Anna Pollert's study of "low-skilled" female workers at an Imperial Tobacco factory.[21] This is an interesting case study, as it has been held up as an example of nonhegemonic direct control and used as a critical case with which to attack Burawoy's workplace regime framework.[22] However, the hegemonic tendency is in fact clearly evident. Here too, union membership had, since the Second World War, been encouraged by the company. Moreover, "the company prided itself on its good labor relations, co-operation rather than confrontation." Supervision was, in fact, much more subtle than it had been twenty years earlier; strict discipline was "not necessary" because the workforce "had their hands tied . . . by the incorporation of trade unionism into management." As one worker reflected, it was "not so strict in here. I expected a factory to be . . . real strict."[23]

Although there was a clear tendency during this era for UK workplace regimes to develop a compromise equilibrium institutionalized through mechanisms that concretely coordinated the interests of capital and labor, there was no guarantee that workplace regimes would take this form. For instance, sociologist Miriam Glucksmann (a.k.a. Ruth Cavendish) provides evidence of how the tendency toward concrete coordination of interests among low-skilled female factory workers broke down. While the speedometer factory she studied operated a closed shop, and a bonus system also existed, the extremely poor and worsening terms and conditions, along with the harsh discipline by supervisors, meant that there was no hegemonic compromise equilibrium.[24]

The End of Hegemony

In the 1970s, core capitalist countries such as the UK were gripped by a crisis of relative profitability as information technology made possible global product markets and increased competition. The solution to this crisis lay in the transition to "flexible accumulation." This required the overcoming of "rigidities" brought about by the regulation of employment, labor, financial, and product markets that lay at the heart of the hegemonic era.[25] A consequence of attempts by firms (with state backing) to curtail such rigidities is that the late twentieth and early twenty-first centuries have been marked by an extraordinary decline of unions in the UK, especially in the private sector. Not only have union membership and collective bargaining coverage declined dramatically, but so too have the scale and scope of labor movement collective action, most obviously strike activity. By 2013, collective bargaining coverage had declined dramatically in the private sector to just 16 percent.[26] Even where employers have continued to recognize unions and nominally engage in collective bargaining, there has been a process of "procedural individualization" of employment relations, whereby collective mechanisms for determining terms and conditions of employment are weakened or abolished. Procedural individualization can, arguably, be equated with the de facto de-recognition of unions.[27]

In the context of the disintegration of the compromise equilibrium upon which hegemonic workplace regimes were based, the question then arises as to how control is maintained in flexible low-end service sector workplaces. It is this question that this chapter seeks to answer with regard to the UK. To do so it presents an in-depth ethnographic case study to investigate the contemporary internal state of an exemplar UK firm, referred to in the chapter as PartnershipCo.

Investigating Workplace Control in the UK

Over the space of a year in 2012–13, I observed union organizing at four PartnershipCo hypermarkets. Five days of union organizing, three union team meetings, and a union branch meeting in a hypermarket were also observed, and the meetings recorded. I met with two senior members of the union leadership and collected documents, such as the staff policy handbook, union collective agreement, union representative scheduling guide, and union rep flexible scheduling guide. Toward the end of my research, an opportunity to gain a deeper insight into the lived experience of work at PartnershipCo presented itself, and I undertook two months of participant observation at the Mulling Point hypermarket (a pseudonym) in North London. The Mulling Point store had a workforce of approximately 200 employees, and this participant observation involved working 8.5 contracted hours per week as a shelf stacker. Work issues were also discussed with colleagues in the canteen before the shifts began and during the train commute to work. In order to complement the observational, experiential, and documentary data, thirty-nine semi-structured interviews were held with thirty-five PartnershipCo informants (workers, labor union reps, and labor union officials).[28]

PartnershipCo was (and continues to be) a dominant retailer in its domestic oligopolistic retail market, and is also one of the largest global retailers, with operations in dozens of other countries. PartnershipCo had hundreds of thousands of employees in the UK and used its size to take advantage of significant economies of scale and to squeeze producers. However, the rise of online shopping represented a major challenge, as it reduced one of the company's main competitive advantages—owning numerous hypermarkets. Therefore, while making large profits, PartnershipCo had also experienced recent pressures to cut costs.

Workers' Power and Rights at PartnershipCo

In sketching the internal state at PartnershipCo, it makes sense to begin by considering the bargaining power of the workforce and the rights to which they were entitled. Workers at PartnershipCo recognized that their livelihoods were highly dependent on their employers. Indeed, they had little confidence that they had adequate alternative sources of income with which to replace lost wages, in the form of either sufficient savings or state benefits. The workers who felt slightly less dependent were those who had second jobs to fall back on. The global economic crisis and resulting high levels of unemployment had created a pervasive view among many informants that there were few realistic alternatives available to them.

They did, however, have some employment rights that were codified through legally binding written contracts. The forms that these contracts could take were specified in the collective agreement with the recognized union. Accordingly, there were three types of contract that workers could be employed on:

> Temporary: Used to cover peak trading times and limited to a maximum of twelve weeks' employment. These contracts required that workers be

given only one week's notice before termination, except in cases of gross misconduct, where no notice was required.

Permanent full-time (36.5 hours a week) or part-time (a minimum of 4.5 hours a week): Workers employed for more than a month on one of these contracts, except in cases of gross misconduct, were guaranteed four weeks' paid notice with an additional week's notice for every year of service after their fifth year, up to a maximum of twelve weeks— representing considerably more protection than the statutory minimum.

Flexible: These contracts could be temporary or permanent, but a worker employed on one would receive only ten to sixteen core hours of work per week. Workers could then be "flexed up" with additional hours that fell during a period in which they had declared themselves available for work. As long as the workers were given twenty-four hours' notice, they could not refuse these additional hours. PartnershipCo's policy stated that additional flexed hours should only amount to approximately 60 percent of a worker's core hours.

The protections granted to workers through their contracts and enshrined in the collective agreement curbed managers' ability to elicit compliance through fear of dismissal. In addition, use of temporary contracts—which provided workers with much less employment protection—was limited by the collective agreement. Moreover, as detailed in part 2, the additional training and recruitment costs associated with temporary workers made the extensive use of such workers unattractive to PartnershipCo. This meant that a significant core/periphery distinction, which is central to many existing accounts of "flexible despotism," was not present.

However, reality did not always reflect the policies enshrined in the collective agreement. Managers at the workplace level occasionally flouted these rules, usually with regard to flexible contracts (as documented in chapter 3). At Mulling Point, where I worked as a shelf stacker, management also did not follow the rules surrounding temporary employment. Temporary staff taken on over the peak Christmas period were not given written contracts to sign, nor were they informed of their employment status. Workers who were in fact employed on a temporary fixed-term basis had their employment status incorrectly described by managers as being "flexible" in that either party could end the employment or alter the shifts worked by giving five days' notice. This caused much confusion among workers, including myself, especially as none of us were ever informed of the end date of our employment or told that one even existed. In fact, I discovered that I was a temporary worker accidently only when I asked my manager to provide me with a copy of the contract for my records at the end of my fieldwork. To my surprise it included a fixed end date! Up to this point, it had been repeatedly implied to me that demonstrating a high level of performance would result in my position being made permanent.

This use of temporary contracts to audition workers for a permanent position was clearly contrary to their intended use as laid out in the collective agreement. However, a recurring theme of life at PartnershipCo was the struggle surrounding enforcement of company policies. This struggle sometimes led to a striking disparity between the official company policies and how PartnershipCo's workplace regime was constituted in practice. Nevertheless, it is clear that the employment status granted to workers at PartnershipCo provided them with considerably more employment protection than the UK statutory minimum.

Labor Unions, Conflict, and Integration

On the face of it, workers at PartnershipCo appeared to have a high level of associational power via their union and the existence of collective bargaining. A "partnership" collective agreement was at the heart of PartnershipCo's internal state. Partnership agreements center around employer support for unionization and employment security while unions in return agree to support flexibility and productivity and to focus their campaigning on issues that provide mutual gains for both workers and employers. Industrial relations expert John Kelly suggests that partnership agreements can be classified according to an "employer-dominated" or "labor parity" typology that is determined by the balance of power between the employer and the union.[29] The findings presented below suggest that the agreement at PartnershipCo was an employer-dominated agreement. The fact that PartnershipCo had seriously considered de-recognition before opting for a partnership, combined with the fact that the union was reliant on PartnershipCo for the majority of its membership, adds credence to this view.

Over the previous half decade, the union had experienced strong growth in both membership and density. Both the interviews and observation of union recruitment indicate that this was in part a result of the union's heavy emphasis on recruitment. However, the union's efforts were also facilitated by the access to workers that the collective agreement guaranteed. At the time of the research, union density at PartnershipCo stood at over 60 percent nationally, nearly five times the sector average of 13 percent.

Many of PartnershipCo's company policies had been collectively agreed with the union and codified in the 142-page Partnership Agreement. This agreement outlined the nature of the relationship between the union and PartnershipCo. The agreement ensured union involvement in consultative committees at store, regional, and national levels, and created a pay consultation and agreement mechanism. Grievance and disciplinary procedures and the process for discontinuing or changing a worker's job role or hours were also covered by the agreement. These procedures guaranteed workers the right to be represented by union reps at all the stages. In addition, union reps themselves had the right to be represented by full-time union officials. The formal role of union reps during the above processes was to help support the workers, to speak on their behalf, and to act as a witness. A large body of other company policies existed and were made available to union reps and officials. Furthermore, all individual workers were, in theory, made aware of the basic policies and rights that these policies conferred upon them through the seventy-five-page employee handbook. Union officials and reps explained during the research interviews that much of the union's work went into making sure that both managers and workers were aware of company policies and followed them.

These company policies provided union reps and officials with leverage on a wide range of issues, especially as they often had a better grasp of them than their managers did. However, the focus the union placed on enforcing these policies also meant that no matter how unjust or inflammatory an issue was perceived to be by the workforce, the default position of union reps was that if it had been carried out by managers according to the stated policy, then it was legitimate. This emphasis on enforcing the company policies confined any struggle between workers and managers within a narrow framework. Moreover, the policies that constituted this framework were not all the result of bilateral agreement between the union and PartnershipCo. In effect, union reps and officials explained that their role was to ensure that the company policies were followed, rather than to promote collective questioning of the fairness of these policies. Thus, they did not seek to campaign or mobilize around injustices, even when they themselves felt that a company policy was unjust (such as the precarious scheduling discussed in chapter 3).

We can see, then, that at PartnershipCo there were some hegemonic practices by which the union and collective agreement functioned to maintain control by keeping contentious issues off the table. Therefore, the greater potential associational power of workers at PartnershipCo, compared with workers at ConflictCo in the United States, was limited to the spheres of workplace politics sanctioned by the company and institutionalized by the collective agreement. In other words, conflict was focused almost exclusively on whether managers followed PartnershipCo's policies correctly. Workers lacked structural power, but they did have some degree of associational power. This restricted managers' ability to secure control through traditional despotic threats of job loss.

Surveillance

A key factor determining the ability of managers to secure control by punishing workers for transgressions is the effectiveness of surveillance. If managers are unaware of workers' behavior in the first place, they cannot take action against it. However, as highlighted in the introduction, it is not only the actual surveillance of workers that is important for control. Building on the work of Michel Foucault, a number of researchers have argued that high levels of workplace surveillance lead workers to self-enforce and internalize the values of their managers and firms. Such claims have tended to overstate the power of surveillance and understate workers' ability to find novel means of resistance. Nevertheless, surveillance is important in shaping forms of resistance.[30]

The degree of surveillance at PartnershipCo was variable and far from comprehensive. Some jobs had greater degrees of technological surveillance, such as online delivery drivers whose route and progress were tracked by GPS. Pickers in the online-only stores had strict pick rates (i.e., rates at which goods were picked off the shelf, scanned, and placed in the box for distribution) that were monitored and enforced by managers. Cashiers in brick-and-mortar stores had their scan rate monitored to ensure that they were processing goods through the checkout fast enough. If the scan rate dropped below a certain level, they would be disciplined. However, at the same time, they were also expected to carry out customer service tasks, such as asking if the customer had a loyalty card, packing customers' bags, and generally providing emotional labor. These customer service tasks and emotional labor were monitored via the use of mystery shoppers.

Customers themselves can also be an active component of surveillance in retail work.[31] However, in practice at PartnershipCo, unless a worker was deliberately rude, it was unlikely a customer would take the time to make an official complaint. After a few weeks of working at PartnershipCo, I myself had few qualms about letting the customers see my annoyance as I told them not to mess up the shelves I had just sorted and arranged. In fact, my line manager set an example of how to deal with customers who asked where products were located by fobbing them off with vague directions so that the "more important work" of getting stock onto the shop floor could be continued.

A hint at the future of workplace surveillance at PartnershipCo may be gleaned from the fact that a union official informed me how, in a few of his stores, PartnershipCo was trialing a device that measured the speed at which stock was being stacked by hand on the shelves. But this form of surveillance was some years away from being widely implementable. The majority of the surveillance at the time of the research in 2012–2013 remained dependent on managerial presence on the shop floor. At certain times, this could be significant; at others, it was only a minor element of the internal state and not an overbearing experience.

Moreover, the perception of surveillance via closed circuit television (CCTV) cameras at PartnershipCo did not loom large in the experience of the workplace regime. There were plenty of cameras, but the feeling was that there was usually nobody monitoring them, especially in terms of surveillance of the labor process. Lacking video cameras and, as yet, task management technology, managerial surveillance at PartnershipCo was on the whole perceived as variable and intermittent rather than constant. In particular, the level of managerial surveillance was felt to vary depending on a manager's relationship with a particular worker, how trusting they were, and how busy the store was.

Disciplinary Procedures: Rationalized Discipline

A central company policy shaping the pattern of control in a workplace is the disciplinary procedure. It is, therefore, worthwhile looking at these policies in more detail. At PartnershipCo, the collective agreement specified in detail the burdensome procedures that managers were to follow when disciplining workers whose behavior or job performance had "fallen behind the required standard." In doing so, it limited the manner in which managers could use the formal disciplinary mechanism to secure control in the workplace.

The disciplinary procedure at PartnershipCo provided workers with a number of important protections against arbitrary managerial discipline. It was also a costly procedure for managers—it was arduous, time-consuming, and potentially embarrassing. Managers had to record all acts of discipline in order to move the worker to the next stage. Another manager had to carry out an investigation and keep notes on all meetings. The worker being disciplined and their union representative would have access to these notes, along with written notice of why the worker was being disciplined, how they could avoid being further disciplined, and the time frame in which they had to improve.

The fact that workers had the right to have a union rep present and could appeal a decision meant that managers were forced to demonstrate that a satisfactory investigation had been undertaken and that they had followed due process, showing that there was a just cause for discipline according to fairness and precedent. During appeals against the first three stages, the investigation and rationale would have to stand up to interrogation by a union rep and, during the final stage, to interrogation by a full-time union official. Moreover, this interrogation would be heard by the manager's own line manager and, at the final stages of appeal, by a senior manager from outside the store.

Embarrassment in front of a more senior manager was thus a potential cost for a manager who decided to discipline a worker without good cause or who did not follow the disciplinary procedure correctly. This provided a large amount of scope for union officials and well-trained union reps to protect workers from managerial discipline, especially through the appeals process. For example, union reps and officials explained how they could shield workers from manager discipline by demonstrating that the procedure had not been followed correctly or that the decision was not consistent with other similar cases. For these reasons, it was felt that the union's institutionalized role in the disciplinary process provided workers with a relatively large degree of protection from the threat of dismissal. Jeff (a union rep) explained how PartnershipCo "isn't the worst employer. To get sacked from PartnershipCo is very very hard and on the whole they do follow the procedures because we have 168,000 members and they are pretty good but only because of the union influence."

The collective agreement then provided reps with an effective tool with which to limit managers' scope for despotism by reducing manager discretion and rationalizing discipline. Anna (another union rep) explained:

> When you say to a manager "Have you read the collective agreement?" and they say "no," that's when you know you've got them 'cause if you say "actually if you go on to page nine, chapter three, and you'll see that what I'm telling you is correct and what you're saying is not correct" and then they suddenly flick around for it in the drawer and they say "oh, that's right" . . . Without it there would be disciplinaries going right, left and center and there would be people losing their job right, left and center . . . It is all stated there in black and white and it's all clear about disciplinaries, what levels of disciplinary, how to move it to a disciplinary, how to issue a warning and all that, how many verbal warnings and written warnings and all that. Whereas some managers don't want to give a verbal; they want to go straight to written and they want it to be their final written, but they can't do that . . . and a lot of managers don't realize until you point it out to them, but that's the best tool, having that partnership agreement and that's why I think it's good that all reps get a copy of that partnership agreement.

Individualization of Indignation: The Grievance Procedures

Another policy central to shaping workplace control is the grievance procedure. Formal grievance complaints place a particular manager's behavior under scrutiny and may even result in managers themselves facing sanctions. Therefore, the degree to which the internal state limits or aids workers in their ability to raise complaints above the heads of their immediate superiors can have a powerful impact on the pattern of control. In most workplaces, the formal grievance procedure provides an institutionalized mechanism for raising complaints.

At PartnershipCo, the collective agreement specified a detailed grievance procedure. After raising a workplace issue informally with their line manager, workers could raise a formal grievance if their manager had not gotten back to them with a solution in fourteen days. An investigation was then carried out, and the grievance was heard within seven days by their line manager with a union rep accompanying the worker. The worker then had the option to move the grievance to the next stage. If the worker decided to do so, a second hearing would be arranged within two weeks and heard by a senior manager. This procedure provided a means for workers to voice their complaints that managers could not simply ignore.

Tellingly, there was no procedure for collective grievances at PartnershipCo that would have provided a means for workers to challenge management as a united group. Rather, the collective agreement detailed how such issues were to be raised through worker representatives at store-level, regional, and national employee consultation committees. But these committees met irregularly. Moreover, they restricted worker participation, with just a handful of worker representatives attending the store-level committees. Area consultation committees further restricted worker representation, with just one worker rep elected by each store consultation committee. Only a tiny percentage of the workforce was on the national consultation committee, which was elected from each area consultation committee. This process, therefore, detached collective issues—and the reps raising them—from the workplaces. Consequently, workers lacked the collective power with which to successfully influence management. As Lee (a union official) explained: "The way PartnershipCo and the union do our negotiations is through the consultation committee processes . . . and quite a lot of these things [grievances concerning precarious scheduling] are negotiated at the area consultation stage and then pushed down to the stores. It's, you know, if I'm completely honest, it feels like one-way traffic at times from PartnershipCo."

Therefore, the main mechanism for raising grievances, even when they were of a collective nature, was through the individual grievance procedure. This meant

that workers' collective problems were individualized. This made collective responses, which would have had the potential to shift the frontier of control by per-
manently wresting significant power away from managers, difficult to mobilize.
The individualization of indignation was reinforced by the fact that the grievance
procedure required workers with the issue to raise the grievance themselves rather
than a rep being able to raise an issue on behalf of one of their members. A major
frustration for union reps was the difficulty of persuading workers to pursue a
grievance when they felt vulnerable, victimized, and scared. This issue will be revisited in subsequent chapters when discussing why the union and the internal state at
PartnershipCo had little impact on precarious scheduling and when explaining the
lack of collective resistance at PartnershipCo compared with ConflictCo.

The grievance procedure had a hegemonic function, in that it both protected
workers from despotism and also kept issues off the agenda and acted as a brake
on the development of collective challenges to managerial control. For example,
I observed at a rep team meeting how the rule that workers with an issue must
raise the grievance themselves had become elevated to a norm that constrained
union responses to injustice. During this meeting, the assumption that managers would class a grievance as legitimate only if it was raised by the individual concerned effectively stopped the store's reps from attempting a collective response
to a perceived injustice. This was in spite of the fact that the rule could only apply
to individual grievances, as there was no procedure for collective grievances:

> MARK (UNION REP PartnershipCo): What I think is the way forward
> is for us to raise a grievance as a union.
> RYAN (UNION OFFICIAL, PartnershipCo): What you've gotta be care-
> ful of is that they might turn this around, "this as your personal cru-
> sade, it's nothing to do with her, she's perfectly happy because she's
> not raised it as an issue through the [grievance procedure]."
> NEIL (UNION REP PartnershipCo): Yeah but is it a personal crusade?
> Or is it for the fact they have not been engaging and following what
> they should be doing?
> RYAN: It's not a personal crusade but they will accuse you.
> NEIL: Well, that's why we do it as a collective.
> MARK: No, this is like in chess we have to think two or three moves ahead.

This example highlights how the internal state at PartnershipCo entailed a systematic bias that made it difficult for workers to voice their dissatisfaction. In
this way the internal state mobilized bias to aid labor control at PartnershipCo.

Despite the developed grievance procedure, PartnershipCo workers also provided many examples of overt managerial abuse, such as verbal bullying and
threats, indifference, and aloofness. In fact, our store manager at the Mulling Point

store would not even speak to us directly, even when a purposeful hello was directed at him. Instead he relayed orders via our line managers even when he was stood next to us. However, if workers were union members and there was at least one good union rep at their workplace, it was likely that the union would put an end to any abuse. Union reps could protect workers against informal despotism by informing the workers of their rights, thereby empowering them to make use of the grievance procedure. Reps could also protect workers against formal despotism by defending them in disciplinaries. In fact, the interviews suggest that many reps had become active in the union following their own experience of overcoming manager despotism by deploying the mechanisms provided by PartnershipCo's internal state. It was not only a major reason why union members became reps, but was also a major reason why people joined the union in the first place. This is not to deny that managerial abuse continued to be a major issue for many workers, but to emphasize that there were institutional remedies available to curtail managers' despotism. Many workers had found these mechanisms effective, and this had frequently propelled them to become more active in the union as a result.

Concrete Concessions: Profit Share Schemes, Bonuses, and Pay

So far, we have seen that PartnershipCo had a number of hegemonic features that both protected workers from individual managerial despotism and controlled the agenda so as to avoid collective worker challenges to the workplace regime. In this section, we consider the degree to which the interests of labor and capital were concretely coordinated.

Workers' interests were principally tied to their employers through a profit share scheme and a (relatively good) defined benefit pension scheme. Up until the year of the research, it had been customary for workers to receive bonus shares worth a couple of percentage points of their pay. However, during the year of the fieldwork, PartnershipCo decided not to award any shares due to declining profitability. It was clear from the informants that the nonpayment of this bonus was a source of significant outrage, amplified by the perceived unfairness of the replacement cash bonus. This cash bonus would only be received after a further three years' service, with workers who left in the meantime losing the bonus altogether. PartnershipCo suggested that the union had been consulted on this replacement payment, a claim the union strenuously denied. Nonetheless, this caused a great deal of antipathy toward the union.

The collective agreement took pay negotiations out of the workplace, and they were instead carried out at a national level by the National Employee Consultation

Committee. Pay negotiations, therefore, seemed very remote to the average worker on the shop floor. The workers' only input was to cast a vote in the election of representatives to their store consultation committee. These representatives then elected a representative from among themselves to attend a higher committee, which in turn elected one of its own members to attend a higher body to vote on the pay deal and potentially be chosen by the union's national officer to carry out the pay negotiations. The use of this committee system to agree to pay deals, instead of balloting members, as had happened before the partnership agreement, limited direct say on pay to a tiny percentage of workers.

As shown in figure 1, the system of pay negotiations had delivered real pay decreases for four out of the five years prior to the fieldwork (2009 being marked by extremely low inflation;[32] see table 2). As a result, pay in real terms at PartnershipCo in 2012 was around 15 percent lower than in 2007. Moreover, workers at PartnershipCo received smaller real pay rises than the average UK worker every year apart from 2009. This meant that, despite having a union density that was more than twice as high as the UK average, workers at PartnershipCo accepted a decline in real pay between 2007 and 2012 that was worse than that of the average UK employee. With regard to pay, this suggests that since the onset of the Great Recession, collective bargaining at PartnershipCo had served to win concessions for capital at the expense of labor.

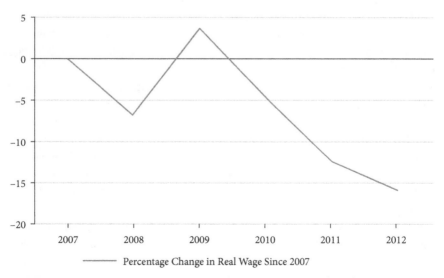

— Percentage Change in Real Wage Since 2007

FIGURE 1. Percentage Change in PartnershipCo Real Wage since 2007

Note: PartnershipCo pay deals 2008–2012 adjusted for Retail Price Index (RPI) UK inflation.
Source: PartnershipCo figures provided by the union.

TABLE 2 PartnershipCo real pay rises vs. average UK pay growth

YEAR	PARTNERSHIPCO BASIC PAY RISE (%)	AVERAGE RPI INFLATION (%)	REAL BASIC PARTNERSHIPCO PAY RISE (%)	AVERAGE UK REAL PAY GROWTH (%)	DIFFERENCE (%)
2008	3.8	4.0	−0.2	0.02	−0.22
2009	2.5	−0.6	3.1	0.08	3.02
2010	2.3	4.6	−2.3	−0.67	−1.63
2011	2.7	5.2	−2.5	−0.78	−1.72
2012	2.0	3.2	−1.2	−0.45	−0.75
Average	2.66	3.52	−0.62	−0.36	−0.26

Sources: Taylor, Jowett, and Hardie, *An Examination of Falling Real Wages, 2010–2013*; PartnershipCo figures provided by the union.

The Union and Normative Control

As we have seen above, while the union provided workers with significant employment security and other benefits, it also institutionalized bias toward the interests of capital and kept certain issues off the agenda. However, the union also played a further ideological role by legitimizing certain aspects of the workplace regime, thereby partially obscuring workers' understanding of their situation. As long as company policy was correctly followed, the union justified controversial management practices such as precarious scheduling.

Sociologist Duncan Gallie's case study of a British refinery during the hegemonic era demonstrates how union reps do not represent a simple one-way transmission of neutral information from workers to managers. Rather, they also transmit information from managers to workers; and what they convey, and the manner in which it is conveyed, will be shaped by the wider political and symbolic practices they encounter.[33] Likewise, industrial relations scholars Eric Batstone, Ian Boraston, and Stephen Frenkel detail how union reps on some occasions act as delegates who reflect the views of their members, but on others they initiate and suppress issues and decide how issues are dealt with, as well as instilling particular priorities and views in members.[34] An illustration of this process at PartnershipCo is provided by Asim, a union rep, who saw his role as helping PartnershipCo achieve flexibility by eliciting a mind-set among workers in which they would be willing to compromise:

> If they haven't got legitimate concerns or legitimate reasons why they
> can't change their hours then the manager will expect and the company
> and the store will expect them to change their hours, so I will try and
> get them in that mind-set. Rather than [have them] say "Oh no I can't

change my hours because I do X." "What is X? Can you be a bit more flexible?" So I try and get them to be a bit more flexible and understand the reasons why they [managers] are trying to change it. You will get individuals who won't want to change their hours no matter what and there's nothing you can do for them . . . apart from explaining to them what the consequences are.

Similarly, John (a union officer) explained that the union could not campaign around precarious scheduling despite the discontent surrounding the issue. All the union could do, in his view, was to seek a compromise through negotiation: "We've [the union] not done any big campaigns on this [precarious scheduling] as we are the big losers; all we can really do is help them [workers] through the process, try and negotiate with the company, go in there with the lad [and represent them] . . . and if the company is reasonable then they will meet us half way and put something together, but it's pointless campaigning on something you can't win on."

One union rep, Toby, had completely internalized the employer's logic that what was legitimate was that which benefited the company's bottom line rather than the needs of the workers he was elected to represent: "There is obviously a business need for it and the union wants PartnershipCo and supermarkets to do well for members and things like that and employment."

This union rep's level of identification with the interests of his employer over the interests of his members was an extreme example. It is, nevertheless, telling of the internal conflicts that other union reps faced, for the union reps commonly saw their role as being to "balance the needs of the business with the needs of the worker."

Moreover, a recurrent view among union officers and organizers was that the campaigns the union encouraged nationally did not deal with the key issues in the workplace, such as the problems caused by flexible scheduling. Though union reps and officers were taught "issue-based campaigning," whereby campaigns are focused on discontentment in the workplace,[35] they did not generally practice it. Mobilization theory highlights the central importance of employers and unions in framing issues within the workplace.[36] In this case, rather than seeking to mobilize around discontentment through campaigning on these issues, the union's campaigns were instead focused on issues that provided mutual gains for both workers and PartnershipCo, including campaigns on lifelong learning and how to deal with customer abuse of staff. As Jimmy (a union representative) described in detail: "We can campaign on a lot of things, one thing is about learning, we campaign on that, about bringing up their educational qualifications, it's free, it's great, it gets people involved, but there is still issues on pay, there is still issues on pensions and if we do realistic campaigns or realistic surveys which are about what really affects us, and what affects us, at the end of the day, is our pay."

The fact that the union did not campaign on major workplace issues such as precarious scheduling reduced the opportunity for it to play an active role in framing issues that were contrary to PartnershipCo's interests. This seemed to be a deliberate element of the union's partnership approach. As Derek, a union rep, explained: "The union attempts to keep away from anything which is contentious; they like to do easy things like looking after children and stuff like that which nobody is going to argue about and nobody's going to say that's wrong . . . or fight racism, the Government or PartnershipCo isn't going to say we disagree with that, but like you say, Sunday trading, PartnershipCo would not like you going into their stores campaigning against Sunday trading . . . so I think they [the union] steer away [from contentious issues]."

Therefore, the union did little to counter precarious scheduling. In fact, it actually aided the smooth operation of firm temporal flexibility through managing the dissatisfaction generated by the insecurity over hours and schedules.

The union also supported increasing the age at which workers could claim their pension (from sixty-five to sixty-seven) and a tightening up of the attendance policy so that workers no longer received sick pay for the first three days of illness. However, this should not be understood as some kind of conspiracy (although this was a surprisingly common view among the workforce); the union was not always willing to act as a conduit for the interests of PartnershipCo. However, it did act according to a logic based on its leadership's understanding of its own organizational interests. Often these interests were deemed to align with those of PartnershipCo as a profit-making enterprise, but not always. Thus, it was not always in the union's own organizational interests to legitimize the workplace regime.

In fact, the high turnover at PartnershipCo required the union to recruit around a third of its membership each year just to maintain its existing membership level. Therefore, a heavy institutional emphasis was placed on recruitment. In order to meet their recruitment targets, union reps framed workplace issues in a way that was detrimental to managerial control—despite not framing their campaigns in such a manner.

I observed how union reps made use of the union's non-work-related benefits, such as promotional offers, when attempting to recruit new members. This might be expected, given the union's general nonconfrontational approach, but union reps also stressed the workplace benefits the union provided. By highlighting what the union could do for workers in the workplace and why they needed to join (whether it was to increase pay through bargaining, protect them in grievances and disciplinaries, or provide legal services), they actually heightened awareness of problems in the workplace surrounding these issues. For example, I observed that Jimmy's recruitment technique was based on stressing how intimidating the disciplinary meetings were for workers, but that the union equalized the institutional power imbalance and protected members by acting as a shield between them and managers. I also observed that Sara's (a union representative) approach was to frame the workers' position as precarious and the union as the only source of security within the workplace. On one occasion, she told a worker, "It was important to be in the union as it gives you 'job security, you never know what's around the corner'" (field notes, PartnershipCo).

On another occasion, I observed a similar approach for recruiting a temporary worker who had been kept on for five months without receiving a permanent contract (despite the company's policy of using this contract only for a maximum of twelve weeks): "Sara told her 'other people have then [i.e., after five months] still been got rid of.' She then focused on the union's legal services for workers going to the Employment Tribunal. The worker swiftly signed up" (field notes, PartnershipCo).

To a coworker who was considering leaving the union, Sara again framed the workplace as highly insecure for nonunion members, telling him, "'It's when you come out of the union that they get you'—she then told a story of someone who PartnershipCo tried to fire rather than making redundant in order to save on redundancy pay and emphasized that this happened as soon as he had left the union" (field notes, PartnershipCo).

While at times the union provided a normative control function, in doing so it followed its own logic, which was not always congruent with the interests of capital. Thus, the union did not always legitimize the workplace regime nor increase workers' integration into the firm. In fact, regarding some issues, union reps in particular would actively increase discontent by stressing negative aspects of the workplace in order to meet their own recruitment goals. A consequence was that, in terms of integrating workers into the workplace, the role of the union was at times dysfunctional.

Despotism or Hegemony?

The presence of collective bargaining and significant union presence at PartnershipCo raise the question of whether the internal state was hegemonic. An answer can be gleaned from the degree to which the relationship between capital and organized labor was of a quid pro quo nature and, thus, whether there existed a true concrete coordination of interests and a stable compromise equilibrium. However, as we have seen, the internal state repeatedly enabled PartnershipCo to benefit from the alteration of workers' terms and benefits. For example, pay negations resulted in the acceptance of declining real wages. The union also supported increasing the age at which workers could claim their pension from sixty-five to sixty-seven. While this was a source of anger among some workers, it was, nevertheless, much less contentious than might be expected, and its rationale was accepted by many. As Paul (a union rep) explained, "Although they changed it [the pension] slightly because of the nature of the stock market and stuff like that, it had to change but it is still one of the best pension schemes in the world."

A further example was PartnershipCo's unilateral decision not to give workers their customary bonus shares. When PartnershipCo communicated this decision, it stated that the union had been consulted, even though this was not the case. The union was evidently used as a rubber stamp for what was a very unpopular decision. However, despite the union's outrage, there were no negative consequences for PartnershipCo in using the union in this way.

We can conclude that the compromise equilibrium at PartnershipCo was in a state of disintegration due to the increasing competitive pressures faced by the company as a result of the growth of e-commerce. The breaking down of hegemony at PartnershipCo was reminiscent of the hegemonic despotism described earlier, in which the absence of a compromise equilibrium meant that hegemonic workplace institutions acted to extract concessions from organized labor. However, that is not to say that this form of internal state was of no benefit to the workers. The union and collective bargaining did provide workers with some associational power that translated into disciplinary and grievance procedures that limited the scope for arbitrary managerial despotism. However, these benefits were situated within a framework that ensured the continual extraction of concessions from labor and thus better enabled PartnershipCo to deal with the challenge presented by e-commerce.

This chapter has also demonstrated how the internal state at PartnershipCo limited the ability of managers to secure control via despotism in important ways. Hegemonic apparatuses rationalized discipline, constrained manager discretion, and provided workers with employment protections. This meant that there was an imperative for control to be secured via other, more subtle means—a dynamic explored in chapter 3. The next chapter will investigate the more despotic internal state at ConflictCo.

INTERNAL STATES IN THE U.S.

This chapter begins by investigating the historical development of internal states in the United States, before presenting a detailed account of the main features of the internal state of an exemplar U.S. firm: ConflictCo. This case study is particularly illuminating given that ConflictCo shares a position similar to PartnershipCo's in terms of its profile and domestic market position, while having a sharply contrasting internal state. As we have seen, PartnershipCo had a number of features that resembled those of the archetypical hegemonic regime, such as a recognized union, collective bargaining, and a fairly stable and harmonious industrial relations climate. ConflictCo, in contrast, represented a more despotic internal state—being famed for its hostility toward, avoidance of, and conflict with unions, along with its low pay and poor benefits. Interestingly, these two firms are reflective of more general differences in the UK and U.S. employment systems. While the strength of private sector unions in the UK has undergone a dramatic decline over the past thirty years, UK unions, nevertheless, remain significantly stronger than their U.S. counterparts. The UK also features greater statutory labor rights and protections than the United States. These differences are discussed further in the book's conclusion.

Market Despotism in the United States

In 1789, Samuel Slater risked treason to bring Richard Arkwright's water frame to New England. The first automated cotton mill followed shortly in 1793, as did

English factory discipline. With a constant oversupply of ethnically divided and desperate low-skilled workers, the workplace regimes in the nascent U.S. cotton industry quickly developed from paternalistic workplace regimes into the exemplar of Burawoy's market despotism.[1] Workers suffered strict overseers, low pay, and intense work. Lacking collective organization, they found that their only option was to accept the working conditions or leave the factory.[2] The rest of industry remained fairly small-scale but, nonetheless, of an equally oppressive nature, with workers being personally overseen by their entrepreneur owners.[3] Capital intensity and the size of factories increased with mechanized mass production in the late nineteenth century, bringing further deskilling[4] and more hierarchical workplace structures.[5]

This greater concentration of workers within increasingly hierarchical workplaces, along with constant threats of deskilling and continuing low pay, led to collective resistance through unions, as it did in Britain. However, here workers met with high levels of repressive violence. For example, two strikes at companies owned by the world's richest man, John Rockefeller Jr., resulted in mass killings: the 1914 Colorado miners' strike, which culminated in the deaths of at least fifty people, including eleven children, during the "Ludlow Massacre"; and, the following year, the Standard Oil of New Jersey strikes, which took the lives of at least nine workers.[6]

In total, between 1872 and 1914, an estimated 500 to 800 strikers were killed in the United States.[7] This violence was seemingly enabled by the fact that the vast majority of workers in key industries were foreign-born, and therefore denied democratic rights. For example, around 57 percent of iron and steel workers and between 60 percent and 73 percent of miners were classed as noncitizen "alien labor." In total, by 1920, around half of the white male working class were noncitizens who lacked democratic recourse in the face of oppression. Moreover, foreign-born workers who took part in strikes, or who were considered labor militants, could be deported. In fact, this was the fate of over 600,000 "alien radicals" who were deported during the first thirty years of the twentieth century. This made immigrant workers "cautious of joining unions, and it made a number of unions equally wary of organizing foreign workers."[8]

Labor organizers were also painted as outsiders with dangerous, foreign, and un-American beliefs, such as antireligious anarchism and communism. In the face of this supposed attack on American values, patriotism demanded that "respectable Americans" support law and order—in other words, the violent repression of the nascent labor movement.[9] Weakened by the violent onslaught of employers and the state, and marked by ethnic divisions, organized labor remained feeble during this period.[10]

It was not only strikes that were met with brutality; even more routine changes to the organization of the workplace were backed by violence. For example, in one case, a foreman punched and threatened workers with clubs in order to enforce a new piece rate. In the face of their organizational weakness and the coercive power of their employers, the main response of workers was simply to leave the workplace and try their luck elsewhere.[11]

Hence, the internal state faced by factory operatives was one characterized by the foreman's authority backed by the threat of dismissal and fines. As labor historian David Montgomery sums up, no matter their "task or what the method of payment . . . the working hours were subject to the virtually absolute authority of a foreman . . . Hiring and firing, assignment to tasks, setting the pay rate (by day or by piece), determining who got laid off or told to stay overtime, and the resolving of disputes all lay in the foreman's domain."[12]

However, labor turnover came to be seen as a considerable problem for employers, some of whom began experimenting with more paternalistic workplace regimes as a solution. Sky-high labor turnover led Henry Ford to introduce his famous five-dollar day in 1914. As sociologist Huw Beynon explains: "The motor industry at the time was a hire-and-fire industry. There were no seniority rights. Everyone was employed day-to-day. The plants were run by the iron hand and arbitrary justice of the foreman . . . Labor turnover rates were extremely high . . . In 1913 Ford required between 13,000 and 14,000 workers to run his plants at any one time, and in that year over 50,000 workers quit."[13]

These experiments in paternalism collapsed in the 1930s, due to the insecurity brought on by the Great Depression, causing "massive strike waves [that] assaulted production apparatuses as the sources of economic insecurity."[14]

Depression, Conflict, and the Development of Hegemony

The Great Depression of 1929–1939 rocked the world economy, and the great wave of insecurity that swept over the United States as a result intensified conflict between capital and workers. Workers struggled for protection against insecurity through campaigns for collective representation and state social insurance.[15] Moreover, during this period of heightened conflict, highly integrated continuous-flow production (such as assembly lines) developed in a number of industries. This greatly increased the bargaining power of workers, as small numbers of striking workers could shut down entire plants. This created an environment that was highly favorable for the formation of unions.[16] At a similar point in time, monopoly capitalism was cemented. Monopoly capitalism meant that giant corporations were able to capture greater profits due to their domination of the economy and constriction of product market competition.[17] Therefore, employers had greater financial means with which to provide concessions to their respective labor forces. In this environment, the regulation of class conflict and the further stabilization of competition became appealing to the newly enlarged industrial sector.[18]

However, workers' diminished purchasing power was leading to worsening crises of overproduction,[19] while elites feared that violent strikes would descend into full-blown rebellion and even working-class revolution.[20] Consequently, firms had an interest in increasing the wages of the workers employed by other firms in order to boost the market for their products. However, only an external body, the state, could achieve the creation of a minimal social wage at all firms, while also regulating conflict and competition. Thus, capital, labor, and elites all had an interest in increasing wages and reducing industrial conflict through the state interventions of the 1930s and 1940s, which established and solidified the conditions for hegemonic workplace regimes. As Burawoy puts it, "Anarchy in the market [during competitive capitalism] leads to despotism in the factory . . . Subordination of the market [during monopoly capitalism] leads to hegemony in the factory."[21]

The formation of hegemonic regimes was eased by lessons employers had learned from earlier failed paternalistic experiments. In particular, employers recognized that formal grievance and appeals procedures did not threaten their managerial prerogative. In fact, they increased worker satisfaction while resolving problems that, if left to fester, could act as sparks for collective action. Grievance procedures also individualized dissatisfactions, ensuring that they were less likely to become a collective matter. They also provided an independent check to ensure that supervisors and managers were following company policies. Additionally, employers learned that such independent checks were beneficial, as they rationalized behavior and legitimized control. Thus, these rules were legitimized and became akin to "law" within the workplace, despite being imposed by management on workers.[22] Apparently, even John D. Rockefeller Jr. became "a lifelong proponent of industrial relations and, in particular, collective employee voice" following the carnage and accompanying public outcry resulting from the Ludlow Massacre and the Standard Oil of New Jersey strikes.[23] As in Britain, the shift toward hegemonic regimes was finally cemented following the Second World War.[24]

As mentioned earlier, the role of the state was key to this transition. By introducing Social Security in 1935, the state increased workers' labor market bargaining power, as workers were no longer solely dependent on their wages for their survival. Additionally, legislation also provided institutional support for union recognition and collective bargaining. These increases in workers' labor market and institutional powers meant that workers were finally able to influence the regulation of labor within the workplace.[25] Legislation was also introduced that restricted the hours of work and established standards for health and safety.[26] These state interventions constrained management's freedom to discipline workers and thus shaped workplace regimes. At the macro level, there existed a "tripartite exchange among governments, unions, and business enterprises."[27] Governments and big business accepted unions, and governments also promoted full employment, while businesses passed on a share of profits from productivity gains to workers so that real wages grew. In return, unions accepted the managerial prerogative (i.e., the right of managers to manage).

From the late 1930s onward, workplaces in the United States were increasingly marked by bureaucratically organized rules, disciplinary and grievance procedures, and wage structures. These practices routinized many management functions and rationalized control. However, managers and supervisors were now also directed by rules and had supervisors themselves, so they could no longer formulate ad hoc punishments. Rather, they could only apply the company's regulations. If workers did not agree with their supervisor's or manager's treatment of them, they could now seek redress through the union or the company's appeal process. Thus, the "appeals process partially relieved the worker from the foreman's capriciousness, especially where a strong union could enforce the workers' rights."[28]

The End of Hegemony

As discussed in the previous chapter, in the 1970s hegemonic regimes in core capitalist countries came under pressure due to increased global competition. This caused a growing crisis of relative profitability in the United States and elsewhere. The response in the United States, as in the UK, was the move toward flexible accumulation and thus the destruction of the perceived rigidities that accompanied hegemonic internal states. The demise of hegemonic internal states in the United States can be seen most clearly in the decline of collective bargaining. In the 1950s, U.S. collective bargaining covered around a third of private sector workers, but by 2013 this was down to just 7 percent.[29]

Investigating Control at ConflictCo

In order to study control in the U.S. retail sector, I participated in and observed union-led organizing drives at six ConflictCo stores in the Los Angeles and San Francisco Bay areas from mid-February to mid-March 2013, and again in December 2013. I attended two weekly union organizer meetings, two worker activist meetings, two worker activist national video conference calls, and three community ally meetings. Documentary data, such as the staff policy handbook, staff magazine, and newspaper articles, was also collected. This experiential, observational, and documentary data was supported by forty-two semi-structured interviews with thirty-three informants (including workers, a former manager, union organizers, and one senior union official). The ConflictCo worker informants were drawn from a dozen stores, five in the Los Angeles area and seven in the San Francisco Bay area.[30]

Despotism "At Will"

ConflictCo was one of the dominant retailers in both its domestic market and in the world, and also had a huge domestic workforce of over a million, with around 100,000 employees in California alone. Like PartnershipCo, ConflictCo used its size to achieve economies of scale and squeeze producers. However, as in the UK, the rise of e-commerce represented a major threat and created pressures to cut costs. ConflictCo's workforce were highly dependent on the firm for their livelihoods, often being drawn from areas with high levels of unemployment, and lacking savings and alternative options. This dependence was compounded by precarious scheduling, which made it difficult for workers to secure a second job or engage in education or training activities in order to improve their employability (this is discussed in greater detail in chapter 4). Like the workers at PartnershipCo, this dependence was frequently given as a reason for the acceptance of poor working conditions.

Not only were workers highly dependent on ConflictCo, they were also offered little protection by the state. The most important law shaping the dynamics of workplace politics at ConflictCo was *at-will employment*, which operates in most states in the United States. This created an employment status in which workers lacked an implicit or explicit legally binding employment contract. Accordingly, managers were free to end a worker's employment at any time for almost any reason without notice. Workers, equally, had the right to end their employment, but, in reality, the lack of labor market opportunities and dependency on ConflictCo made doing so an unattractive option for most. Moreover, ConflictCo was keen to make workers aware of their weak employment status. For example, most of ConflictCo's company policies included a disclaimer at the end of them stating: "This information does not create an express or implied contract . . . Employment at ConflictCo is on an at-will basis, which means that ConflictCo or the associate can terminate the employment relationship at any time for any reason or no reason, consistent with applicable law."

All of the informants emphasized how managers were keen to make clear to workers that they could easily be fired. How such threats translate into control is fairly obvious, but Akira (former worker, ConflictCo) illustrated it particularly clearly: "Managers tell you you're replaceable . . . 'Either you can do it this way or you can do it the other way—out the door.'"

This power was amplified by managers directly linking these threats to the weak labor market position of the workers. Andre (a worker) provides a lucid but typical example of the common manner in which managers heightened workers' insecurity by playing on the ease of their replacement: "They'll tell us that 'we get 400 applications a day, and this is the job, if you don't want to do the job we'll replace you with someone who does.'"

Managers' ability to routinely dismiss workers at will was not merely hypothetical, and their threats were not merely rhetorical. Informants described how managers did, in fact, frequently dismiss workers without difficulty. This despotism translated directly into control, as Omar (a worker) made clear: "They'll hire people and they will like fire like three of your friends, so they'll have you worried like oh man they're hiring people, they might fire me so I've gotta get on with my job and make sure I don't do anything wrong."

In fact, between the two fieldwork trips undertaken for this study, three of the informants were dismissed following their involvement in the worker association. Thus, the lack of employment protection granted to workers by "at-will" employment status provided managers with an important source of control. Managers could mobilize this as a means of control via threats to dismiss workers and replace them with more compliant individuals. Additionally, managers' personal relations with workers were experienced as being dictatorial and abusive, with workers being humiliated in front of coworkers and customers. Managers routinely patronized, shouted at, and insulted employees, for example, calling them lazy, incompetent, stupid, and worthless. Managers also frequently threatened workers with disciplinary action and job loss. The degree to which these sources of despotic control were tempered by other elements of ConflictCo's internal state is developed below.

Union Hostility and Conflict

ConflictCo as a company was extremely hostile to unions and, in the past, had even closed a store following a vote for unionization. A prominent human rights organization had gone as far as to claim that ConflictCo breached U.S. workers' right to freedom of association. ConflictCo set its workplace policies and rules unilaterally with no worker or union input. According to the "ConflictCo Policy

Guide," behavior at ConflictCo was supposedly dictated by over seventy policies that prescribed everything from how grievances were to be raised and discipline administered to the dress code and how drug screenings would take place. However, the workers were not provided with a physical policy book. Instead, employees could access and print off these policies only through the workplace intranet.[31] Without having them physically to hand, it was difficult for workers to know the details of the policies, and they were unable to look them up without arousing their manager's suspicions.

Informants claimed that the policies were frequently changed by head office without notification, and that managers used these changes as a way to discipline unsuspecting workers. The workers' lack of knowledge regarding the policies also meant that managers could break those policies with impunity and, thus, impinge on the few rights that ConflictCo's internal state granted them. Without knowledge of the policies, informants suggested that it was often impossible to raise grievances: workers were unaware whether or not a manager was breaking a policy in the first place. It also meant that it was difficult for workers to avoid being disciplined, and they also struggled to defend themselves. In general, the policies were unknown and said to be highly unstable. Reflecting this, the informants displayed little trust in the company's policies as a set of neutral rules created to ensure the fair and efficient conduct of both workers and managers.

The Worker Association

At the time of the research in 2013, there was in fact a union supporting ConflictCo workers in building a worker association, but only a small minority of workers had joined it. However, this union-backed campaign at ConflictCo (detailed in chapter 6) had provided workers with a degree of associational power. The campaign achieved this by creating negative publicity around working conditions and, specifically, the retaliatory victimization of workers. Following the success of the worker association at gaining media attention, Ali, a senior union organizer, argued that managers "would have to be dumb to retaliate against workers now."

The worker association had also filed a large number of successful claims of unfair labor practices with the National Labor Relations Board regarding managers' retaliation against their members. Workers explained how these tactics had often been effective at stopping obvious forms of managerial retaliation, such as threats, disciplinaries, and dismissals. This combination of collective and legal action had, according to the informants, considerably reduced managers' scope to use blatant despotic methods of control, especially when dealing with members of the worker association. However, such associational power was capricious, being reliant on the degree to which managers feared that workers and their union supporters would be able to leverage media or state intervention.

The Framing of Injustice

In contrast to PartnershipCo, the internal state at ConflictCo did not actively integrate the union within its structures, which produced a fractious industrial relations climate. As a consequence the union and the worker association that it supported attempted to frame workplace issues in a manner that was highly hostile to the interests of capital. According to John Kelly, dissatisfaction at work, while a necessary condition, is not sufficient to trigger collective action, as this dissatisfaction must be transformed into a sense of injustice. Injustice can be understood as a "breach of legal or collective agreement, [of] rights or of widely shared social values."[32] Therefore, in trying to mobilize the workforce toward collective action, the union and the worker association sought to frame the conditions leading to workplace dissatisfactions as illegitimate and, thus, unjust. For example, I observed how Nick, a union organizer, would inform workers during organizing drives that "because ConflictCo is the number one retailer, we think it should treat its associates [employees] like it's the number one employer."

Another frequent strategy was the comparison of pay and conditions at ConflictCo with those of unionized retailers. This strategy was employed particularly successfully by those organizers who had a background in retail, and I myself found this a successful strategy for engaging ConflictCo workers during my participant observation of organizing. Joe explained how it was hearing a leader of the worker association from another ConflictCo store talk of the poverty of ConflictCo workers that sparked feelings of injustice and anger in him, and led to him becoming a leader of the worker association: "My sister Akira was talking about . . . how you [as a ConflictCo worker] have like three cards: a [ConflictCo] discount card, a state-aid card and . . . a credit card and that just made me mad and got me really active."

Managers sought to reduce opportunities for union organizers to undertake this framing by having them ejected from stores, in some cases by the police. The ability of workplace activists to frame issues was also curtailed by managers separating them from their workmates and increasing managerial surveillance of their activities while at work (see below). There was, though, no evidence that surveillance led workers to internalize the firm's values and aims, as famously suggested by Michel Foucault. There were in fact some notable acts of resistance at ConflictCo, which are further detailed in chapter 6.

In particular, social media provided union organizers and worker activists with an important space in which to engage in their own framing of working conditions. The worker association's Facebook group had 22,000 likes in May 2013, and it provided an accessible space beyond the workplace in which such framing could be undertaken. A typical example of the way the worker association attempted to frame ConflictCo's pay as illegitimate through posts on their Facebook page is one from April 23, 2013, that highlighted how the CEO's pay was 1,000 times that of the average ConflictCo worker.

Unlike at PartnershipCo, the union did not have a partially hegemonic role in terms of controlling the agenda, mobilizing bias, or framing workplace relations so as to limit conflict. Instead, ConflictCo aimed to limit conflict and ensure control through more despotic means. As already mentioned, informants expressed a strong sense of being under surveillance in the workplace, and it is to this observation and monitoring that we now turn.

Surveillance

An atmosphere of surveillance was created at ConflictCo through three forms of monitoring: information technology, CCTV cameras, and managerial presence on the shop floor. Workers explained how they felt they were being monitored by two forms of information technology: task direction software, which monitored their speed at restocking shelves, and scan rate software, which monitored their speed on the checkouts. The task direction software, called *My-Guide*, had preprogrammed time frames for basic tasks, such as putting out a specific number of pallets of goods in a specific department. Managers could also create their own time frames for less standard tasks, such as facing up (neatening up the stock on the shelves). The program would then flag up a worker's productivity to management if he or she exceeded the specified time allowance. At that point, a manager would come and check on why the worker had fallen behind. The My-Guide system was experienced as an effective but resented source of surveillance, illustrated by the fact that workers referred to it as the "my-slave system."

Scan rate software was based at the checkouts in order to monitor the speed with which a worker scanned products. Workers had to reach a minimum speed and were rebuked by managers if they failed to do so. These software-based forms of surveillance were utilized in combination with in-store video cameras, so that if workers were not reaching my-guide or checkout productivity targets, managers could check their behavior and verify the workers' excuses. There were a large number of cameras, some of which were thought to be dummies, but the workers were unsure which ones. These cameras were ostensibly there to protect against customer theft, but they played a particularly strong role in creating a perception among workers of being constantly watched by management. In some cases, video recordings were used as the basis for disciplinary action, but workers were not given access to the supposed evidence.

Finally, there was also surveillance simply through managerial presence. Managers touring the shop floor were perceived to be watching out for workers' minor indiscretions and lack of productivity. Workers also felt that managers purposefully made them aware of their presence through verbal reminders, such as casual hellos or more formal comments on their progress. This atmosphere of surveillance was effective at discouraging and limiting the hidden forms of resistance that were common at PartnershipCo, and which are discussed in greater detail in chapter 6. However, the power of surveillance was based on the fear it instilled in workers rather than constituting a Foucauldian process in which workers became passive as a result of internalizing the norms of their employer. Workers' views were no less hostile toward their employer than those at PartnershipCo, but ConflictCo's workplace regime denied them the space to display resistance without fear of punishment.

"Coaching for Improvement": Tyrannical Discipline

In this climate of surveillance in which workers lacked employment rights and union protection, discipline was supposedly rationalized through a procedure called "coaching for improvement." According to this company policy, a manager could "coach" (i.e., discipline) a worker by issuing a written notification of a problem with the worker's performance or conduct, and how to correct it. In the next twelve months, a manager could then serve that worker with a second written "coaching," followed by a final written coaching. The worker then had to meet with the manager to discuss the coaching and write a plan for how he or she would correct their behavior. In line with the lack of employment protection provided by the at-will employment practiced by ConflictCo, the manager was free to dismiss workers for their performance or conduct after this third level of coaching without notice or redundancy pay. In addition, dismissed workers would not receive unemployment benefits, as the state viewed the workers as responsible for losing their job. However, the disciplinary procedure provided managers with an extra freedom in that they could skip levels at their discretion. This meant that they could give an employee a third-level warning immediately or skip any levels in between. Moreover, no burden of proof was required, and at no point would the worker be allowed an independent representative or even a witness.

This disciplinary procedure, then, combined with the at-will employment status, placed a huge amount of discretionary and unaccountable power in the hands of managers. Managers were free to choose to "coach" any workers who failed to "meet reasonable expectations" in their job performance and conduct. Informants had been disciplined for minor indiscretions as wide-ranging as not having clocked off at the time they were supposed to, poor attendance, not wearing the correct pants, having spoken back to managers, breaking a policy they had been ordered to break by a manager, and not having worked at a fast enough pace—even when working with an injury received on the job. As one worker, Omar, put it: "You can get a coaching for anything man, 'cause it is so crazy. Yeah there has been some cool people fired over some bullshit reasons, good people."

Unsurprisingly, this disciplinary procedure was not experienced as being a rational application of managerial control. Rather, it was perceived by informants as being applied unequally and unfairly, based on favoritism or as a means to retaliate against workers who attempted resistance. It was also felt to be used to "churn" those workers whose length of service meant that they had become relatively expensive, a typical view being that of Ashlyn (a worker): "I think sometimes they [managers] just do whatever they want to do to whoever." The only way workers could appeal a coaching was through what was known as the "open door policy," but, from the workers' perspective, this "open door" grievance procedure, as detailed below, was just as problematic.

An Open Door to the Sidewalk?

In most workplaces, the formal grievance procedure provides an institutionalized mechanism for raising complaints. At ConflictCo, the grievance procedure was called the "open door communications policy." According to this policy, all workers were "encouraged and expected [to] bring suggestions, observations, problems or concerns to the attention of any supervisor or manager without fear of retaliation."

The complaint was then meant to be investigated and followed up on a periodic basis until it was resolved, and its resolution discussed with the worker. The grievance procedure was highly individualized, with workers even lacking a right to be accompanied by a coworker to act as a witness, let alone being entitled to a representative. There was also no provision for collective grievances. Beyond having to discuss their decision with a worker, managers retained complete discretion over how and when to deal with a complaint. The only means of appeal available to workers was to use the same process to take their complaint to a higher level of management—theoretically, all the way up to the CEO.

It was widely felt among the informants at ConflictCo that even this biased procedure was not followed; it was referred to as the "broken" or "closed door" policy, as having been "nailed shut a long time ago," or that it was in fact "an open door to the sidewalk." The source of this antipathy toward the grievance procedure was that it lacked the institutional oversight with which to ensure that managers carried out proper investigations. Workers felt that managers simply based their decisions on their preconceived opinions. Managers were perceived to ignore complaints with which they disagreed, not bothering to investigate them properly if raised by a worker they were not sympathetic toward. When workers tried to take their complaint to a higher level outside of their store, including, in one case, up to corporate board level, the complaint was also disregarded. The result was that workers saw little point in using the procedure.

Moreover, workers were hesitant to make use of the open door policy because they had little confidence that confidentiality would be maintained or that they would be protected against the supposedly "strictly prohibited" retaliation. Managers were thought by the informants to have close personal bonds with each other and therefore to share information about workers' complaints, leading to retaliation against the workers. Therefore, neither the disciplinary nor the grievance procedures at ConflictCo provided workers with institutionalized protection from abuse, leaving workers reliant on the variable power of the worker association to protect them by leveraging media or state action.

Concrete Concessions: Profit Share Schemes, Bonuses, and Pay

Having considered the despotic nature of discipline at ConflictCo, let us now consider the degree to which the interests of workers and the firm were concretely coordinated. Mechanisms such as pay rises, bonuses, and a profit share scheme may have provided workers with a stake in ensuring the profitability of ConflictCo through their own productivity. However, ConflictCo had never fully embraced the kinds of hegemonic practices that were common in other U.S. workplaces in the postwar period. This can be seen by the fact that ConflictCo had never provided its workers with a defined benefit pension plan. Rather, ConflictCo created mechanisms that on the surface appeared to be analogous to those of hegemonic internal states but that in fact provided only minimal concessions to the workforce.

ConflictCo began providing workers with shares in the company in the 1970s in order to counter threats of unionization. However, after first reducing the amount that the company paid into the worker shares scheme in the mid-2000s, in the early 2010s the scheme was scrapped in order to cut costs. ConflictCo moved instead to matching workers' contributions to a 401(k) retirement plan and paying a quarterly store bonus, although workers could still use their pay packet to buy shares in ConflictCo through a stock purchase plan at a discounted rate. According to the informants, as the pay was so low and variable (as discussed in the next chapter), many workers (including a number of the informants themselves) were forced to sell the shares they had built up in the past in order to make ends meet in the short term. Many other workers simply could not afford to invest in any meaningful way in the first place. According to the informants, those workers who could afford to contribute to a 401(k) could afford to do so only very minimally. Thus, even these workers felt that they did not have adequate savings to cover their retirement.

If a worker's store met performance targets, the worker would receive a quarterly bonus. However, this bonus did little to create a sense of shared interests with ConflictCo, as workers tended not to understand how the bonus related to store performance. Those workers who did understand the connection still did not attribute the store's performance to their own productivity on the shop floor but rather to forces outside of their control. For example, at one store, workers blamed their lack of a bonus on the store being affected by bad weather that had caused a power outage and necessitated renting a generator. At another store, located in a high-crime area where a customer had been shot during a robbery a few months previously, the lack of a bonus was attributed to the high level of theft by customers. Therefore, when a store failed to qualify for the bonus, it created feelings of injustice among workers that were heightened by the awareness that the bonuses of neither store managers nor executives were related to the same performance targets as their own.

Employer-based health insurance is a typical means by which U.S. corporations have historically attempted to tie their workforces' interests to their own: if workers leave or lose their job, they also lose their health care. However, ConflictCo never fully embraced this model, limiting its health insurance coverage by making it expensive and restricting it to full-time employees. While only around a quarter of the worker informants were without employer-provided health insurance themselves, dissatisfaction with its restrictiveness and cost ran much wider, with all but one of the worker informants raising it as a source of considerable discontentment.

That there were few concessions being granted to workers at ConflictCo is further demonstrated by the fact that starting wages were declining in real terms.

For example, at one store, Mary (a worker) showed me her first pay slip from nine years previously. It was nearly 10 percent higher in real terms than the starting pay of current workers at the store. According to the pay policy, pay rises were decided unilaterally by ConflictCo and were performance-related. Pay rises ranged from zero to sixty cents an hour, which workers received only after eighteen months of service. Performance was evaluated annually, and if the workforce's performance was normally distributed, then 14 percent of workers would receive no annual pay rise at all, with most workers receiving a rise of just forty cents an hour, or around 5 percent of starting pay. However, this rise was a flat figure rather than a percentage, thus its relative worth declined as workers' pay increased with service. This meant that the most loyal workers actually received a lower percentage pay rise with each year's service.

Language, Ritual, and Personality Cults

ConflictCo's internal state had propagated an environment of despotism and fear. Moreover, it was one in which few concessions were offered to workers so as to tie their interests to those of the firm. ConflictCo therefore tried, although quite unsuccessfully, to ensure control and limit resistance by directly shaping the values of workers. As detailed above, ConflictCo was extremely hostile to unions, and the union was not directly integrated into the internal state. ConflictCo instead relied heavily on propaganda and ritual in an attempt to directly shape the workforce's values and cognitions. By "propaganda" I mean the provision of information to workers that was biased, partial, or misleading in order to promote the firm's interests.

Much of ConflictCo's propaganda focused on the portrayal of the values of ConflictCo and its founder as pro-worker, these values being emphasized in communications such as store posters and magazines. Leonardo, a ConflictCo worker, made clear that these were not neutral sources of information: "In the break room they have all those kinds of magazines and all these stories and things about ConflictCo and the founder and they never say anything bad about ConflictCo [laughs]."

In fact, despite having been dead for twenty years, the founder was featured on six of the pages (including covers) of the most recent edition of ConflictCo's employee magazine. These features amounted to four pages' worth of content. For example, one page featured a photo of the founder stroking his dog, with the following text in large print: "Let's go for it! Let's take care of our associates [workers]; **Let's take care of our people,** and they'll take care of our customers."

Another page, headed "Top 10 Things to Know about ConflictCo" and featuring a large photo of a smiling worker, included claims regarding ConflictCo being "a big family" that offered "competitive pay and benefits" (including the claim that the average worker earns more than five dollars per hour over the federal minimum), and highlighting "the opportunity for advancement"—especially for women. Perhaps the page that went furthest in displaying personality cult–like elements was headed "The Founder Moment" and went on to ask workers to vote for their favorite moment involving ConflictCo's founder. The moments workers were asked to vote on included the founder getting married, receiving a medal from the president of the United States, doing the ConflictCo cheer (see below) on the company's in-house TV channel, and doing a public dance.

There was also an Orwellian focus on company language and terminology, with employees being termed "associates" and being encouraged to become symbolic shareholders. As we have seen, the grievance policy was called the open door policy and the disciplinary procedure coaching for success. This terminology supposedly reflected the founder's official "rules of business." These emphasized the sharing of profits, partnership with and appreciation of employees, and Conflict-Co's "core business belief" in listening to all its workers.

All workers had to undertake anti-union education activities during their orientation. Worker informants explained that this consisted of a computer module and a video in which ConflictCo "workers" (it seems likely they were, in fact, actors) gave their opinions on unions, unanimously depicting them as only interested in taking workers' voices and money without providing anything in return. In response to the rise of the worker association, the informants at active stores explained how ConflictCo put notice boards above the time clocks and screened continuous slide shows that equated the worker association with unions. Pamela (a worker) provides an illustrative account of the messages these screens conveyed: "ConflictCo had at the two time-clocks televisions on each side and it's constantly streaming about the worker association and the union and how evil they are and how many jobs they have lost and how many stores have closed because of the union and how you shouldn't have to pay anyone to speak for you and you shouldn't have to be involved in anything like that when you have an 'open door' policy."

Nicola, a former assistant manager, also explained how she was trained to discourage unions by telling workers negative stories about them.

"The ConflictCo Cheer"

The internal state at ConflictCo also sought to reinforce a notion of the workplace as an environment in which workers were happy through a mandatory collective ritual. Anthropologist Laura Bear demonstrates the importance of rituals at work with the example of Indian shipbuilders' practices surrounding the iron-working god Vishwakarma. Her account provides an illuminating example of how rituals can deeply and powerfully shape the ways in which workers relate to and understand their work.[33] At ConflictCo, a ritualistic cheer was a central component of the informants' work experience. The "ConflictCo cheer" took place three times a day to coincide with the beginning of the three shifts. Workers were supposed to enthusiastically spell out ConflictCo along with phrases such as "We are number one!" and "Whose ConflictCo? My ConflictCo!"

The Destabilizing Effects of Normative Controls

Let us now consider the effectiveness of these direct normative controls at ConflictCo. The success of the anti-union propaganda in shaping workers' attitudes was a common explanation for why more workers had not joined the worker association. However, it was widely felt by most of the informants that these negative views could be overcome if it were not for the anti-union propaganda being effective for a second indirect reason, that is, that this propaganda made very clear that ConflictCo was highly opposed to unions. This, combined with their insecurity and the high levels of surveillance, resulted in workers being extremely fearful of being seen to have anything to do with unions.

Thus, the anti-union propaganda put about by management was very effective regardless of whether or not it truly was a form of brainwashing (as some believed), because it made the rules of the game clear to workers. Nearly all the informants explained how it was fear that was the major barrier to collective organization, rather than workers' attitudes. Some worker informants stated that their coworkers would no longer even speak to them after they had joined the worker association for fear of guilt by association. This high level of fear was supported by the participant observation of store organizing, and was clearly illustrated by my attempt to discuss the worker association with workers on the shop floor during a store visit. When I spoke to a male Filipino worker in his forties, he said, "I can't talk to you about that, my manager is just over there and he'll hear me"—his body language clearly showed he was extremely scared (field notes, ConflictCo).

Akira, a recent employee who was now working as an organizer for the worker association, summed up how this anti-union training created a generalized fear that nearly all the informants felt to be both prevalent and a major barrier to collective organization: "You're being threatened, if you want your job, stay away from this basically. It's a death word. You go in there and start talking about organization [and] 'Oh union! Union! Get Out!' Yeah, alerts go off [in workers' heads]."

It therefore seems clear that the power of this anti-union propaganda lay in it clarifying acceptable worker behavior (i.e., hostility to unions) rather than in its ability to truly obscure reality and shape workers' attitudes. Thus, the anti-union propaganda acted as a conduit of fear rather than truly shaping workers' wants and beliefs. Without this underlying fear, and the surveillance and coercion provided by the internal state, workers would have had no reason to conform with the propaganda and would at least have been open to alternative frames of understanding. However, sociologist Michael Mann explains that when institutionalized ideologies seem to no longer hold true, people are likely to look for alternative accounts that fit better with the reality they experience. Therefore, any attempts to rely exclusively on propaganda and ideology to maintain control are unlikely to succeed.[34]

In fact, there was evidence that by reinforcing the supposed values of ConflictCo—as embodied in the founder—the use of propaganda actually reduced control. Workplace regimes that stress symbolic representations that are contradicted by reality actually destabilize the regime and have been found to undermine control.[35] At ConflictCo, declarations of the "good" pay of the "average" worker were simply not believed by the informants because they clearly contradicted the workers' actual lived experiences. As such, they sparked feelings of injustice and outrage, typified by Vincent's (a worker) claim: "Another unjust thing is ConflictCo's constant lying and broken promises."

The emphasizing of ConflictCo's and its founder's values, when the reality so clearly contradicted them, only reinforced the perception that the current situation was unjust. Moreover, it placed the blame for that injustice squarely at the feet of the firm's executives. Workers were constantly reminded that their grievances existed in contradiction to the clear wishes and ideals of the revered founder. This meant that even though none of the informants had actually worked at ConflictCo while the founder was alive, they all firmly believed that the founder was a "great man who listened, respected and cared about ConflictCo's workers." Others explained that he was a "really nice guy," treated workers like part of a "family," would be "turning in his grave," and would even, despite his famed hostility to unions, be "pro-union if he was alive to see what ConflictCo has become." One worker even believed the founder had won the Nobel Peace Prize. Workers thus saw the cause of their troubles as emanating from the death of the venerated founder and the betrayal of his legacy by his heirs, who still majority-owned the company.

ConflictCo's emphasis on the founder's values, then, legitimized opposition to ConflictCo's current leadership. Matthew, a worker, illustrated this point particularly clearly:

> There's a lot of like propaganda and examples around the store that try to, you know, like "wow that's what we are like, that's the way it is here. Yeah!" You know, but everybody knows in reality that when you walk up to the court it is not like that at all. "The founder says" is actually a big poster board in our backroom which has pictures of the founder in three different poses and it has quotes next to them and one of them says, you know, "To really run the store you should be listening to the people on the floor, which is the workers." And that itself isn't being done today and that's why I get more and more fuel to put on the fire, because of stuff like that. I know the founder, I've heard from a lot veterans about the founder and, in their opinion, they really believe that he's turning in his grave right now because of how ConflictCo is treating its workers and ConflictCo has basically turned in the opposite direction since the founder died.

Likewise, the informants felt that most workers were not enthusiastic about having to participate in the ConflictCo cheer, and many tried to avoid it. Brad, a worker, explained in detail the effect the cheer had on him. He also highlighted how he and his coworkers would use customers to resist participating:

> It's actually mandatory. There are a lot of people who don't want to do it, but you have to, if you're at the meeting you have to do it, so a lot of people avoid the meetings, so when they page or announce it on the overhead, and I know I do this and a lot of workers will do this, we'll find a customer that needs help just so we can say, "I was helping a customer so I couldn't go," and if it's the smallest thing we'll find something to do, people don't want to go, 'cause they don't want to chant . . . [Managers] say they do it to make it more of a fun environment . . . but the fact of the matter is that the way the chant is set up it's, you know, you come to work at somewhere like ConflictCo that treats you terrible and you're forced to chant how fantastic and happy a place it is, it actually feels like a brainwashing procedure . . . keep telling yourself it's OK and it will be, when really it's not, because in the chant we talk about how it's our company, it's our ConflictCo, it's the greatest place ever, but it's, like, no it's not . . . [But] it pressures you to comply . . . you feel like a child.

Leonardo, a worker in his sixties, was more succinct: "I never go to the meetings, because it's all bullshit."

Vincent explained why it increased his sense of injustice and outrage: "The cheer is retarded . . . It makes me hate them even more . . . because I know there's a hidden agenda to it, you know it's like to get you pumped up about a company that doesn't care about you. If this company gave me full benefits and a full-time position and I made a good amount of money an hour, then yeah I might do the ConflictCo cheer."

Other workers distorted it by chanting "Can you pay us some more please!" or shouting out the name of the worker association.

In summary, the symbolic and normative aspects of ConflictCo's internal state were largely ineffective, as they so sharply contradicted workers' actual lived experiences of the workplace regime. While anti-union propaganda was an effective barrier to collective organization, this was due more to its making clear to workers that they were expected to behave in a hostile manner to unions. The effect of this propaganda was thus to instill a fear of unions among the workforce. However, this power rested on the coercive nature of the internal state and its ability to secure control rather than on the effective obscuring of reality and shaping of workers' attitudes toward unions. Moreover, the propaganda and collective ritual that emphasized the supposed values of ConflictCo and that were claimed to be embodied in the founder actually destabilized the regime and reduced control. They not only highlighted the disparity between the symbolic representation of ConflictCo and reality; they also justified resistance to those currently in control. So we see that at both PartnershipCo and ConflictCo, the ability of the symbolic apparatuses of the internal states to impose control through the obscuring of workplace relations was limited and dysfunctional in important respects. At PartnershipCo, this was due to the union and especially its workplace reps' attempts to meet the union's recruitment needs. This meant that these actors often framed workplace relations in ways that were not conducive to labor control, that is, as insecure and exploitative. In contrast, at ConflictCo the attempts at directly shaping the values of workers, through language, propaganda, and ritual, were largely ineffective and in fact legitimized opposition to the current management.

Limits to Despotism

It is clear that, unlike the PartnershipCo internal state, ConflictCo had few elements synonymous with hegemonic regimes. Workers faced a high level of arbitrary discipline, while managers had few constraints placed on them by the unstable and opaque company policies, including the disciplinary procedure. Moreover, the internal state lacked any mechanisms that workers could utilize in order to seek protection from abusive managers or improve their working conditions. Workers were denied a collective voice through a union and were also deprived of an individual voice through a functioning and effective grievance procedure. Managers were felt to simply ignore, or even retaliate against, workers who raised grievances through the open door policy. When added to an employment status that provided workers with few protections and a high level of surveillance, this resulted in an internal state that provided managers with a huge amount of coercive arbitrary power over workers. This power often manifested itself in verbal abuse, threats, and bullying. Moreover, workers gained little in the way of material concessions in terms of pay or benefits, and ConflictCo clearly had little concern with constructing a compromise equilibrium.

Instead of providing workers with concessions that would tie their interests to the firm's, ConflictCo attempted to achieve quiescence via the direct shaping of workers' values. This ideological process took two forms: propaganda and ritual. However, these attempts at symbolic shaping of worker cognition were largely ineffective, and actually served to heighten skepticism toward management and legitimize resistance by highlighting the gap between the firm's claims and reality. At the time of the research, the inherent despotism of the ConflictCo internal state had been, to a degree, checked by a union-backed worker association (discussed further in chapter 6). The legal and media campaign that this group had successfully waged acted to limit the scope for managers to utilize blatantly despotic means of control. This meant that at ConflictCo, just as at the more hegemonic PartnershipCo, there was an imperative for control to be secured via other, subtler means, which we discuss in chapter 4.

Part 2
THE DESPOTISM
OF TIME

This part of the book focuses on the allocation of labor at PartnershipCo and Con-flictCo. In doing so the findings highlight that the kinds of mechanisms synony-mous with the internal labor markets of the hegemonic era were largely absent at both companies—there being little evidence of workers being shielded from the external labor market. For instance, neither firm made use of seniority rules to protect established workers from insecurity, there was little real job mobility, and pay was close to the legal minimum in the respective external labor markets. In fact, the relatively low pay of workers, compared to management, and the huge profits of both firms were sources of perceived injustice at both. As already high-lighted in this book's introduction, the shielding of workers from the external labor market has been argued by Michael Burawoy to be crucial for enabling he-gemonic workplaces and the creation of consent. However, even at the more progressive PartnershipCo, we find little evidence that the existence of an inter-nal labor market was central to the production of consent.

In the absence of the hegemonic effects of internal labor markets, part 2 in-stead investigates an element not considered by Burawoy—namely, working time.[1] Despite the highly divergent political and economic contexts and the contrasting internal states of the two cases, both operate with high levels of temporal flexi-bility. In both cases this was achieved via manager-controlled flexible scheduling and was experienced by workers as damaging to work-life balance and as a source of precarity and insecurity. In fact, the experiences of precarious scheduling were remarkably similar, despite the existence at PartnershipCo of union-backed policies and procedures that were meant to result in flexible scheduling being a "two-way process."

The high levels of precarious scheduling at both firms provided managers with a powerful mechanism by which they could arbitrarily discipline workers. The use of flexible working time in this way is termed "flexible discipline." Managers at both firms could use their control of scheduling to punish specific workers by changing their hours so that their schedule clashed with family or social activities. Alternatively, managers could simply cut a worker's hours so that these hourly paid workers could no longer make ends meet. The power of flexible discipline meant that control could be secured without recourse to traditionally despotic techniques.

Flexible discipline had other advantages for managers, in that it was impossible for workers to be certain that they were being punished or whether managers were genuinely responding to changing demand. At PartnershipCo this meant that control could be achieved "with a smile" and without the damage to the "psychological contract" (the unwritten expectations regarding employment) caused by threats of dismissal. At ConflictCo the inherent ambiguity and subtlety of flexible discipline were particularly useful for undermining the worker association, providing managers with a means of disciplining workers who became active in the worker association—one that was very hard to prove as being a form of retaliation. Other benefits for managers of this form of control were that it is less rigid than the binary of dismissing / not dismissing a worker and could be rescinded and modulated by providing more hours or predictability, making this a very flexible form of control.

Unsurprisingly, scheduling was perceived as operating according to favoritism, and, therefore, flexible discipline was not only a mechanism for the punishment of individual workers. It also operated as an active source of overall control in which workers generally tried to gain managers' favor through increased productivity, so as to avoid being a victim of this form of discipline.

DESPOTIC TIME IN THE UK
Overcoming Hegemonic Constraints

In this chapter, we explore the despotic use of working time to achieve control at PartnershipCo. In his influential studies of workplace control, sociologist Michael Burawoy highlights the importance of the internal labor market in shaping workplace regimes. The term "internal labor market" refers to the shielding of employment relations from the external labor market through mechanisms such as seniority policies, employment protections, internal promotion ladders, and differentiated job structures based on skill and knowledge development. However, as Burawoy recognizes, his research objectified as timeless what was actually a historically specific workplace organizational form. In fact, as highlighted previously, internal labor markets represent a particular institutional form that was dominant during the relatively brief hegemonic era, starting in the 1930s and 1940s. The importance of internal labor markets diminished from the mid-1970s onward, being dismantled through concession bargaining and the procedural individualization of employment relations. Internal labor markets are, however, just one means by which tasks are allocated within firms. This chapter focuses instead on an element of work organization that Burawoy did not consider: the regulation of working time.[1]

The starting point for this analysis is the view that working time is not determined technologically. Instead, its regulation is determined through a process of conflict and struggle over the definition of "working time"—and its distinction from, and relationship with, "free time." As historian E. P. Thompson states: "Mature industrial societies of all varieties are marked by . . . a clear demarcation between 'work' and 'life' . . . This is a place of far-reaching conflict . . . not a simple [historical] one of neutral and inevitable technological change, but one of exploitation and of resistance to exploitation."[2]

This chapter highlights the degree to which a new flexible definition of working time has taken shape in the twenty-first century. Doing so sheds light on the role of working time in securing workplace control. In particular, the chapter will illustrate how flexible scheduling at PartnershipCo was found to be highly manager-controlled, even in the presence of institutionalized working time regulations. The negative impact of flexible scheduling on job quality and well-being is also demonstrated. This is shown to provide managers with an additional powerful yet subtle means of securing workplace control through coercion. Specifically, flexible scheduling offers managers a simple, readily available, and unaccountable way to threaten and punish specific workers with worse hours and shifts, as well as requiring all workers to actively maintain the managers' favor through being "good employees." This chapter, therefore, focuses on the role of flexible scheduling in enabling coercion in the workplace through flexible discipline. Chapter 5 will then focus on how flexible scheduling also enables the misrecognition of workplace relations through "schedule gifts," that is, the granting of additional work hours by managers in order to help workers meet their material needs by increasing their earnings. Additionally, managers' alterations to schedules can help provide for workers' social needs by improving work-life balance.

The Shielding of Labor from the External Labor Market

At PartnershipCo, an internal labor market was not significant in the creation of worker consent. As already mentioned, the internal labor market refers to the shielding of labor from the external market through administrative rules and procedures—particularly the notion of seniority. The fieldwork highlighted the limited efficacy of an internal labor market in the creation of worker consent at PartnershipCo. This supports the literature, which suggests that there has been widespread dismantling of internal labor markets and growing procedural individualization of employment relations.[3] In particular, there were no seniority rules whereby those with the longest service at the firm would be protected from redundancy. However, in one important way workers at PartnershipCo were sheltered from the external labor market in that they experienced little employment insecurity although they did often experience schedule insecurity (discussed in detail below). As Jimmy, a union rep, explained: "I think people are concerned not so much with worry about [losing] their jobs; new people are concerned about their [flexible] contracts as they don't offer any [schedule] security . . . [over] the hours they are doing. The older workers know the score; they know it's a secure job."

Discounting Wages

Absence of a strong internal labor market and the exposure of labor to the external labor market can also be seen in the fact that pay did not diverge much from the minimum wage. Wages were, therefore, low, with starting pay being below a living wage, and had been declining in real terms for a number of years. However, while some informants were very angry about pay and understood that in real terms it was deteriorating, it was inequality that really generated a sense of outrage. As noted by Jimmy: "The gap between the bottom and the top is horrendous and if you worked it out in cans of baked beans . . . how many we have to sell for her [the store manager's wage] and how many we have to sell for us, it really puts it into perspective, and should we be paid more? Yeah!"

And according to Jeff, also a union rep: "The injustice, the sheer profits that they're getting . . . look at the people at the top . . . we're working for one of the biggest companies in the world, let alone in the UK, and getting paid a pittance . . . When people see the directors at the top earning literally millions and that's without their bonuses and us at the bottom getting £7 an hour, £7.50 an hour, and you know it just doesn't seem fair when we are doing most of the work . . . These guys are getting paid millions and only coming into the office for three days a week. So yeah I would say anger sums it up."

For some informants, this sense of injustice was heightened by their belief that board-level management were responsible for running PartnershipCo badly. These workers, therefore, felt that the board was thus culpable for the business requiring that workers' pay be squeezed. Sandra, another union rep, commented: "I think the reason we got 2 percent [for a pay raise], a lot of it, was Partnership-Co's fault . . . it's us that's suffered again 'cause of their mistake and it does make you kinda angry."

However, other workers were more accepting of the pay at PartnershipCo. This was largely due to the fact that, although for many workers pay was below a living wage and had been declining in real terms, it was still better than the pay at comparable retail employers. Additionally, not all workers recognized that a "pay rise" below inflation represented a pay cut in real terms. Some informants were, therefore, happy with below-inflation pay rises since, to their minds, this still constituted an increase in their pay. Given the wider economic situation, this made them feel relatively lucky. What is clear, however, is that while some workers accepted their pay, it was not a mechanism by which much active consent within the workplace regime was generated. In fact, it was a source of discontent for many workers at PartnershipCo. For example, at the Mulling Point store where I worked for two months, PartnershipCo's own staff survey found that 52 percent of the workforce felt that their pay was unfair.

Furthermore, there was little opportunity for genuine mobility within the job structure, given that there was little incremental difference between pay grades for hourly paid workers. There was also very little likelihood of advancement into salaried management. Therefore, on the whole, there was little evidence that internal labor market–type elements were significant hegemonic features of the workplace regimes that aided labor control through producing consent. The allocation of labor to particular tasks was based on the principle of functional flexibility. This meant that most staff were trained in multiple roles and could be shifted by managers from their primary tasks to secondary ones as needed. For example, at a moment's notice shelf stackers could be ordered to stop what they were doing and to go operate a checkout. This lack of task discretion led to working time being experienced as intense and insecure. Let us consider the role of working time in securing workplace control in more detail.

Precarious Scheduling at PartnershipCo: Flexibility beyond Contingency

Experiences of flexible scheduling at PartnershipCo highlight the importance of the conceptual distinction between "manager-controlled flexibility" and "worker-controlled flexibility."[4] Manager-controlled flexible scheduling is of principal benefit to employers, whereas worker-controlled flexible scheduling is beneficial to employees. Research suggests that despite frequent employer claims to the contrary, flexible scheduling cannot be both manager-controlled and at the same time worker-controlled.[5] The findings presented below clearly demonstrate that there was a high level of temporal flexibility at PartnershipCo, which was achieved through manager-controlled flexible scheduling with little evidence of worker influence. This was despite the fact that there were institutionalized workplace mechanisms that aimed to unsuccessfully ensure that flexibility was both manager- and worker-controlled.

Flexibility: "A Two-Way Process"?

The collective agreement between the company and the union covered many aspects relating to scheduling. Most importantly, it stipulated that PartnershipCo's employment relationship with its hourly paid store workforce was to be limited to three forms: standard, temporary, and flexible. Standard workers were employed on contracts that guaranteed them fixed core hours (36.5 if full-time and no less than 4.5 hours if part-time) with overtime being voluntary.[6] If managers wished to change workers' fixed core hours, they had to follow a strict "labor matching review process"—also codified in the collective agreement.

The union's policy booklet on labor matching reviews explained that "change is constant and is driven by many factors including new technology, customer demands, the economic climate and new business initiatives . . . [Labor matching] is the policy used to manage this constant change by making variations to [an] employees' contracted hours . . . [And] identify[ing] where hours are needed in store."

Following the labor matching review process, which included a twenty-eight-day consultation with the affected worker, PartnershipCo would issue contractual notice (ranging from four to twelve weeks, depending on length of service) unless the worker agreed in the meantime to alter his or her hours. The outcome of these labor matching reviews could vary from small alterations to existing shift patterns (such as moving the shift an hour earlier or later in the day) to more major ones (such as moving a shift from a weekday to a weekend or modifying a daytime shift to a night shift). The most extreme alteration observed was the complete transformation of a particular job role from days to nights. However, as discussed below, even the less extreme adjustments could have serious consequences for work-life balance.

Despite the official policy stipulating that such reviews were not to be carried out frequently or utilized in relation to short-term changes in demand, informants perceived them to be very frequent, apparently affecting each worker between two and four times a year. Moreover, the review period could drag on for many months and in some cases lasted twelve months or more. Review periods were in fact experienced by employees as a virtually constant process, with the outcome being hard to predict. For example, Sandra described in detail during an interview how this procedure was used in reality: "All of a sudden you will get called into an office. 'Right, we need to have a chat with you,' and you'll be all stressed about it . . . [But] you won't hear nothing for two months and then three months and then four months . . . [and] a year down the road they then say they have to do it again."

The consequence of labor matching reviews was that contractually guaranteed core hours were, in fact, amenable to high levels of manager-controlled flexible scheduling. In addition, it was widely perceived by the informants that managers were not holding proper consultations in which they were willing to listen to workers' concerns and come to a compromise. Union reps and workers recounted how managers would instead intimidate workers into changing their hours to such an extent that workers were afraid they would be dismissed or lose their job if they were not compliant. Susan (a union rep) explained during an interview how this fear formed a barrier to the union's influence: "People do feel compelled to do it and don't really have a choice in it, if they still wanna job because it's that whole canopy of 'you're lucky to have a job' . . . That's the biggest thing, people go to them [the union] and then they get half way through the process and they think 'hang on a moment, I could lose my job through this, I don't want to do this anymore,' they sort of get a little bit scared."

Another union rep, Rosie, elaborated on how managers' subtle threats heighten such feelings: "You get told that there are plenty of people out there who need jobs, so it's more bribing than anything else."

Asim, a union rep, made it clear that, in some cases, this fear was achieved less subtly and was clearly in contradiction to PartnershipCo's policies: "People have been told, wrongly, that they can be sacked for it if they don't change their hours."

Furthermore, while company policy stated that labor matching reviews should not result in reduced core hours, workers would "voluntarily" reduce their hours in order to remain in their current department and job role. As Neil, a union rep, explained: "It was all these shifts cobbled together, and it wasn't a job. But what it allowed them to do was cut hours . . . So it's been a way of cutting costs; people have cut their hours because they want to stay in their department."

In much of the literature, temporal flexibility is suggested to be a feature of nonstandard, atypical, or contingent work. Yet what the findings at PartnershipCo demonstrate is the fact that in a 24/7 economy, firms can extend flexible scheduling to standard, permanent, and full-time workers who will generally experience this not as flexibility but as a source of precarity.

TEMPORARY CONTRACTS: THE LIMITS OF NUMERICAL FLEXIBILITY

Temporary workers principally provide firms with numerical flexibility: the ability to respond to changes in demand by quickly altering the size and composition of the workforce. PartnershipCo had previously combined the temporal flexibility provided by labor matching with the numerical flexibility provided by temporary workers. Temporary workers were employed on fixed-term contracts of up to twelve weeks to cover peak periods of demand, such as Christmas, but this combination of temporal and numerical flexibility had proved inadequate. The guide to flexible contracts explained that the labor matching review process had proved too time-consuming, ill-suited to short-term changes in demand, and not flexible enough to cope with recurring shifts in demand. Furthermore, using temporary staff brought with it additional costs in terms of recruitment and training and, in the case of online-only stores, agency fees. Therefore, the year before the fieldwork was undertaken, a new temporally flexible employment status was introduced. The aim of this new employment contract was to increase flexibility.

FLEXIBLE CONTRACTS: THE MOVE TOWARD GREATER TEMPORAL FLEXIBILITY

This newly created flexible employment contract covered full-time and part-time employees. Full-time workers were contracted for 36.5 hours, but these hours were not set. The hours could be scheduled at any time (excluding Sundays, which by law had to be voluntary) the workers had indicated that they were available to work during their interview. While workers were free to stipulate their preferred availability, managers would take into account whether the workers' availability suited the company's needs before employing them. As such, providing greater availability increased the chances of being hired. These full-time flexible workers had to provide at least fifty hours' availability each week. The worker's schedule was supposed to be drawn up at least four weeks in advance but could officially be altered with as little as seven days' notice in "exceptional situations."

Flexible part-time workers had to provide up to forty-eight hours per week of availability to work (although they would only work up to 36.5 hours). Part-time flexible workers were then contracted to work a minimum of 7.5 core hours per week and three hours per shift, although the guide to flexible contracts makes clear that PartnershipCo considered the ideal number to be ten to sixteen hours per week. These workers could then be "flexed up" with additional hours during their availability periods. Officially, these additional flexed hours should only have equated to a maximum of 60 percent of the workers' core hours. For example, if they were employed for ten core hours, their flexed hours should have been no more than six additional hours. Importantly, flexible part-time workers were supposed to receive notice of their extra hours at least seven days in advance, but in "exceptional situations" could be provided with just twenty-four hours' notice. However, the policy explicitly stated that this was not to be the norm. Additional flexed hours were allocated to match demand during busy periods. If workers refused to work at times when they were officially "available," then in the first two instances they received a warning. After a third refusal, they would face disciplinary action.

Beyond Numerical Flexibility

According to PartnershipCo's guide to flexible contracts, the implementation of this new flexible employment status was at the discretion of individual stores. However, it also made clear that a mixture of standard, temporary, and flexible workers was needed in order to respond to changes in demand while managing payroll budgets effectively. Flexible contracts were expected to limit the need for temporary workers to three peak trading periods (Easter, summer, and Christmas), and even during these periods, the payroll costs of temporary workers would be restricted to around 10 percent of the normal payroll. For new stores, the guide to flexible contracts explained that the ideal model was to reduce core contracted hours to 80 percent of the payroll costs. This was so that the remaining 20 percent of the payroll could be allocated to additional hours in order to match short-term changes in demand. This would require approximately 45 percent of staff to be on flexible contracts and was also considered to be the ideal model for existing stores to move toward. The transition toward this ideal was gradual, as existing staff could not be transferred to flexible contracts unless they applied for a new job role. That said, by January 2013—that is, only a year after flexible contracts were introduced—the union rep guide noted that flexible contracts were becoming increasingly common.

Despite plenty of evidence of part-time flexible contracts, there was no evidence at the fieldwork sites that full-time flexible contracts were being used. This was presumably because part-time flexible workers presented greater potential for flexibility through the combination of flexed time and overtime, as discussed below. Although the sampling was not randomized, this suggests that the vast majority of the workers employed on flexible contracts at PartnershipCo, in the London area at least, had part-time employment status. Consequently, the discussion below regarding workers employed on flexible contracts is limited to this part-time flexible work.

The guide to flexible contracts emphasized that the flexibility of these contracts was "two-way," in that they enabled both manager-controlled flexible scheduling and worker-controlled flexibility, as workers could request not to work reasonable hours that fell during their availability if they had not yet been scheduled. According to the guide to flexible contracts, this would provide workers with schedules that "suit people's lives . . . allowing staff in our stores to work hours that can be flexible enough to meet their individual needs."

SHORT HOURS CONTRACTS: COMBINING OVERTIME AND FLEXED TIME

On paper, being employed on a flexible contract at PartnershipCo was quite different from being a standard part-time worker. Rather than working compulsory flexed time, standard part-time workers could be offered voluntary overtime paid at the standard rate. The proportions of flexed time and overtime within a store were meant to be roughly equivalent. The practice of achieving flexibility through both traditional overtime and compulsory flexed time required that both part-

time and flexible workers be hired on contracts that guaranteed them only minimal core contractual hours. This meant that demand could be matched through
fluctuating additional hours. Consequently, part-time contracts and flexible contracts operated as complementary forms of "short hours contracts." In fact, a
common theme of the interviews was the similar proportions of contracted hours
and the additional hours that both part-time and flexible employees actually
worked.

Additional hours were an important feature of the workplace, with standard
part-time and flexible workers having, on average, thirty-six hours of work a week
but being contracted, on average, for just nine hours a week. Although the standard part-time workers were not contractually obliged to accept any additional
hours offered, in reality it was unlikely that those employed on short hours contracts would refuse them, despite the fact that they were only being paid at the
same rate as core hours. The nature of these low pay and short hours contracts
meant that workers often had a material need for additional hours. For example,
all of my teammates at Mulling Point frequently worked overtime despite com-
plaining about how hard it was to work a nine-hour shift and that their bodies
were aching. Moreover, this precarious situation of potentially not having enough
hours to make ends meet was heightened by a perception that refusal to work
overtime would result in additional hours not being offered in the future. Derek,
a union rep, explained this situation lucidly during an interview: "People will do
their utmost to do the extra hours and will allow themselves to be bullied into
working days they don't really want to work or shifts that they don't really want
to work. A lot of them are actually struggling to get childcare in place and things
because they are terrified of not getting any more shifts and being stuck with this
three and a half or seven hours a week, which they've gotta live on . . . so I've
known managers to say 'look if you don't do the shift tomorrow, I won't offer
you any more again.' They are blatant about it."

A further important difference of flexible contracts compared to traditional
part-time contracts was that unlike overtime, flexed time was meant to require
at least twenty-four hours' notice. This contractual protection was also perceived
to be disregarded, however. As Mike, a union official, explained during an interview, "They don't use the rules and try and take advantage: 'you will come in tomorrow.'"

PartnershipCo's policy that additional flexed hours should constitute only
60 percent of core hours also made little difference, as it was frequently bypassed
through the use of traditional overtime. This meant that overtime / flexed time
could constitute three-quarters of a worker's total weekly hours. This is, however,
well below the most extreme example. Jimmy (a union rep) stated that workers
were being contracted for less than four hours a week but typically working

thirty-six hours, meaning that overtime / flexed time was increasing their hours ninefold.

Given that these contractual protections and company policies regarding flexed time were habitually disregarded by managers, from the workers' perspective the differences between being employed on a standard part-time (short hours) contract or a flexible short hours contract were minor—despite the former in theory guaranteeing more worker control over additional hours worked. Instead, both were understood by workers as entailing precarious scheduling, as they experienced little notice of unpredictable and irregular additional hours, along with the disappearance of uncontracted hours that they had become accustomed to working.

In terms of maximizing scheduling flexibility, overtime and flexed time had contrasting advantages and drawbacks, and this made them highly complementary. This is why PartnershipCo aimed to have them utilized in equal proportions. The main advantage of overtime was that workers did not have to be given any notice. Thus, workers could be offered overtime with even less than the twenty-four hours' notice contractually required for flexed time, providing the flexibility to respond to real-time changes in demand. For example, I observed that it was common for members of my team of shelf stackers at Mulling Point to be offered overtime for the following morning during our evening shifts or even to extend the shift currently being worked. In an illustrative example, Rio was asked to extend his shift as he was putting on his coat to go home.

The obvious disadvantage of overtime to the company was that workers had discretion as to whether they accepted or rejected the additional hours. So overtime, at least in theory, could leave demand unmet. Conversely, the advantage of flexed time was that workers could not decline additional hours if given twenty-four hours' notice, so demand was guaranteed to be met. The drawback was that managers had to anticipate and plan for the increased demand at least twenty-four hours in advance. Flexed time also added a level of complexity to scheduling, which increased with the number of workers employed in this way.

The Impact of Precarious Scheduling on Job Quality
The Impairment of Work-Life Balance

The flexible scheduling at PartnershipCo fell a long way short of the claimed "two-way process" that supposedly enabled workers to meet their individual needs. Rather than constituting a harmonious combination of manager-controlled and worker-controlled flexible scheduling, it was in fact almost entirely manager-controlled. This form of flexible scheduling had a deleterious effect on job quality. Specifically, it diminished workers' work-life balance by affecting their ability to plan their time, and consequently impacted their family life. A characteristic experience was that of Sara, a union rep: "Now that Paul [another PartnershipCo worker] is living with me and he has the Saturday off, I've already set aside Saturday as a day for me, Paul, and my son to do something as a family . . She [Sara's manager] now wants me to work Saturdays . . . it's all up in the air."

A recurring concern raised in the interviews at PartnershipCo was the impact that precarious scheduling could have on childcare responsibilities—this was especially a concern for female workers. As noted by Asim, a union rep: "They balance their work life with their family life, i.e., dropping their kids off or having careers and when suddenly the business is like 'you have to change your hours again' it affects them, it affects them immensely because they have to start it all over again, they have to balance their family life because they don't want to lose their job, so they have to make a lot of sacrifices."

Primary childcare was not the only type of caring impacted. Low-income families could not afford professional childcare and therefore relied on family members such as grandparents. One of the major demographics employed at PartnershipCo was older people who were likely to have grandchildren. Similarly, the ability of workers to care for their aging parents was also adversely affected. This was important, as the labor matching policies at PartnershipCo considered only primary care as a "justifiable reason" for not changing hours.

The inability to plan one's life also acted as a barrier to social activities. The unpredictable nature of their schedules caused workers to experience their lives as being in disarray. The experience of Susan (a union rep) was indicative of this: "You plan something, and then they say 'oh can you come in and do something different,' and you feel compelled to do it. So you're changing all everything around."

Susan also explained how the instability impacted her family: "It's very hard moving things around . . . I've got a partner, so it's having a normal life out of here, he works in an office, Monday to Friday shifts, nine to five sort of thing, so it's having a normal life outside of here and [PartnershipCo] don't realize that I'm afraid, they think you are just here for them."

Derek, another union rep, detailed how it was not only the irregularity of the hours that played havoc with workers' home life but also the unpredictability of not knowing when you would be asked to work: "You can get up one day and think right I'm not working today and then get a phone call, you've not got anyone to look after your kids, or whatever, you might just be going shopping . . . to do your weekly shop, get a phone call, you've gotta come into work and they daren't say no, and especially women with children they've then gotta run round looking for someone to look after their kids."

A further difficulty for workers was that the unpredictability of their schedules made it hard to work a second job, which workers often desperately needed as their guaranteed hours were so low. As Bryah (a union rep) made clear: "They give you that ten hours [which is in your contract] but then they call with twenty-four to forty-eight hours' notice to come and do the job and if you have a second job, then there is a problem for you to come in and do that."

Schedule Insecurity

The unpredictable scheduling and its consequences for work-life balance and workers' income created a pervasive sense of insecurity. This supports the proposition put forward by a number of social scientists that insecurity related to working time can be an important contributor to job insecurity.[7] Workers experienced insecurity over future changes to their hours, as Jimmy, a union rep, explained: "There is no sort of hour security . . . you work an average of forty hours a week or thirty-six and a half hours a week and then when the overtime cuts come in, you are only on seven hours a week."

Or as Rosie (a union rep) put it, "You're never secure; you're never secure in your hours."

The source of uncertainty and worry was a sense of workers not knowing what the future holds for their schedule, whether they would be able to work the hours they were given and, if they could, how this would impact their life. It was the uncertainty about what the future held, rather than the general requirement to change schedules, that was most problematic, and this was amplified by poor communication of the changes. Susan explained how a lack of communication increased schedule insecurity: "One minute you walk in and you know what you're doing, and the next minute you walk in, and you don't . . . It's OK if you can accommodate that [change in hours] but sometimes it's with the not knowing."

This schedule insecurity was described by Tony, a union official, as being the biggest issue facing retail workers at PartnershipCo: "Insecurity, that's a big challenge . . . Are they gonna change their hours, are they going to have their hours reduced . . . The biggest issue is usually that."

Precarious scheduling created a pervasive sense of subjective insecurity at PartnershipCo. This is supported by over half of the workers who were asked responding that they felt that their working hours would get worse over the following twelve months. Furthermore, the vast majority of employees agreed that they felt insecure about the future of their job, despite none of these workers thinking it likely they would lose their job in the next year. This insecurity, combined with its potential impact on work-life balance, could be very stressful. Sandra (a union rep) explained how "they put a lot of stress on people . . . I used to be in tears."

Flexible Discipline: The Subtle Securing of Control

As discussed above, the flexible nature of scheduling at PartnershipCo resulted in many workers' schedules varying widely in both the number and timing of their hours, week in, week out. The near-total control by managers of this scheduling had a damaging effect on workers' work-life balance and led to workers experiencing a pervasive sense of schedule insecurity. This placed a great deal of discretionary power in the hands of managers.[8] Managers had the power to cause distress to specific workers simply by altering their schedule to unusual times, or times that clashed with childcare, social activities, education, or a second job. Alternatively, managers could cut the number of hours workers received and thus drastically reduce their income, or could increase the instability and unpredictability of their schedule. In these ways, managers not only had control over workers while they were in the workplace but also wielded a significant influence over the workers' home lives, as Tony (a union official) explained: "If I challenge [managers] . . . I might not get the overtime . . . or might not get my Sundays, or the hours I'm doing at the moment are perfect [as] I can finish at two, I can go home and pick up the kids . . . if I make a fuss I might have that taken away, or I'll have my hours changed, so if I keep my head down and do as I'm told I'll keep those hours."

Of course, flexible scheduling is instigated for profit maximization rather than control. Nevertheless, it does place a large amount of power in the hands of managers who can potentially use their discretion to cause significant suffering to specific workers. In reality, how frequently managers took advantage of this situation is impossible to infer conclusively from the data available. However, the informants certainly perceived that this happened, and with regard to control, it is this that matters.

For their part, managers pleaded innocence, informing workers that they had no choice but to alter their schedules due to staffing needs being set by head office on the basis of projected sales. While this was often not believed by the workers whose schedules were being affected, the inherent ambiguity of securing control via scheduling presented managers with a major advantage. For example, over a number of years, a worker's schedule may be relatively stable until he or she does something that displeases management. At this point, workers can suddenly find their schedule altered, their hours cut, and their working time highly unstable and unpredictable. In this situation, it seems extremely plausible to them that they are being disciplined. It is, nevertheless, possible that the change is a coincidental result of alterations to projected sales by head office, and that their manager is simply responding to this new reality in the best way they can.

That the majority of workers experience some degree of instability in their hours made it even harder for them to distinguish for certain whether such alterations were acts of discipline or not and, consequently, almost impossible for workers to know whether to blame their manager or the whims of market forces. Importantly, since schedule changes can always be disavowed as having been required by supply and demand, this makes them an ambiguous form of punishment and thus less damaging to the "psychological contract" than threats of dismissals. Colin illustrated this particularly clearly when he stated that, despite being very distressed that his job had been changed to nights, he did not blame management: "I do understand they need [to meet] certain [customer] demand and obviously, I'm just the unlucky one that mine happened to go to nights."

Precarious scheduling enabled control to be secured without recourse to standard despotic practices. Thus, a high level of workplace control could be accomplished "with a smile." This was important, as the scope for more traditional means of discipline was curtailed by the hegemonic apparatuses discussed in chapter 1, such as employment protections and the developed disciplinary and grievance procedures policed by the union. Nonetheless, workers felt reliant on their managers' mood and were afraid that if they displeased them, their schedule would suffer as a consequence. Derek explained that "they are terrified of not getting any more shifts and being stuck with this three-and-a-half or seven hours a week, which they can't live on . . . Being desperate for some extra hours, they depend on the mood of the manager for their income . . . Once your face doesn't fit you don't get any more hours."

Within the constraint of ensuring that staffing needs were met within their labor budget, managers had the capacity to give workers they liked more hours (including upgrading their contracts to full-time status), the shifts they wanted, and greater schedule stability. Moreover, scheduling was a zero-sum game: any benefits one worker gained were at the expense of others who, as a consequence, would receive either fewer, less stable, or less desirable hours. Unsurprisingly, scheduling was perceived as operating according to favoritism. Logically, therefore, workers tried to gain favor with their manager, in some cases by boosting their productivity by undertaking extra tasks or working off the clock. For example, at Mulling Point I observed how Denise, a worker who often received overtime, tended to start work fifteen minutes early and continued working after her shift had finished.

Conclusion: The Power of Flexible Discipline

This chapter has demonstrated that the operation of an internal labor market at PartnershipCo was not a significant source of consent. However, the despotism of working time aided the securing of workplace control, by increasing the arbitrary power of managers. Managers were perceived to use their discretion over scheduling to instigate flexible discipline, which could cause misery for specific workers by simply scheduling them to work at times that clashed with their home life, by cutting their hours, or increasing the instability and unpredictability of their hours. A benefit to managers of this mechanism of discipline was its subtlety. This subtlety was especially beneficial, as the scope for traditional despotic methods of control was constrained by the presence of hegemonic apparatuses such as employment contracts, developed disciplinary and grievance procedures, and union presence. The following chapter moves on to consider whether precarious scheduling operated as a similar mechanism of control at ConflictCo where the internal state more closely resembled market despotism.

DESPOTIC TIME IN THE U.S.

Undermining Worker Organization

The previous chapter highlighted the power of precarious scheduling at PartnershipCo. This chapter explores whether similar practices existed at ConflictCo, despite its contrasting context and internal state. One way that PartnershipCo and ConflictCo diverged significantly was with regard to insecurity. While workers at PartnershipCo experienced little employment insecurity, this was not the case at ConflictCo. It was clear that workers at ConflictCo were highly fearful of losing their jobs. This was a consequence of ConflictCo's internal state, which made use of "at-will employment," meaning that there was no redundancy policy, and managers were free to decide themselves which workers to keep on. Those who lost their jobs received no redundancy pay or notice. There was, therefore, a great deal of employment insecurity among the informants. If flexible discipline is found to be central to the operation of control at ConflictCo, despite the availability of traditional forms of discipline, then it significantly strengthens the case that this is a vital feature of workplace regimes in the twenty-first century. This chapter begins by investigating the existence of internal labor markets at ConflictCo. It then turns to investigating the flexible nature of time in this workplace regime.

Discounting Wages

As was the case for PartnershipCo, the absence of a strong internal labor market can be seen in the fact that pay at ConflictCo was set at only fractionally above the minimum wage in the external labor market. Also as at PartnershipCo, pay at ConflictCo had been declining in real terms, but here low pay was a major source of outrage among workers. Their low pay was commonly seen as an injustice due to how hard they worked. Omar (a worker) illustrated the relationship between the intensity of the work and discontent with the pay particularly clearly: "There are people . . . who bust their ass for ConflictCo . . . twenty-cent raises every year, what is that? . . . and these assistant managers, as lazy as fuck, disrespecting people, getting [a] $1,500–$5,000 bonus a year. And it's just not fair . . . the workers who are making this company the money are getting cheated, are getting discredited and getting disrespected; it just irritates me, man."

For other workers, the perception of injustice sprang from the disparity between their low pay and the profits made by ConflictCo—much of which flowed directly to the executives and shareholders. For example, Vincent (a worker) explained how his pay was so low that he was unable to afford a separate bed for his child. Vincent felt that "the thing that is most unjust is the wages that they pay us. This is a multibillion-dollar company, they make billions of dollars in profits a year, my store alone this Black Friday made over a million dollars just in that day. You know this company can afford to pay me a livable wage . . . I should be able to afford a stove or at least payments on a stove . . . We [he, his wife, and two small children] all sleep in the same room over here as I can't afford a bed in that one. Here in America the poverty line for a family of four is $20,000 and I make close to $16,000 and I think that is the most unjust thing."

That ConflictCo made such high profits served to highlight to workers that their low pay was not inevitable, as Mary (another worker) articulated clearly: "I'm just angry and disgusted at ConflictCo. It could be such a good place for the community, the environment, their workers, and they choose not to be, they just have to have all that money for themselves."

Furthermore, there was little opportunity for workers to increase their wages through genuine mobility, as advancement into salaried management was highly unlikely. Within the pay structure, there was also little incremental difference between pay grades for hourly paid workers. The highest and lowest hourly skill-based pay grades were differentiated by just $1.70 per hour. Workers also received a premium of around $1 per hour if promoted to supervisor and, on average, received a raise of forty cents (5 percent of the standard rate) every year after their first eighteen months. After 6.5 years Andre's hourly pay had increased by $3; after ten years Mary's had increased by $6; and likewise, even after twenty years, James's had also only increased by $6.

Therefore, on the whole, there was little evidence that internal labor market–type elements significantly shielded workers at ConflictCo from the external labor market or were a source of consent. We will, therefore, move on to consider the allocation of working time in securing workplace control—which, as we have already seen, was a significant mechanism of control at PartnershipCo.

The Worst of Times: Flexibility "At Will"

Working time at ConflictCo was shaped by California's at-will employment law; that is, the quantity and timing of scheduling were entirely at the discretion of management. Legally, employees had the "reciprocal" discretion not to accept the hours they were offered, and to end their employment relationship without notice. In reality, however, workers had very little ability to reject their scheduling by either ending or threatening to end their employment due to the restrictiveness of unemployment benefits combined with the high levels of unemployment and underemployment. This meant that scheduling flexibility at ConflictCo was achieved simply through managers' direct scheduling of hours on a three-week basis, based on the head office's projected future customer demand.

ConflictCo's flexible scheduling was experienced by all the worker informants as requiring frequent and unpredictable changes to their schedules. Overwhelmingly, informants felt that these changes led to a large variance in their hours. Some workers even stated that they would often not be scheduled for any hours one week, but then twelve to thirty-eight hours other weeks. Hours frequently varied week by week by a factor of two or three, with the average week by week difference within the three-week schedule period being around twenty hours. This was even the case for those workers who were officially "full-time." The informants explained how full-time status was ignored, one worker stating that full-time employees were getting as few as ten hours a week. If workers did not receive full-time hours (at least twenty-four hours), then they lost their full-time status and officially became part-time. In the process, however, they lost access to employer-provided health insurance (although most workers already lacked the required hours or found the deductibles and/or premiums too high to access it).[1] Shift patterns were also irregular beyond the changing quantity of hours, with little pattern to weekly shifts. Typically, it was felt that this made the scheduling even more random and unpredictable.

During recruitment, ConflictCo would require workers to fill out an availability survey of the hours they could work. The informants suggested that, in reality, workers had little choice but to indicate full availability, otherwise they would not receive adequate hours or even be hired in the first place. The three-week schedules were frequently altered after they had been set, sometimes only one day in advance. The unpredictable nature of these changes to schedules was heightened by a lack of communication. Additionally, there was no faith in the grievance procedure as a means to improve communication and ensure that schedules were set on a three-week basis. In fact, some workers found out about changes only when they were disciplined for nonattendance, or turned up at work only to be told that they were no longer working that day.

Scheduling at ConflictCo was, for many workers, on a zero hours basis. Part-time workers were not guaranteed a minimum number of hours, while full-time workers were not guaranteed full-time hours and could unilaterally have their full-time status revoked. Workers had very little influence over this flexible scheduling, either formally (owing to the lack of collective representation) or informally (through individual discussion with a manager). A typical managerial attitude was reported to be along the lines of "Well, you can either work or go work somewhere else." Without independent oversight or enforcement, managers even ignored ConflictCo's company policy that schedules be set on a three-week basis, which was the only constraint on their ability to schedule workers at will.

The Impact of Precarious Scheduling on Job Quality

The Impairment of Work-Life Balance

Precarious scheduling at ConflictCo had a negative effect on workers and reduced job quality. Specifically, it impaired workers' general work-life balance, reducing their ability to plan. Rachel (a worker) summed up the overall impact on work-life balance: "Your schedule is such a yo-yo you can't have a life."

The uncertainty that precarious scheduling entailed made it very difficult for workers to plan their social lives, as Brad (another worker) explained: "You can't plan anything . . . It affects you whether you're single, married with kids, whatever, because it does just take all the organization out of your life."

The unpredictable nature of working time was also a major barrier to workers' attempts to carry out other essential tasks, especially if they had other jobs. As Andre (a worker) explained: "You don't know what days you're gonna have off so what days you might actually get paid, and I have a job where I work during the day as well [as nights at ConflictCo], so it kind of just makes it that much harder because now I don't know which day off I'm going to have to run errands."

This unpredictability impacted workers' general family life, for example, spending time with children and partners and undertaking family activities that required advance planning. Even if workers did manage to have their schedule changed so that they could spend time with their family, this carried the risk of an unaffordable cut in hours. A recurring concern raised in the interviews was the impact that flexible scheduling could have on childcare responsibilities—a particular concern for female workers. This could cause serious repercussions if parents were required to leave children unattended, leading, in some cases, to the intervention of social services.

Insecurity

Not knowing how many hours would be allocated to them each week made it difficult for the workers to predict their income and thus caused difficulty in confidently planning their expenditures. This difficulty was aggravated by the fact that precarious scheduling could result in some workers facing weeks in which they worked a very low number of hours. During such periods, the financial hardship encountered could be extreme, requiring workers to resort to extraordinary measures such as using food banks, taking on debt, lapsing on rent and utility bill payments, and even losing one's home and having to move in with relatives. Rachel explained how manager-controlled flexible scheduling caused income insecurity among hourly workers: "You are just wondering like, 'Oh my God, are they going to change my hours, are they going to cut my hours next week, am I going to have enough money for my rent next week?'"

Kim (a worker) made clear that it was not just the unpredictability of hours but also the inherent instability of their income that caused workers problems: "It adds a lot of stress to it because you never know what your pay is going to look like, you know it's a problem trying to pay stuff and your pay is never steady, you know your pay goes up and down because ConflictCo plays around with your hours; that causes a lot of stress, it's very stressful."

The effects of precarious scheduling were particularly pronounced at ConflictCo because the hourly rate was so low. Joe (a worker) elucidated how low pay combined with unstable hours was a source of fear: "I don't make a lot of money and I only work thirty-four hours, twenty-four is nothing, so yeah I'm scared."

The fact that income insecurity and working-time insecurity combined into a more general insecurity surrounding scheduling can be seen by the fact that the vast majority of workers interviewed felt that the quality of their working hours would get worse over the next twelve months. The majority also agreed or strongly agreed that they felt insecure about the future of their job. Typically, this schedule insecurity was said to have caused stress and anxiety and depressed well-being. For example, Brad explained how the fear of not being able to afford food or rent or of being unable to pay his bills led him to feel depressed: "At first [I felt] depressed because they are things I have to deal with every day. The very real concern that if my hours got cut how am I going to feed myself, how am I going to pay my bills, keep a house over my head, keep the gas in my car to get to work in the first place."

Likewise, Akira (a former worker at ConflictCo) explained that she required therapy to deal with the stress and anxiety caused by precarious scheduling: "A whole lot of stress and anxiety . . . It's sad, it's heart breaking, I did a lot of crying, you know I have to hold back tears mostly every time I talk about it. I've had a lot of therapy just from working at ConflictCo, mental therapy for stress management, anxiety management, just from working there."

Ali (a union official supporting the worker association) suggested that this stress, anxiety, and depressed well-being might manifest as psychosomatic complaints: "It's very stressful, you know there are many employees who might never have had problems with anxiety or depression but when they start working at ConflictCo they have to start going to the doctor and get, you know, medication, or if they had these existing conditions it's made it a lot worse, whether it is high blood pressure, so you know it's affecting people not just mentally but physically as well."

Flexible Discipline: Subtly Securing Control at ConflictCo

As at PartnershipCo, the flexible nature of scheduling resulted in workers' schedules varying widely in both the number and timing of hours week by week. Managers at ConflictCo had near-total control over this scheduling, which had a damaging effect on workers' work-life balance and led to workers experiencing a pervasive sense of schedule insecurity regarding future changes to their hours. As at PartnershipCo, managers not only had control over workers while they were in the workplace but also over their family and social life, as Francisco (a ConflictCo worker) explained: "If they change your time every time that you go to work, and they change your day off, that means that they own your life already because they let you work any time they want, any day they want and you know you can't even plan for your life."

The extension of this power beyond the realm of the workplace led another worker, Brad, to equate manager-controlled flexible scheduling to slavery: "I would compare it almost to feeling like a slave because your power to control your own life is taken from you; they are going to make you [work] whenever . . . they want."

Not only did manager-controlled flexible scheduling provide managers with this discretionary power over workers' lives, but managers could use it to punish workers if they were not flexible, productive, or obedient enough. This created fear among the workforce: if they displeased their managers, their hours would be cut or schedules altered. Akira (a former worker) elaborated this common theme:

"You're disciplined like a child; like you would punish your twelve-year-old: 'I'm going to take your hours, I'm gonna take your days because you spoke back.'"

The subtlety of this manner of control proved especially useful for surreptitiously disciplining workers who joined the worker association, thus undermining the union-backed campaign to wrest a degree of control from management. Many workers at ConflictCo felt that this was a barrier to the growth of the worker association. Kim (a worker) explained why: "If I go to an event [organized by the worker association], and I'm out there and they [managers] find out, I will find out the next week over that I've been slashed ten hours or so and my hours would have been steady at thirty-two hours for like a couple of months, and then all of sudden an activity comes about and my hours get slashed."

In fact, a similar experience led Becky (a former worker) to quit her job at ConflictCo, leaving her unable to claim unemployment benefits: "I was continuously being active in the worker association, and I was going to rallies and protests and in June or July 2012 there was the China Town rally, so I went to that and . . . two weeks later . . . I went to the computer to look at my schedule, and my hours had gone down from thirty-eight down to eight, and I wasn't even scheduled for one of the weeks, and at that exact moment, my manager was on the phone to someone and saying, 'Are you available to come for an interview at 11 A.M. tomorrow?' So I heard that, and it was kinda a slap in the face, so I left."

As Valentina, one of the lead union organizers supporting the worker association, explained, it was very difficult for workers, the worker association, or the union to combat this form of punishment: "It's hard to distinguish if it is complete retaliation or if it is just what ConflictCo usually does . . . Their schedule is X, then they do something publicly, and their schedule changes . . . they are probably trying to mess with you because they know that you can't work that shift . . . But that's not something that you can necessarily prove . . .'cause then we'd have to make the argument that their hours have never changed before and that's not the nature of retail."

Moreover, dismissing someone is rigid in its immutability. Conversely, cutting or altering a worker's schedule can easily be rescinded, making it a much more flexible and permanent means of control. This flexibility also means that the punishment can be modulated and reduced over time, unlike the binary nature of dismissal/nondismissal. Manager-controlled flexible scheduling, however, was not just a tool that managers could utilize as and when they needed in order to punish specific workers. It also constituted an active and constant "structuration"[2] of the workplace environment, meaning that all workers needed to constantly strive to maintain the favor of managers. As Brad (a worker), put it, "Pretty much everyone feels that if you are on the good side of a manager they will give you more hours, give you better shifts."

As discussed in the previous chapter, the fact that managers had the ability to cut or offer workers additional hours and set shifts meant that workers had an interest in attempting to gain favor with their manager. José, a union organizer, claimed doing so was common among the workers he spoke to: "Some workers do try and do that [gain a manager's favor by doing extra tasks]. I spoke to someone the other day who was like: 'When I first started I used to do a lot of extra stuff for ConflictCo and the time came for them to cut hours and I went to the manager who I'd done all this extra stuff for.'"

Nicola, a former assistant manager at ConflictCo, supported the workers' view that managers at ConflictCo used their control over schedules as a way to secure high productivity: "If they are part-time and they have performance issues, I know that managers would look at giving that person less hours than a worker that performed better."

This process of gaining favor also personalized this mechanism of control—which had important implications for the obscuring of the labor process, discussed in the next chapter.

Conclusion: The Power of Flexible Discipline

This chapter demonstrates that, as at PartnershipCo, the operation of an internal labor market was not a significant source of consent at ConflictCo. It then shows that, despite the divergent internal states at PartnershipCo and ConflictCo, both operated high levels of manager-controlled flexible scheduling, which translated into precarious and insecure scheduling for workers. The precariousness of such scheduling in turn aided the securing of workplace control. As at PartnershipCo, a major strength of this mechanism of control for managers was its subtlety and ambiguity. However, at ConflictCo this subtlety was particularly useful for managers, as their scope for blatant despotic methods of control had been reduced by negative publicity surrounding working conditions in their stores. In particular, flexible discipline was a useful tool for undermining the worker association, as it was very difficult to prove that temporal flexibility was being used in this way. Other benefits for managers of flexible discipline were that this method of control was, by its nature, less rigid than formal and informal threats of dismissal. Punishing workers through alterations to schedules could easily be modified and rescinded simply by managers offering workers additional hours or reducing the variability of their schedule.

This chapter has also highlighted how flexible discipline operated in a similar fashion at ConflictCo and PartnershipCo. This was despite the fact that managers at ConflictCo had more traditional despotic tools at their disposal than those available to their counterparts at PartnershipCo. This similarity in the face of highly divergent industrial relations climates, employment protections, and welfare systems demonstrates that flexible discipline may operate as a mechanism of control across vastly different contexts. The control engendered by flexible scheduling is not, however, simply a disciplinary tool that managers wield as and when they need, in order to punish specific workers. It also constitutes an active and constant structuration of the workplace environment according to which all workers constantly strive to maintain the favor of managers. The following chapter moves on to consider the dynamics of the work at PartnershipCo and ConflictCo, and the implications of precarious scheduling for the obscuring of exploitation—and how this too aids control.

Part 3

THE DYNAMICS OF WORK AND SPACES OF RESISTANCE

The final part of this book provides more detail on what it was like to work at PartnershipCo and ConflictCo. In particular, chapter 5 focuses on the nature of the labor process at the two firms. Parts 2 and 3 looked at the cases separately and in succession. Doing so was useful so as to draw out the differences between the more progressive regime at PartnershipCo and the more reactionary one at ConflictCo. However, the common characteristics of the work mean that in part 3 they are best considered together, so as to capture the slight differences that were present. The work at both firms mainly entailed stocking shelves and serving customers, with the use of functional flexibility causing similar (high) levels of work intensity and stress as workers attempted to juggle the physical and emotional demands of their jobs.

As highlighted in the book's introduction, previous research has demonstrated that workers can subvert intense labor processes such as these by creating work games that provide them with "relative satisfactions." These work games have been argued to aid workplace control by obscuring exploitation through focusing workers' attention on "winning" the game and thereby producing greater profits for their employer, rather than questioning the exploitative social relations in which they are located. However, at ConflictCo there was no evidence of work games operating in this way. This was not entirely unexpected, as the internal state of ConflictCo most closely resembled that of market despotism (although, as chapter 2 explains, a worker association had been able to win the workforce some respite from blatant acts of despotism). Workplace regime theory suggests that work games are a feature of hegemonic rather than market despotic regimes, as it is the former that provide workers with enough security and certainty to absorb themselves in work games without fear of management retaliation, unsustainable work intensification, or job loss.[1]

More surprisingly, work games were also absent at PartnershipCo, where the internal state included some institutions that resembled those found in hegemonic regimes and that provided workers with some protections and security. That work games were not important features of the regimes of ConflictCo and PartnershipCo might be explained by the high levels of schedule insecurity, making it impossible for workers to focus their attention on turning the labor process into an engaging game.

In the absence of work games at ConflictCo, workers instead turned to highly individualized acts of escapism through music, either listening to it on headphones or singing and humming to themselves, as well as attempting to laugh to themselves about the grim situation that confronted them. Escapism was also the prime way in which workers at PartnershipCo sought to relieve the daily grind of their work. But unlike at ConflictCo, where workers feared high levels of surveillance and harsh discipline, at PartneshipCo the greater security and protection afforded to workers by the internal state meant that they could engage in informal acts of collective escapism. This escapism in the form of "having a laugh" was usually based around the assertion of masculinity and femininity through horseplay, bullying, and flirtation.

While this escapism made working at the two firms more bearable, it did not obscure exploitation. In fact, it was the flexible discipline outlined in part 2 that again aided control by laying the basis for the misrecognition of exploitation at both ConflictCo and PartnershipCo. Managers at both firms had the ability to arbitrarily improve or worsen workers' schedules in terms of both the quantity and quality of their work hours. This situation meant that it was imperative that workers both attempted to win their managers' favor and plead with them for changes to their hours. When managers accommodated workers' needs by providing them with different hours or alternative schedules, workers experienced it as an act of kindness that needed to be reciprocated through hard work. In this way the account of "schedule gifts" in this book develops on the sociological literature on gifts, in particular, the classic studies of Marcel Mauss and Pierre Bourdieu as well as recent research by Ashley Mears.[2] Schedule gifts are shown to bind workers to managers, through the creation of social debt and the moral obligation to repay perceived acts of kindness by managers in helping workers improve their schedules. In this way, flexible scheduling leads exploitation to be misrecognized and experienced relationally in terms of gratitude and moral obligation toward those in positions of power.

Chapter 6 investigates the room available for resistance at ConflictCo and PartnershipCo. In doing so, it demonstrates that the control afforded by flexible scheduling was not complete and was also susceptible to breakdown. At PartnershipCo the insecurity of scheduling seemingly fueled union membership; however, given the hegemonic role of the union, discussed in chapter 1, this did not actually lead to collective resistance. Instead workers engaged in forms of what anthropologist James C. Scott has termed "'hidden resistance."[3] While the potential for such acts to markedly challenge managerial control was limited, they do, nevertheless, highlight that the control enabled by precarious scheduling is not complete and that it could potentially fuel acts of collective resistance. In fact, ConflictCo provides an example of how precarious scheduling can fuel new forms of collective action at work.

At ConflictCo the high level of surveillance and fear of harsh managerial reprisals limited the kinds of hidden resistance that were common at PartnershipCo. Yet a small minority of workers had overcome their fear and been mobilized by a union-backed worker association. This worker association had been able to make use of social media in combination with direct action to successfully improve working conditions at ConflictCo. This success was despite the worker association's relatively small number of members, the weak structural power of these workers, and the extreme hostility of ConflictCo toward worker organization. Therefore, this mobilization demonstrates how even in the face of the despotism entailed by precarious scheduling it is possible for workers in the twenty-first century to resist, and that the workplace regimes of this era may be unstable.

THE DYNAMICS OF WORK AND SCHEDULING GIFTS

In the previous chapters, flexible discipline was shown to be a powerful means by which control could be secured at both PartnershipCo and ConflictCo. This chapter will investigate how control at the two workplace regimes was aided by the obscuring of exploitation. The chapter will proceed by describing the main characteristics of retail work at PartnershipCo and ConflictCo. In particular, the nature of the labor process will be detailed. The chapter will then provide a brief history of work games, that is, the manner in which workers create games that make their work more enjoyable but that also lead them to become complicit in their own exploitation, for winning these games invariably entails producing additional profit for their employer. The chapter will then move on to discuss the absence of work games at PartnershipCo and ConflictCo. In place of the mystifying effects of work games we find that flexible working time aids control as a consequence of "schedule gifts" obscuring exploitation. Schedule gifts resemble Pierre Bourdieu's discussion of the misrecognition that formed part of the gift-giving ritual among Kabyle peasants in northern Algeria. Schedule gifts are found to be crucial for understanding control in the on-demand economy.

Work Dynamics in Low-End Retail

At both PartnershipCo and ConflictCo stores, the job content and labor processes were similar. Although there were a range of jobs being undertaken, the two main job types can be categorized as shelf stacker and cashier. The shelf stacker role involved restocking shelves on the shop floor with products from the stockroom and the "facing up" of shelves. Facing up required that goods be moved to the front of shelves in order to make the shelves appear well stocked at all times and to make the shop aesthetically pleasing. Facing up also eased the shopping experience by making products more visible and easier for customers to reach. This was my job for two months at PartnershipCo's Mulling Point store.

Cashiers at ConflictCo and PartnershipCo operated large checkouts with conveyor belts for moving goods, bar-code scanners for their identification, and cash register software for the calculation of the required payment and change. Because the roles demanded quite different levels of physical labor, cashiers tended to be older and shelf stackers generally younger. However, functional flexibility required permanent shelf stackers to be trained to operate checkouts during busy periods. This meant that shelf stackers could be called away from their shelf-stacking responsibilities at any time that extra checkout operators were needed.

"Cracking the Whip and Not Giving a Shit"

Functional flexibility of this kind caused shelf stackers much frustration and stress, as their work was still evaluated in terms of the level of completion of their shelf-stacking tasks. As Ashlyn, a worker at ConflictCo, explained: "I hate it, I do not like to go up there and handle money, I don't like being up there. It takes time away from my department, you know, and I tell them, if you want me to be cashiering do not expect me to come into my department and have it zoned [faced up] and have no go backs [products that require putting back on the shelf]. You know I can't do it, I'm telling you right now I can't do it, I'm just telling you I can't do it. If you want me to have my department zoned and everything I can do it, as long as I'm not at the cashiers."

A discussion with two ConflictCo workers in the LA area, Sophie and Megan, that I noted down in my fieldwork diary demonstrated this point clearly: "The call went out for her [Sophie] to go on the tills, a circumstance which she was very despondent about, saying, 'How am I going to get all this done when I'm getting called to the checkout all the time?' Megan responded, 'Oh no, you've had your checkout training. I'm trying not to have mine, otherwise I'll never get my work done and will be shouted at by the managers.'"

At PartnershipCo, functional flexibility caused similar problems. Nick, a union rep at PartnershipCo, put it as follows: "There is a lot of this multi-skilling going on now . . . It's getting harder to work there now."

During my participant observation, working as a shelf stacker, I noted how glad I was that I myself was not checkout trained: "Whilst I was working on the toilet rolls a bald manager, who I didn't know, came over and asked if I was check-out trained. I replied that I wasn't, to which he responded, 'Oh, you are one of the lucky ones.' If I had been [trained] I would never have completed my shelves."

Cashier and shelf-stacking roles required some emotional labor, such as smil-ing and being friendly with customers, and in the case of shelf stackers, helping customers to locate products. Yet physical and emotional labor often came into conflict, as the manager doing my induction training remarked: "You see, with PartnershipCo it is like they want us to be like robots, everything is controlled, every task only takes an exact amount of time which is measured and this [a video illustrating customer service] reminds us that we need to be human when deal-ing with customers."

However, those elements of the work that required more qualitative evalua-tion invariably took a back seat to elements that could be measured quantitatively, such as the speed at which shelves were stacked and faced up and how much pro-duce was processed through the checkout. Paul, a union rep at PartnershipCo, discussed the difficulty of doing both: "The work rate that you're expected to do on checkouts . . . is phenomenally high but then they also want you to give good customer service, but if you want me to speed up and get things done then I'm not going to be able to give good customer service."

As discussed in chapter 1, my experiences at PartnershipCo demonstrated that, in the context of low-end retail, the importance of the much commented on tri-adic relationship among workers, managers, and customers was of secondary im-portance to worker-manager relations.[1] This meant that the emotional labor of customer service was clearly of much less importance to managers than the phys-ical labor of handling and moving goods around the store so that customers would be able to locate and purchase them.

At both firms, most job roles allowed little employee control or discretion over how and when these work activities were carried out, leading to workloads that were experienced as high and intense. Work intensity was also felt to have in-creased in recent years at both firms, representing an additional source of dis-satisfaction. A common phrase at PartnershipCo was "doing more with less." Nick (a union rep at PartnershipCo) explained this common theme concisely: "They are putting a lot of pressure on everybody to work harder, faster, with less people . . . People are getting pushed and pushed and pushed all of the time . . . A lot of people are under a lot of pressure."

Work intensity also put workers under a great deal of emotional strain, as Mary (another union rep) explained: "Well I'll tell you how bad it has got, because we've got a supervisor who came out of this room two weeks ago in floods of tears; it was unusual for her to be like this so I took her to the toilet, and she said, 'I can't cope with my role as a supervisor anymore, it's just too much.'"

Likewise at ConflictCo, a chief source of discontentment was the perception that workloads and the intensity of the work had increased in recent years. A worker, Pamela, illustrated this theme particularly clearly: "In general there is not enough staffing, not enough hours, not enough time in the day to accomplish what they demand out of every worker in that place."

A number of informants claimed that the intensity of work was so high that it was damaging their health. Akira explained what happened to her while working at ConflictCo: "We could never get that job [cosmetics] done, we were defeated before we came to work . . . So I tried to start working harder and I worked my-self into a hospital."

As noted in chapter 2, ConflictCo shelf stackers called the "my-guide" task management program "my-slave." The idiom of slavery was also employed by black workers to describe the general work intensity at ConflictCo. For example, Twanda stated, "They work you like a slave."

Andre also used particularly lucid imagery of slavery to describe the conse-quences for worker health: "We have a saying 'cracking the whip and not giving a shit' . . . They just want to keep on pushing you, and pushing you, and pushing you, and pushing you, to see how hard they can push you until you break."

At PartnershipCo the work intensity was also felt to have increased in recent years, and this was a source of dissatisfaction. During my participant observation of shelf stacking at PartnershipCo, I found that the workload was constantly too high to be achieved in the time allocated, requiring a very high work rate to reach anywhere close to what the managers expected of us. Some members of my team even resorted to working off the clock at the start and end of their shifts. The phys-icality of this "service work" should also not be underestimated, consisting as it does of lifting, pulling, and pushing quite heavy boxes of products, as well as rip-ping up packaging, all at a fast pace.

Previous research has highlighted the ingenious ways in which workers have been able to use their agency to subvert intense labor processes such as these and create work games that can transform arduous work into a source of relative sat-isfaction. These work games not only enable workers to develop new sources of enjoyment in the workplace but also involve an element of consent to exploita-tion in that "winning the game" usually entails producing higher levels of profit for their employer.[2]

Work Games

Hegemonic regimes in both the United States and the UK made work games viable due to the employment security this type of regime provided. At the same time, the constraining of managerial despotism provided workers with a degree of what sociologist Andrew Friedman has described as responsible autonomy from managers' direct control.[3]

Workers initially devise and enter into work games in order to counter the weariness, tedium, and arduousness of work and to make time pass quickly. Although workers initiate these games independently, managers play an important role in ensuring their sustainability.[4] However, in market despotic regimes "the piecework game becomes a self-defeating spiral of labor intensification . . . The game itself produces conditions that make the game more difficult to play." This is because workers lack sufficient bargaining power to ensure that the rules of a game become stabilized and thus that the game is reproduced. In such situations, if there is too much uncertainty and fear, then work games lose their ability to be engrossing. There is therefore only limited scope for the obscuring of labor processes via work games in despotic regimes.[5]

Hegemonic regimes, on the other hand, provide conditions that are more hospitable to the constitution of work games, as they restrict the scope for managers to practice arbitrary discipline. The internal state and the internal labor market protect workers from capricious managerial discipline, providing them with the appropriate level of certainty and security necessary to become absorbed in work games. Furthermore, social pressure provides a powerful incentive to play the same game with the same rules as everyone else. Continual peer-to-peer evaluation into how well each individual is playing "the game" makes it difficult to opt out without also being ostracized by colleagues. However, "the very act of playing the game simultaneously produce[s] consent to its rules. You can't be serious about playing a game . . . if, at the same time, you question its rules and goals."[6]

Burawoy illustrates the process through the game of "making out" that was played by workers he studied in a machine shop in the 1970s. This piece rate game entailed skillfully producing large quantities of parts and thus producing the output on various machines, which would result in the workers' earnings being maximized. However, if workers produced too much, then the piece rate for that job would be rerated by management, thus making it harder for everyone to earn a living on that job. For this reason getting a job rerated by producing too much would earn the scorn of the rest of the workforce. Therefore, winning the game of making out required a skillful and delicate maintenance of an output just below what would lead to a job's piece rate being altered. "Making out," however, became an end in itself beyond that of making more money, with "operators constantly shar[ing] their piecework experience as a chief item of conversation, and always in terms of 'making money,' [but] they were, in reality, communicating 'game scores' or 'race results,'"[7] and therefore "the difference between making out and not making out was thus not measured in the few pennies of bonus we earned but in our prestige, sense of accomplishment, and pride."[8]

In addition to Burawoy, a number of researchers have identified the importance of work games. For example, as Burawoy points out, sociologist Donald Roy found similar "making out" work games in the same machine shop thirty years earlier.[9] Roy also details a work game in a garment factory that involved cutting certain quantities of particular colored shapes so that the die used to produce them would require filing down and thus provide the worker with a change of activity as a reward. However, this game was not collective and was, consequently, less gripping for workers.[10]

During the hegemonic period similar games were also identified in the UK. For instance, Huw Beynon discovered at Ford a game that he dubbed "working back the line." This game consisted of a process whereby workers "worked back the line" by working faster than the assembly line required so as to "make their own time" in which they could rest and socially interact.[11] Another example is provided by Pollert's study of female workers at an Imperial Tobacco factory. At this factory, workers also tried to cope with the drudgery of their work through escapism and "having a laugh," but Pollert also demonstrates how this provided the basis for a work game: the game of flirting, teasing, and poking fun at male supervisors. This game proved highly absorbing because it "was a complex, tense balance between confrontation and collaboration: complex, because class control was mediated by patriarchal control, and neither side of the relationship could separate them; tense because if either side went too far in the sexy word-play, if the girls' flirtations turned to disrespect or the charge hands['] sexist cajolery went too far, the rules of the game could snap." Moreover, for the workers, "failure in the game [ineffective flirting or going too far] leads to the sanction of being more likely to receive arbitrary victimization."[12]

Work Games in Contemporary Workplaces

Despite the era of hegemony and employment security coming to an end in the 1980s, a number of researchers have identified work games as continuing to play an important role in the obscuring of workplace relations. For example, fast-food workers have been found to engage in sales games.[13] As noted in the book's introduction, this is surprising, as Burawoy argued that security was important for making these games absorbing, and employment security is not something often associated with the fast-food industry. Indeed, these games often lack a financial incentive, with the only compulsion being the social pressure to play. This means that these games might not be absorbing. For example, at a call center most workers soon became uninterested in the learning game they engaged in and instead quit their job.[14] This game, therefore, did little to generate commitment among the workforce. Contemporary work games have also been found in factories and casinos where workers do have some security.[15]

It was highlighted in the book's introduction that given the importance of flexible working time, there might be potential for games structured around time to play an important role in the maintenance of workplace control. In addition to the game of "working back the line" at Ford (already discussed), other time-based work games have been uncovered, albeit not in the service industry, for example, at a Chinese textile factory and a UK chemical plant.[16] Given these examples, drawn from various contexts, it was expected that work games would continue to play a central role in workplace control in the twenty-first century and that at firms making use of temporal flexibility these games would be structured around time.

Work Games at ConflictCo

Previous research has documented some potential for work games to obscure exploitation in service sector settings, including in fast-food restaurants and call centers, but most successfully in casinos where workers had greater security. Given the importance of temporal flexibility, discussed in part two, and that previous research has highlighted examples of work games involving working time, it might be expected that such games would exist at PartnershipCo and ConflictCo. Yet, there was in fact very little evidence for the importance of work games, involving time or otherwise, at either ConflictCo or PartnershipCo. ConflictCo did not systematically incentivize work games through the provision of bonuses or even symbolic prizes.[17] Without this material support, the development of work games was left to the creativity of workers to spontaneously devise games for themselves. Indeed, some informants explained how they tried to constitute their work as a race, either with regard to their scan rate when operating the checkouts, or regarding the speed at which they could empty their pallets of goods when restocking shelves. They even occasionally discussed their scores and strategies with their coworkers.

However, these attempts at the creation of games were undermined by managers. For example, managers were meant to give out badges to checkout operators who achieved fast scan rates, which would have enabled workers to keep score of who was winning this game. However, the badges were not distributed by their managers, undermining the purpose of the game. In another instance, managers told workers that the number of pallets they put out was unimportant, as the amount of stock on each pallet varied. Thus, the basis of the game was again undermined, and the workers were deprived of a means of keeping score. Instead of focusing on the race to put out pallets and thereby breaking the work down into measurable goals that could have provided a form of relative satisfaction, the workers' attention was refocused onto a constant stream of intense work.

The fact that managers were seemingly undermining a potential means by which exploitation could be obscured demonstrates that patterns of control are unlikely to be a conscious priority of management. This supports Paul Edwards's view that control will often not be the consequence of deliberate managerial strategy but rather develops out of a complex, and often unconscious, interplay between agency and structure within the workplace.[18]

Earlier it was highlighted that the "learning games" that call center workers have been found to play are not very effective. Workers tended not to find them absorbing, for the only compulsion to play is the social pressure created through interaction with customers. Most workers thus refuse to continue playing and instead quit the work.[19] At ConflictCo, however, there appeared to be little compulsion to even begin to play such learning games, as the workers did not seem to experience any intense social pressure to become competent in their interaction with customers. In fact, workers at ConflictCo did not struggle to be proficient in their customer interactions—though given that these interactions were of a fairly routine nature, there was little need for employees to work hard at becoming better at serving customers. Thus, there was no basis for learning-type games.

Escapism at ConflictCo

Without work games to occupy their minds, escapism and humor were central to workers' lived experience of ConflictCo. Sociologist Huw Beynon documents escapism and humor as pertinent psychological coping methods.[20] For those on the shop floor, this escapism was principally achieved through using headphones to listen to music—despite this being against company policy. John, a shopping cart collector at ConflictCo, discussed his coping method: "I just do my job. When I get to my job site I just put my headset on and listen to my radio on my phone, on my earphones, and get my job done."

The importance of this escapism for productivity can be gleaned from the fact that this was one of the few rules that managers allowed workers to break. As Matthew (a worker) explained: "Even though it's against policy and they [managers] say it, . . . they don't over-enforce it, apart from when overnighters fall behind, [then] they usually come out and reinforce it and say 'no more music' and we'll go a little while and then somebody will have the courage to play the music and then it just all gets going again."

The unlucky workers whose job made listening to music through headphones impossible had to detach themselves from the reality of the workplace in other ways, one of which was to create their own music by singing or humming to themselves. Another way, as Beynon found at Ford and sociologist Donald Roy found in a garment factory, was by "having a laugh" through horseplay and lighthearted worker interaction.[21] As Mary, a worker at ConflictCo, put it: "You just have to laugh, just laugh it off, because if you dwell on it, it just brings you down."

Work Games at PartnershipCo

In Burawoy's account of work games, he argues that too much workplace uncertainty is a barrier to the development of games.[22] Thus, it might be expected that the employment protection provided by the hegemonic apparatuses at PartnershipCo would create a more hospitable environment for the constitution of work games than at ConflictCo. However, here too, workers' only tactic for making their situation more enjoyable was escapism from the daily grind of work. Listening to music was said to be an advantage of the job for online delivery drivers, but for in-store workers the principal manner in which escapism was achieved was, again, through "having a laugh" so as not to dwell on the everyday reality. As we saw in part 1, workers perceived there to be a lower level of surveillance at PartnershipCo than at ConflictCo, and workers at PartnershipCo were also less fearful of being fired for misconduct as long as they had the support of a union rep.

A consequence of this lower level of employment insecurity was that the workplace regime provided space for the pursuit of escapism through informal group formation and a degree of autonomy from officially sanctioned behavior through horseplay, messing around, and flirting with each other. Ackroyd and Thompson argue that having a laugh, horseplay, and banter in the workplace often revolve around the assertion of sexuality.[23] In fact, among male workers at PartnershipCo, "having a laugh" could involve a quite predatory and aggressive affirmation of masculinity. Jeff provided an illustrative example:

> So you know when you get a group of guys together and they are just going to start beating the crap out of each other. Well in my store you get a lot of messing around, you know, not on the shop floor but downstairs you'll get, how can I put it, horseplay, I suppose . . . So there was this one guy, a guy called Dahn, who we, well, I should say for the record

that I wasn't involved, he got tied up with the sort of red ties that come on the cages, completely tied up, I mean totally tied up, literally hogtied [laughing], put in a cage, and left in a chiller for about half an hour. So yeah we were all stood outside and he's going "let me out, let me out!"

Paul also explained how he and his coworkers would make time go faster by "messing around," such as throwing boxes at each other. Paul was also certain that managers were not concerned by such antics as long as the work was completed on time.

Conversely, for female workers, messing around involved the assertion of femininity, which could have a more explicitly sexual dimension. Sara explained: "A lot of what I'm about to tell you, we should in theory get told off for but we don't. So I've got Norman, so we have tickle fights . . . and it's just hilarious and we have so much banter, people would say it is sexual harassment, but it's not, it's just banter, the fact that the guys know that I'm flirtatious and the rest of it, so they'll say 'alright darling' and we'll have hugs."

Jeff and Sara had a clear understanding that management tolerated this messing around and "banter" because it improved the workers' ability to carry out emotional labor when dealing with customers.

While these findings at PartnershipCo and ConflictCo parallel findings of escapism at Ford and among the garment workers studied by Roy, they differ from Pollert's findings, drawn from female tobacco workers, for whom "having a laugh" did develop into a work game.[24] This may have been due to the "laughing" at ConflictCo being an individual experience, while "having a laugh" at PartnershipCo did not tend to be a tense competition between worker and manager. Instead, it was nonrisky and inter-worker. In fact, workers avoided contact with managers so that they would be free to "have a laugh." For example, Laura, a worker at PartnershipCo, explained the existence of the "managers' table" in the canteen as being a consequence of workers wanting to "have a laugh," which they could not do in the presence of managers: "The manager is a nice guy but I don't want to eat bloody lunch with him, I want to have a laugh" (PartnershipCo, field notes).

Explaining the Absence of Work Games

It is not possible from the data available to infer the exact reason for the absence of absorbing work games at PartnershipCo and ConflictCo. Perhaps the work activity was simply ill suited to the formation of such games compared to the semi-skilled manufacturing and less routine service work previous researchers have studied. Alternatively, the specific workplace regimes may have been unconducive to work games for some reason. Maybe the managers were less interested in allowing work games to develop, or perhaps precarious scheduling generates too much uncertainty for enthralling work games to take hold. Certainly, as the previous chapter highlighted, workers were worried about what the present held for them due to the unpredictable nature of their schedules. Consequently, it is conceivable that they preferred to try to transcend their present reality through escapism, rather than focusing on the anxiety of their current situation by engaging in work games.

As Gabriella, a worker at ConflictCo, put it: "How are you gonna make your job more enjoyable . . . You are always worried, how many hours am I going to get this week, you know, can I afford to pay my bills . . . you always worry."

Which raises the question: In the absence of work games, was exploitation simply left unobscured?

Schedule "Abuse" and Schedule Gifts

At ConflictCo, the continued loyalty of other workers was often explained figuratively through idioms of "domestic violence" and "Stockholm syndrome." For example, Gabriella explained her coworkers' loyalty as being due to the fact that "people are scared and are used to the abuse already. It is like when you are in a relationship, an abusive relationship; it is the same cycle. They get used to the abuse and they don't want to say anything."

When questioned further as to why employees at ConflictCo work so hard when they are treated so badly, Gabriella returned to this theme of workers becoming used to being treated in this way: "Why [do] we work so hard? Because we get used to the abuse, that's why we cannot see it [the abuse] anymore."

Another worker, Tim, also suggested that his coworkers' loyalty was like domestic abuse because they blamed themselves for the abuse they faced: "They go 'oh it's my fault that I'm being pushed around,' battered wife syndrome kind of thing."

Rachel (another worker) also spoke of the psychological effects of workplace abuse: "You have to remember that ConflictCo has fifty years of treating their associates like this. You can't take away [the psychological effects of] fifty years of mistreating their associates that quick, it takes a while."[25]

Emma, a recent employee who was now working as a union organizer, elaborated further on the power created through abuse: "If you're in an abusive relationship, a lot of people stay because they get used to it, and they still stay loyal to that one person who keeps knocking them down every day. That's kind of the same thing as with ConflictCo. It might not be a personal relationship but it's that exact thing, you get used to them knocking you around. It's just a commonplace thing and you end up staying. You don't think there is anything different, or you don't know anything different."

The references to domestic abuse should not be taken literally, of course, but instead understood as attempts by the informants to describe a situation that seemed paradoxical to them, one in which their coworkers seemed to have positive feelings toward their abusive employer. This idiom of an "abusive relationship" was applied specifically to the experience of precarious scheduling, and it is this element of abuse and how it can be obscured that we will now develop further.

Sociologist Ashley Mears has forcefully argued the need to go beyond work games and what she calls the "situational construction of consent," and instead place even greater emphasis on the relational nature of control. Mears highlights the manner in which "meanings of work are also shaped through relationships and social ties beyond the accomplishment of work activities."[26] In particular, she draws on Marcel Mauss's seminal work on gifts to demonstrate the powerful role of feelings of obligation in enabling exploitation. As discussed in the book's introduction, sociologist Pierre Bourdieu developed Mauss's argument further by demonstrating that the power relations underpinning gifts are, in fact, often misrecognized by both the giver and the receiver. For Bourdieu, the power of gifts lies not only in the obligation for reciprocation but in the inability of the less powerful party to reciprocate. Bourdieu's concept of misrecognition provides a sophisticated account of how abuse can simultaneously produce consent. Bourdieu states that misrecognition is "the gentle, invisible form of violence, which is never recognized as such, and it is not so much undergone as chosen, the violence of credit, confidence, obligation, personal loyalty, hospitality, gifts, gratitude, piety—in short, all the virtues honored by the code of honor."[27]

Bourdieu illustrates the process of misrecognition through the exchange of gifts among Kabyle peasants. He argues that gifts that cannot be reciprocated bind debtor to giver through moral obligations while shrouding the gifts as a gesture of generosity. This is not to say that there is a deceiver or a deceived but, rather, that there is a collective denial of the reality of exchange. For example, a master who gives his servants gifts is, Bourdieu contends, deceiving himself about his true motives just as much as he is deceiving his servants. In fact, misrecognition is even held to be beneficial to the dominated, as it enables them to perceive themselves not as subjugated and oppressed but rather as the lucky and honored recipients of gifts. As shall be demonstrated, schedule gifts aid control by providing a means by which the securing of control through flexible discipline is simultaneously translated into the obscuring of exploitation.

Chapter 4 demonstrated that manager-controlled flexible scheduling at PartnershipCo enabled the securing of control without recourse to standard despotic practices. Thus, a high level of control could be accomplished "with a smile." This was important, as the scope for more traditional means of discipline was curtailed by the hegemonic apparatuses in operation at PartnershipCo—such as the developed disciplinary and grievance procedures policed by the union.

At ConflictCo, managers also had a discretionary capacity to improve workers' schedules. Manager-controlled flexible scheduling, however, was not just a tool that managers could utilize as and when they needed in order to punish specific workers. Workers felt compelled to attempt to avoid and reduce the harmful consequences of precarious scheduling by going to see their manager and pleading with them in person to alter their schedule or provide more hours. Leonardo, a worker at ConflictCo, explained that if you did not complain to a manager then you did not get enough hours. A more detailed account of this common experience was provided by another ConflictCo worker, Joe: "Before they used to cut my hours but now I can go to a manager . . . There are times they've scheduled me for sixteen hours, and I went to her and she fixed them."

Vincent, a ConflictCo worker, provides an illustrative example of the level of desperation this pleading could amount to: "I'm always constantly asking for a full-time position . . . I've told my store manager, 'It's literally getting hard for me to put food on my table and pay my bills. Can I get a full-time position?'"

As we have seen, precarious scheduling caused significant harm to workers. Moreover, having to beg managers for schedule gifts, in the form of more hours or alterations to schedules, acted to hide the nature of flexible scheduling as a mechanism of control. The requirement for workers to go to their manager and ask them directly for help personalized the scheduling experience, which otherwise would have been a remote and mechanical practice. Without this personalization, the scheduling experience would have consisted of little more than the workers collecting a printout of their schedule, which had been drawn up according to predictions of demand calculated a hundred miles away in the head office. When managers acceded to workers' requests and accommodated their needs, it therefore appeared as a personal act of kindness.

As Gabriella explained: "It's just temporary fixes, but then the person feels so grateful that the manager has given them the hours. But next week you have to worry again."

This kindness, however, could not be repaid directly and thus had the potential to create an emotional debt, as Seb (another worker) noted: "Sure I have [felt grateful] . . . not [to] management in particular . . . but when a particular manager says, you know, 'Sit down, let's take a look at your schedule and see what we can do,' then I'm grateful to that guy or gal."

Moreover, any individual acts of managerial kindness could only ever be temporary fixes owing to the need to schedule workers flexibly to meet demand. Accordingly, the workers' gratitude could be regenerated on a weekly basis.

Investigating the misrecognition of this process required more experiential and textured observation of interactions in the workplace, which was made possible through my participant observation as a worker at PartnershipCo. During my time working as a shelf stacker at the Mulling Point hypermarket, I observed that managers would encourage workers to beg them for additional hours, making vague promises that more hours were available or soon would be. For example, as documented in my field notes, one manager claimed: "'I always have some overtime so let me know if you want any'—this was despite my entire work team being employed on less than nine hours a week and all desiring more hours and, in some cases, to be made full-time."

Such claims understandably created an expectation among workers that more hours would be available to them. For example, one of my coworkers claimed that he had only taken the job based on the assumption that he would be getting more hours. Another poignant example is provided by Jackie, a worker I had met during our induction training two months previously. On my way into the store on my second to last day of working at PartnershipCo, I met Jackie, who was having a cigarette break. As I noted in my field diary:

> [I] asked her whether she was getting many hours. She replied that she'd not since Christmas and that "it's strange because you speak to the staff and they say their department is short but when you ask the manager they say there isn't any at the moment but keep putting your name down for overtime. I'm just getting a few hours here and there." I asked her what they'd said when she was first taken on and she replied that "originally they'd said I would get a full day on Sunday, and then my manager said a few weeks ago that it would only be three hours, but next Sunday I've not got any. So I don't know what's happening . . . my manager just keeps on saying 'just carry on until February' and then he'll get his new budget from the store manager."

Similar expectations were created at other stores, as Bryah, a union rep at a different store, explained: "The way they say it is that 'we employ you for ten hours but you may get twenty-five hours a week'—you may—it may not always happen."

In order to explore the effect of the capricious, unsettled environment created by these vague promises of more hours, it is instructive to compare my own experience with that of my closest work colleague. Rio would get the train to and from work with me, providing good opportunities for us to discuss work. Rio was a black man in his early twenties and from one of the most deprived areas of London. Rio did not share the university education of our manager, and before starting at PartnershipCo he had been unemployed for a year, forcing him to move back home with his mother. Despite my own best efforts not to work overly hard and to be considered an average worker, I was, nevertheless, a favorite. Favoritism manifested itself in the fact that, like other favorites, I was routinely offered additional hours while Rio was not. Rio was desperate for additional hours and had told our manager during his interview that the core hours on which he was hired were insufficient for him to make ends meet. In fact, he claimed to have explicitly told the manager not to take him on unless PartnershipCo could provide him with additional hours. At the same time, the manager offered me schedule gifts, offering me additional hours and allowing me to rearrange my schedule even when this broke company policy.

For my part, my personal commitment to not working hard was undermined by the realities of being a favorite in a workplace practicing manager-controlled flexible scheduling. To take one example: I was scheduled to work on both Christmas Eve and New Year's Eve at a time when it was company policy that no one be granted leave on either of these days. This was a major problem, as I needed to travel on Christmas Eve to be with my family on Christmas Day. I had also booked a holiday over the New Year before being employed by PartnershipCo. However, when I brought these problems up with my manager, he casually replied that it was "no problem" to change my hours on Christmas Eve and to take New Year's Eve completely off! Moreover, he appeared genuinely concerned by my predicament. When this manager then came to check on my progress on the work tasks (which he had personally set me), I felt guilt that I had not achieved what he had asked of me. I found myself feeling an emotional debt to him and a moral obligation to increase my work effort.

What this example demonstrates is the manner in which scheduling gifts obscure the role of precarious scheduling in securing control. I was not outraged by the general organization of the work, which meant that my coworkers and I should have so little control over our working time. Nor did I feel guilt or sympathy for the worker who would have to take my place on Christmas and New Year's Eve. I felt gratitude to the manager and identified with his interests (the completion of the work tasks he oversaw). Thus, precarious scheduling is not only a mechanism that forces workers to accede to managers' wishes; it also actively integrates workers into achieving managerial aims. It binds workers to work hard for their manager through a sense of gratitude and obligation to repay them for their "kindness."

Even with a sociological understanding of the exploitative nature of labor processes and my commitment as a researcher not to work hard, the work no longer appeared to me as just paid labor, but rather as a moral obligation to my manager due to his acts of "kindness." Under such conditions, employment is not experienced as simply the impersonal exchange of X money for Y labor, but rather relationally as the need to repay what appear to be managers' acts of compassion, caring, and friendship. Manager-controlled flexible scheduling was thus a powerful yet subtle mechanism of control at both ConflictCo and PartnershipCo: securing control by extending arbitrary managerial power, and obscuring exploitation through misrecognition of workplace relations. Bourdieu found that the economic relations (gift exchange) of Kabyle peasants also obscured the domination of that very same economic system. Likewise, at PartnershipCo and ConflictCo, manager-controlled flexible scheduling not only enabled the securing of exploitation through discipline but simultaneously obscured this process.

The exchange of gifts in this way could be understood as a type of game, one that takes place over an extended period of time and that is hierarchical as opposed to the horizontal games identified by Burawoy and others.[28] However, Burawoy argues that work games produce consent because participants focus on winning the game, rather than challenging the socially sanctioned rules and goals that constitute them.[29] In contrast, when engaging in gift exchange, actors are not aware of any socially constructed rules and goals guiding their actions—beyond the expectation of reciprocation. Instead actors collectively misrecognize the creation and maintenance of social indebtedness as acts of kindness, gratitude, and reciprocation. This misrecognition makes the experience of gift exchange in the workplace quite different from the conscious playing of games. For example, workers at PartnershipCo and ConflictCo did not keep score of their schedule gifts, nor did receiving schedule gifts become an end in itself, beyond that of meeting material needs, in terms of achieving a high score so as to win the game.

The argument above does not, however, rest on an assumption that managers purposefully manipulate workers through scheduling gifts. They could just as well bestow these gifts out of genuine concern and a desire to help. In fact, Bourdieu argues that gift exchange requires that the dominators deceive themselves just as much as the dominated.[30] Additionally, Bourdieu argues that misrecognition is particularly important in the absence of formal institutions that can maintain domination through integration and mobilization of bias. Likewise, the findings presented in this chapter support the importance of misrecognition via schedule gifts for maintaining control when hegemonic institutions are absent, partial, ineffective, or dysfunctional. However, the next chapter investigates the consequences of relying on this misrecognition when it is not concretely underpinned by institutions within the workplace. It demonstrates that this form of control is inherently unstable and susceptible to breakdown, and that it can itself be transformed into a source of injustice that may lead to resistance.

Summary

Focusing only on discipline and coercion entails a one-dimensional view of control. However, when a complex division of labor exists, surveillance, and thus discipline, become difficult and costly. Therefore, workplace control also tends to require legitimization and the creation of consent. This chapter has investigated the dynamics of ConflictCo and PartnershipCo and explored whether work games aid control in our exemplar twenty-first-century flexible workplaces. Following the insights of Burawoy, it was expected that this control would be obscured through work games, perhaps games involving time. However, uncertainty and fear of arbitrary managerial discipline via flexible scheduling may have presented barriers to the development of satisfying work games. Consequently, rather than focusing their attention on the uncontrollable suffering of the present through engaging in work games, workers preferred to disconnect from the present via escapism. This was the case at ConflictCo, which more closely resembled the despotic regimes that, Burawoy argues, provide too little certainty and protection for workers to engage in game playing. Surprisingly, though, it was also the case at PartnershipCo, which had many elements that Burawoy equates with the hegemonic regimes that, supposedly, gestate work games by providing stability and security. This is perhaps due to the fact that while workers at PartnershipCo experienced fairly high levels of employment security, there was, nevertheless, a great deal insecurity caused by the prevalence of precarious scheduling.

In any case, the focus on work games has been criticized and the need to place even greater emphasis on the relational nature of control has been stressed. In the absence of the hegemonic regimes identified by previous research as being critical to ensuring the maintenance of control, alternative means of workplace control were required at both PartnershipCo and ConflictCo. One such means—precarious scheduling—is not simply a disciplinary tool; it also constitutes an active and constant structuration of the workplace environment according to which all workers constantly strive to maintain the favor of managers. At PartnershipCo and ConflictCo, control was found to be aided by the misrecognition of schedule gifts entailed by flexible scheduling. Therefore, flexible scheduling does not simply constitute a disciplinary tool as suggested by previous studies; it also simultaneously obscures exploitation by enabling the giving and receiving of these gifts.

Work environments that entail high levels of manager-controlled flexible scheduling require workers to actively and constantly beg managers for their schedules to be altered and more hours granted. The acquiescence by managers to a particular worker's needs is then misrecognized by the worker as an act of kindness that the worker is unable to reciprocate. The inability of workers to reciprocate the schedule gift binds them to the manager through an emotional debt and a sense of moral obligation, while shrouding the manager's act as a gesture of generosity and kindness. In securing and simultaneously obscuring the workplace in this way, flexible scheduling provides a powerful mechanism of control in the on-demand economy. The following chapter investigates the stability of this control through a consideration of worker resistance at PartnershipCo and ConflictCo.

LIMITS OF CONTROL AND SPACES OF RESISTANCE

Previous chapters demonstrated that precarious scheduling has a powerful control function, both securing and obscuring exploitation. However, thus far, developing the argument has led to a fairly all-encompassing image of control at both PatrnershipCo and ConflictCo. There were, however, inevitable limits and contradictions to the control engendered by manager-controlled flexible scheduling at both PartnershipCo and ConflictCo.[1] This chapter investigates these limits and highlights that worker resistance, however limited, did exist. This resistance suggests that control built on precarious scheduling may, at times, be vulnerable to disruption.

"Schedule gifts" obscure exploitation. However, this is not the same as producing consent to it, and workers may carve out spaces in which they can develop novel means of resistance. Importantly, precarious scheduling can at once obscure the nature of the workplace while also sharpening feelings of injustice due to the insecurity it entails. This sense of injustice increases the potential for resistance and threatens the reproduction of control.

This chapter proceeds by first investigating open and hidden resistance at PartnershipCo and the formal and informal forms of organization that facilitated conflict. The contrasting nature of resistance at ConflictCo is then considered. The nature of resistance differed greatly at PartnershipCo and ConflictCo, with hidden forms predominating at the former but proving absent at the latter (where a minority were instead engaged in a campaign of open collective resistance). However, the centrality of flexible scheduling to these differing forms of resistance was common to both cases. Moreover, the success of the worker mobilization in forcing concessions from ConflictCo suggests that social media may provide a means by which acts of open collective resistance, even when engaged in by only a small minority of workers, may provide a significant challenge to employers' control.

Seeking Security at PartnershipCo

In sketching resistance at PartnershipCo, the obvious starting place is the union. Unions provide a clear means by which open resistance can manifest. For example, unions can foment industrial strife, facilitate worker mobilization, and organize acts of collective resistance, such as strikes. At PartnershipCo, precarious scheduling was a key influence shaping how workers engaged with the union. Workers were compelled, as shown in the previous chapters, to seek schedule gifts in order to reduce the negative effects that precarious scheduling had on their lives. However, another strategy workers pursued was to seek the protection of the union. In chapter 3, it was argued that the union was fairly ineffective at constraining precarious scheduling. Nevertheless, it was seen by some workers as a way of providing some degree of greater protection.

As highlighted in chapter 1, the union was thought to be able to increase workers' security through the ability of union reps to provide effective support during the grievance and disciplinary procedures. This sense of added protection and security also extended to flexible scheduling and was cited as a major reason why workers were joining the union. Jeff (a union rep at PartnershipCo) explained that, in his experience, the union's potential to help resolve scheduling problems was a key reason why workers joined. This was, he believed, because workers were themselves so uninformed about their rights regarding manager-controlled flexible scheduling: "This thing of flexi-contracts coming in and labor matching, we've got a lot of people who were on full-time contracts but have had their contracts either reduced or shifted to days that they don't wanna work, and a lot people have joined just on the back of that, just because they are not sure of what their rights are and what they can do, so you know they want the support."

Another union rep, Jimmy, also believed this to be similarly true for workers on flexi-contracts: "They've been employed on these small contracts and as much as some of them are on three and three-quarter hours, they want to know that they are going to have forty hours a week and want a proper contract and they are joining and they want to know that there is someone there looking after them."

Not all union reps agreed that flexi-contracts facilitated recruitment. They highlighted that, in spite of these workers having a greater need of union support, they were also unwilling to commit to paying regular union dues, as they were unsure of their income week by week. Nevertheless, the worker interviews did provide some support for Jeff's and Jimmy's shared view of the importance of union ability to help with scheduling—at least with regard to labor matching. William (a worker at PartnershipCo) explained: "If I didn't want to do it [change his hours], they [the union] would [help me]. I know I'd have someone on my side to help me with that."

Likewise, James (another worker) argued: "You need unions for disciplin[ari]es or if you're just not happy with something they [PartnershipCo] are trying to do, [such as] changing your hours—you can go to the union and they can try and help you. And I would say everyone should join the union as it's a good thing to have behind you."

Precarious scheduling may have been one of the reasons that the union (which represented workers in industries where these practices were common) was growing at a fast rate, having increased in membership by nearly 25 percent between 2007 and 2012. While there is no way to conclusively prove this, it is clear that precarious scheduling was not an insurmountable barrier to union growth.

Schedule Insecurity and Injustice

The fact that precarious scheduling was potentially aiding the recruitment of workers to the union should not, of course, be assumed to constitute resistance, especially considering the union's hegemonic role (discussed in chapter 1). John Kelly argues that the transformation of dissatisfaction into a sense of injustice is central to the development of collective acts of workplace resistance.[2] However, consciousness is contradictory; that is, in striving to make sense of a world that is complex, contradictory, and confusing, people's understanding of a situation will often be fragmentary and contradictory.[3] This also applies to workers' understanding of precarious scheduling.

Precarious scheduling compelled workers to seek schedule gifts that obscured exploitation. However, the schedule insecurity workers experienced could also be understood as a source of injustice. Though workers may have been glad to receive a schedule gift, felt grateful toward the manager who bestowed it, and worked hard to repay that individual manager, this did not mean that they consented to being placed in this situation in the first place. The allocation of overtime was found to fuel conflict at Ford in the 1970s, leading to the emergence of the union shop stewards' committee.[4] Similarly, at PartnershipCo, scheduling was by far the most common issue workers discussed as unjust. The injustice centered on a number of different practices related to flexible scheduling that were deemed to be unfair. These practices included the use of flexi- and minimum-hour contracts and how these contracts did not provide workers with guarantees or rights. For example, Jimmy argued that scheduling should be understood as a human rights issue: "There's a human rights bit in here somewhere because we do have a right to rest, a right to choose when we work."

Another common theme of the interviews was that labor matching (i.e., the process whereby PartnershipCo reviewed its staffing needs and potentially shifted its entire workforce's schedules) was unfair, as it was carried out too frequently or was not applied equally to all workers, alongside more general issues surrounding the effects of flexible scheduling on work-life balance. As Holly (a union rep at PartnershipCo) explained, "It's unfair because we have lives outside of work."

This sense of injustice also led to anger at the workplace regime. For example, Sara (another union rep) explained how the frequent labor matching caused her to feel anger toward her manager: "It just makes me angry . . . that we [the manager and her] dealt with this sort of two months before . . . we had a discussion about my hours so nothing has changed . . . The department ran very well with the hours we had so why does there need to be a change?"

This sense of injustice and outrage was not only generated from personal anguish but could also be sparked by a perception that coworkers were being treated unfairly, as Derek (a union rep) demonstrated in his comments regarding flexi-contracts: "I think that is totally wrong—flexi-contracts—I've met people on contracts for three and a half hours a week . . . and I think it is so wrong, nobody could possibly survive on three and a half hours' pay a week. Then it boils down to you've got your three and a half hours a week plus your flexi hours that they will give you if they need you . . . They should have a proper contract. Some [workers] are very angry about it, but others are just glad to get work."

Yet this injustice and anger did not lead to open collective action, for, as we have seen, the union did not formally campaign on "controversial" issues such as precarious scheduling. The union's resistance to manager-controlled flexible scheduling was limited to ensuring that the company's policies were being followed correctly. Thus, collective injustice was translated into individual actions such as grievances. In the absence of collective action, stories relating to workers' ability to undertake hidden acts of resistance were common. These acts of resistance demonstrate that there were limits to control at PartnershipCo.

Hiding Resistance at PartnershipCo

As discussed in the introduction, the very fact that resistance is undertaken by the weak against the powerful means that those engaging in resistance will often sensibly seek to disguise their resistance.[5] In order to try to uncover hidden resistance, questions were posed during the research in a way that attempted to depersonalize the issue and reduce the deviance attached to such acts. The aim was to enable the informants to draw on their experiences without feeling as if they had to justify such actions or take ownership of them. The questions were also asked in a lighthearted manner, in an attempt to emphasize that there was no moral judgment or condemnation. Only the union reps with whom I had built up a high level of trust over many months of participant observation were asked these particular questions. The typical form of questioning was, "Some people have mentioned [example from previous interview]. Have you ever come across that kind of thing?" This approach yielded data that suggested that workers had a number of strategies by which they could covertly resist managerial control. These fitted into two broad categories: informal output restriction and sabotage.

"You Go Slower"

Workers could informally restrict their output either by deliberately working at a slow pace or by undertaking a kind of informal "work to rule" where they followed the rules strictly but did little more. The high level of informational surveillance provided by scan rates on the checkouts made it more challenging for these workers to reduce their productivity. Nevertheless, Anna (a union rep) explained that acts of hidden resistance were still possible. She even encouraged workers to carry out such acts and protected them from being disciplined:

> You go slower, if they are saying to you "come on, come on," you go that little bit slower and you think "right, I'll bugger you up. You won't hit your targets this week" and when they moan about the scan rate, I say scan a bit slower and all you've got to do when they take you in the office is say "I want my rep in here" and all you've gotta say then is, well, "I was talking to so-and-so for forty minutes. What am I meant to say to the old lady, 'Go on, see you later, get out, I can't talk to you today, I'm being watched'"?

Sara spoke of further ways in which the surveillance of checkout operators could be overcome and explained that workers could increase the disruption caused by their resistance: "If it's a cashier they wait until it is really busy and then they will slow down or they'll go, you know 'I'm feeling sick. I'm going home'— if their sick record isn't too bad, or they'll go 'I need a toilet break.'"

Another union rep also suggested that workers could strategically use breaks, which they would normally forego, in order to cause disruption. Brianca, a union rep at PartnershipCo, suggested that acts of hidden resistance were not limited to cashiers. Workers on the shop floor could employ the emotional side of their labor (which was harder for managers to observe and evaluate successfully) as a way to cover the restriction of their physical labor: "[Workers] would get away with no work . . . [as they would] go and say [to their manager], 'There is none of these on the shop floor and a customer wanted twenty of these so we had to find them' just to piss off the manager."

Union reps encouraged this hidden resistance, but it could also take on a collective character without their encouragement. Stephen Ackroyd and Paul Thompson argue that such acts of "misbehavior" are often based on informal self-organization by workers. According to these theorists, such unofficial collective organization is always present in the workplace as workers seek to expand their autonomy and affirm their identity.[6] For example, Harry (a union rep at PartnershipCo) explained how "a whole bunch of guys will get together and say 'I hate that manager . . . and that guy there is a bloody . . . we hate him!' and they will take out a load of complaints and then they will work slowly and then the work won't get done and he [the manager] has got to answer for it."

Jimmy also believed that premeditated and collective resistance was possible by combining elements of "work to rule" and "go slows": "You can sort of gang together. It's his figures at the end of the day when it's not stocked and everything else, as long as you've sticked by the rules, you are doing your job and he's still not getting it stocked up, and it's him whose gotta answer those questions."

Jeff claimed that he had organized employees to informally work to rule as a response to managers' lack of acquiescence to a worker's demands: "I've gone into a meeting with a member of staff myself, and we've said 'OK, if that is the way you want to play it, from now on we are going to stick to the rules.' They will do their job, do this and then go home . . . and you see that quite often if someone gets frustrated and annoyed by their manager they will stick to the bare minimum of the job . . . There is not a lot they [managers] can do. I would like to see them try."

Sabotage

According to the union rep informants, there were a number of additional and more innovative workplace sabotage techniques. The most readily available method was to damage the stock by "accidentally" mishandling it. Sara explained this tactic concisely: "'Oh look, I just dropped a jar of pickled onions'—it's easily done."

This sabotage could be carried out in a more sophisticated manner so as to hide the culprit. Some of these methods had the additional benefit of reducing output and, once again, customers provided useful cover for these acts: "Yeah, we all done that [purposefully damaged goods] or they used to get a fizzy drink, or eggs or flour, do you know that flour bags are sometimes broken and then 'Oh no, a customer has spilt it all over me.'"

More cunning sabotage tactics removed the worker in question from the scene of the act altogether. One union rep explained how workers would secretly rearrange cages of stock so that when the cage was removed from the elevator it would topple over and damage the stock it held. Other union reps recounted with glee how workers they knew would rearrange perishable goods, such as bread and milk, so that those with the nearest sell-by date would be bought last by customers. Anna explained how effective this resistance could be as a means of harming specific managers: "They [managers] don't like that because that goes on their waste and then they've got to answer for their waste. And what you do as well. I know one girl who used to work on dairy and the manager really didn't like her, and they used to clash all the time, and she'd move all the milk with the next day's date to the back, and the dates two days later forward, so he [the manager] lost over £500 of milk, and he never ever knew it was her. He thought it was just bad rotation from his guys 'cause she never normally done milk . . . and he was called into the manager's office for why his waste was in the red."

Another way that workers surreptitiously increased wastage was to hide products before they were due to have their price reduced, and then place them back on the shelf.

Resistance at PartnershipCo was restricted to these hidden acts of limited potential in terms of truly challenging managerial control. Nevertheless, it is important to acknowledge them, for these acts demonstrate that the control engendered by precarious scheduling was neither complete nor all-encompassing. Furthermore, the insecurity caused by precarious scheduling can aid union growth and a sense of injustice. It is not inconceivable that this could lead to future challenges to control and to the destabilization of the workplace regime. In fact, ConflictCo provides an illustration of just such a challenge.

Raising Labor Standards through Reputational Damage at ConflictCo

The situation regarding hidden resistance at ConflictCo was very different from the one at PartnershipCo. Apart from workers avoiding and subtly distorting the "ConflictCo cheer"—documented in chapter 2—there were few examples of hidden resistance. This was primarily because the level of surveillance and the consequences of being caught were considered to be too high. ConflictCo also differed vastly from PartnershipCo in terms of open collective resistance.

As highlighted in chapter 2, ConflictCo had always opposed unions and had successfully avoided unionization. Moreover, ConflictCo workers felt highly dependent on ConflictCo and perceived themselves to have few labor market alternatives. This sense of dependence was deepened by the fact that unemployment benefits in California were limited. Added to this, the workplace regime left workers feeling highly insecure in terms of both their employment and their schedules, and they were left in little doubt by ConflictCo's anti-union propaganda that the company was very much opposed to unions. Therefore, all of the informants maintained that most workers were very fearful of collective organization, and the vast majority were afraid to even be associated with a union for fear of retaliation.

Yet, a minority of workers had overcome their fear and joined the union-backed worker association. Although the exact number was confidential, the interviews suggested that approximately 1,000 ConflictCo workers in California had joined (of these, around 500 workers were in the LA area and 250 in the Bay area, with the rest being spread out throughout the remainder of the state). In practice, the union and the worker association worked in tandem. The union provided the majority of the financial resources, as well as organizational experience and legal expertise. For example, in the LA area, the union funded ten organizers. However, in order to try to overcome ConflictCo's anti-union propaganda and the legal barriers facing unions, the union attempted to mobilize workers to join only the worker association rather than the union itself.

The association, for its part, did not explicitly seek to engage in the formal collective bargaining that is central to classic conceptualizations of labor unions. This can be partly explained by the fact that under U.S. labor law employers can require workplace certification elections—which in practice have become an extremely one-sided affair—before recognizing a union for collective bargaining. Nonetheless, this mobilization, which included thousands of ConflictCo workers, culminated with around 400 members of the worker association taking part in widely publicized strikes on Black Friday 2012, the busiest shopping day of the year, in protest of low pay and poor working conditions. Throughout 2013, further open collective action took place, with around 200 ConflictCo workers taking part in strikes along with a campaign of civil disobedience leading to over 250 arrests. The main forms of collective action these workers embarked on were dramatic strikes and acts of civil disobedience such as the above, which resulted in workers and supporters being led away in handcuffs by police. The first time this tactic was used was during the 2012 strike, when workers, family, and supporters in the LA area blockaded the road outside a store for two hours before being arrested. The spectacle of these direct actions was heightened by the presence of large numbers of supporters who joined the picket lines.

That this relatively small-scale mobilization represented a threat to control at ConflictCo can be seen by the fact that the company was forced into making some concessions to workers. In 2015, ConflictCo announced that it would raise its starting pay rate, significantly improving the pay of 500,000 workers. This equated to an increase of between 12 percent and 25 percent on what many workers who informed my research were being paid. Additionally, these mobilizations, along with those of fast-food workers that also took place at the same time, have influenced state and local governments to intervene to a greater extent in the employment relationship by raising various local minimum wages. For example, before the mobilization in California, the minimum wage had remained at $8.00 per hour since 2008. However, in September 2013, Democrats in a number of areas, including LA and the San Francisco Bay area, significantly increased minimum wages.

The Power of Social Media and the Aggregation of Solidarity

It was unexpected that this mobilization would be so successful at forcing these concessions from ConflictCo. Unlike the automobile workers of General Motors and Ford during the hegemonic era of the 1940s to the 1970s, workers in the retail sectors have weak associational power, including low union membership and little collective bargaining.

The limited power of retail workers results not only from their low levels of unionization, but also from the difficulty they face in causing major economic disruption. The extensive use of functional flexibility in the U.S. retail sector means that there is little specialization in terms of job roles. Therefore, in the event of a strike, workers from another section or store can quite easily replace striking workers. In order for a strike to threaten significant economic disruption, a high level of participation from workers at a significant number of sites within a geographic area would be needed. If this were the case, however, disruption would still be localized and would have little upstream or downstream impact on other sites, unlike, for example, strikes by energy workers. Even if one chain were completely shut down by a strike, shoppers could easily get food and other goods from one of the chain's competitors. The limited power that accrues to retail workers is attested by the fact that even a five-month strike in 2003 by 59,000 supermarket workers at 850 stores in Southern California was largely ineffective.[7]

Not only did the worker association at ConflictCo lack the structural economic power to cause significant disruption, but it also lacked associational power. Only a tiny percentage of the workforce were members of the worker association, and an even smaller percentage of the workforce took part in open acts of resistance.

To put these numbers in perspective, the membership was spread across 700 stores in California, each with a workforce of around 300. This means that, on average, there were around two or three members at each store where the worker association had a presence. Although membership tended to be more concentrated than this, the handful of strongest stores in the Los Angeles and San Francisco Bay areas still only had a membership of around a hundred workers (a density in the region of 30 percent). It was far more common for the most active stores to have a membership in the range of a dozen to fifty workers (a density in the range of 5 percent to 15 percent), and there were many stores with only half a dozen or fewer members.

The role of social media (e.g., Facebook, Twitter, YouTube) is central to understanding why this mobilization, which had such a low rate of participation, was successful. Social media networks had by 2013 become extensive and enabled high levels of communication between the few workers whose fear of collective organization had been overcome. These workers, while dispersed either spatially in different stores or temporally on different shifts, could connect with each other and with union organizers through social media groups. By engaging in discussions over Facebook, workers were able to learn of situational similarities at each other's stores and to provide each other with practical and emotional support, thus fostering identification with each other's situations. Akira, a recently dismissed worker who was working as an organizer for the association, explained this process particularly clearly: "It is basically an outlet for, not only frustration but also networking . . . seeing . . . what ConflictCo is doing now to other associates and comparing our similarities . . . just being there for one another so you know that you're not the only one going through what you're going through and spreading the word about trying to change ConflictCo and get others to join in."

Tim, a worker, explained the profound effect of realizing that a sense of injustice is shared by a wider collective: "It's a great way for people, especially when they are first starting, to be introduced to the larger scope of things, because there is a difference when you're used to dealing with your individual store and then when you see it is nationwide and you're talking to other people—it kinda blows your mind away. A lot of workers think that the problems they are experiencing are just this store or it's just that manager, but everything else is great. But when they . . . hear or see the same problems they are dealing with being expressed by people in Washington State or New York or Texas they are just, like, Wow!"

As suggested in this quote, a sense of group identity was further fostered by the uploading of videos to Facebook and YouTube. These videos tended to include speeches by charismatic leaders and the undertaking of totemic actions. These connections were possible despite the network being geographically dispersed across a vast country. Bill, a senior union official, explained how social media massively expanded social interaction and strengthened workers' social networks: "It's been transformative . . . there's thousands of conversations happening every day amongst members of the worker association . . . It's totally widely open, people are building their own groups, they are learning from each other, they're supporting each other . . . This campaign wouldn't have been possible five years ago . . . It breaks down the barriers and the walls that people face in life and it's also a place where people can support each other whether they are in the same store or across the nation and, lastly, it's got a natural way that people can become engaged."

Social media was combined with traditional Internet communication, such as online video conference calls, which enabled workers from across the country to link together in order to discuss major issues, provide feedback, and make decisions.

Networking Injustice

As highlighted in chapter 2, online spaces (in particular Facebook, YouTube, Twitter, and Instagram) played an important role in facilitating union and worker framing of the situation. Union organizers and workers used this online space to foster the blaming of the owners and directors as "greedy" and "criminal" and as exploiting the workforce. This can be seen particularly clearly in the following statement by Pamela (a worker at ConflictCo): "ConflictCo has been lying to them [the workers] because their slogan is 'Live better' but who's actually living better? The founder's family, not their workers."

This use of social media was important, as managers sought to reduce opportunities for union organizers to undertake framing face to face by having them physically ejected from stores, in some cases by the police. The ability of workplace activists to frame issues was also curtailed by managers separating them from their workmates and by the high level of surveillance in the workplace.

This framing of workplace dissatisfactions ranged from poor pay and benefits to intense work due to understaffing, favoritism, managerial abuse of workers, and precarious scheduling, all of which were identified by the majority of worker informants as being major workplace issues. It led to the articulation of two main injustices. The first was that pay and benefits were unfair in relation to how hard employees were required to work and how much money the "greedy" executives made. The other major injustice articulated by workers was that ConflictCo was not treating them with "respect" with regard to managers' abusive, and seemingly unequal, treatment toward them.

The importance placed by workers on respect reflected ConflictCo's heavy symbolic emphasis of respect as core to both their corporate values and the business outlook of the company's founder. In framing their dissatisfactions as examples of *disrespect*—something that contradicted the stated core values of ConflictCo and its founder—opposition by workers to those currently in control of ConflictCo was legitimated.

Although not directly reflected in workers' articulations of injustice, it is noteworthy that the irregular and unpredictable nature of scheduling was one of the major dissatisfactions raised by the informants, and was a major demand of the mobilization. For example, the association's declaration stated: "Our schedules are often irregular and inflexible, making it difficult to care for our families."

Additionally, workers often carried placards at demonstrations demanding full-time contracts. The importance placed on the issue of precarious scheduling by those workers who were undertaking open acts of resistance supports the evidence from PartnershipCo that, while manager-controlled flexible scheduling aids workplace control, the schedule insecurity it entails may have the contradictory effect of actually adding to a sense of injustice. Thus, while precarious scheduling enables a new form of control, it also simultaneously destabilizes the workplace regime.

Swarming Collective Action

Social media also facilitated and amplified symbolic collective actions. Not only did social media aggregate and amplify a sense of injustice, but it was only as a result of the association's actions being interconnected through online networks, particularly on Facebook, that they were truly "collective." Strikes are often thought of as being, by their very nature, collective.[8] Yet, when ConflictCo workers took strike action, it was as part of a small workplace group of around five workers at most stores. Sometimes, even lone individuals participated, but, in spite of their physical isolation, these individual workers were connected through online networks.

Social media networks also provided a means of spreading word of the dozens of disparate but simultaneous actions through Facebook "Events," while the lack of rigid organizational or communicative boundaries enabled the expansive networking of support for these actions. This support included other low-wage workers and labor and community groups, meaning that significant solidarity was mobilized both physically and financially. For example, the Los Angeles County Sheriff's Department reported that there were around 1,000 supporters at the main 2012 LA area demonstration. As Ali, a union organizer, put it: "We are much more about taking direct action . . . You know we are taking action now and doing something about it now rather than waiting for the law to do something."

Social media networks enabled traditional and self-generated coverage of these actions to be widely disseminated. For example, the worker association claimed that there were over 300,000 Facebook posts and 60,000 tweets about the 2012 strike. The swarming nature of these actions and their representation through social media further increased media interest. John Arquilla and David Ronfeldt, both researchers of military strategy, argue that a high level of communication technology can enable "swarming" collective action—the strategic pulsing of action from all directions. Swarming is argued to be a tremendous force multiplier, one that industrial relations scholars Charles Heckscher and Françoise Carré posit could, therefore, provide labor with an effective new means of undertaking collective action. Swarming is also seen by Arquilla and Ronfeldt as being a tactic that is particularly well suited to causing reputational damage.[9]

The force multiplier effect of swarming can be seen by the fact that the 2012 strike involved a relatively small number of employees stopping work for a single shift but that it created a significant level of media coverage regarding working conditions at ConflictCo. For example, in November 2011, the only coverage relating to working conditions at ConflictCo in a major U.S. newspaper amounted to just 57 words in one article, whereas in November 2012, there were 2,089 words across six articles. According to a senior union official, the print and website coverage generated by the association alone was equivalent to $24 million worth of advertisements in 2012 and $31 million in 2013. As the president of ConflictCo West explained in a newspaper op-ed, the media coverage made it seem as though the majority of workers were striking.

This suggests that reputational damage provides an avenue by which a relatively small number of workers who are totally denied recognition by their employers can, nevertheless, mount a serious challenge to managerial control. The source of the worker association's power was not the direct economic damage of its strikes (which was insignificant), but rather its ability to undertake direct action that incurred symbolic damage to the reputation of ConflictCo. Hence, it should be understood as an example of what we might call "raising labor standards through reputational damage."

That ConflictCo should be so susceptible to reputational damage is not obvious, however. Sociologist Jennifer Jihye Chun argues that symbolic power is most effective when used against institutions that are sensitive to public opinion, a category ConflictCo, as a low-cost discount retailer, does not seem to fit into.[10] Additionally, ConflictCo is also unusual for a major multinational in that it remains family controlled; consequently, the impact of reputational risk is reduced, as the impact on share price is of less importance. However, ConflictCo had reached market saturation in its traditional markets, and same-store sales had been declining in recent years. This made expansion into metropolitan markets crucial, as this was something it had avoided in the past owing to the presence of unions. However, this expansion could be delayed and even blocked by concerned local authorities, as had recently happened in one major city. Thus, symbolic sources of power could be translated into a political source of power by compelling local Democratic Party politicians to believe that it would be untenable for them to support new ConflictCo developments.

Summary

Precarious scheduling is a powerful source of control by which workplace regimes can both secure and obscure exploitation. However, this chapter has demonstrated that there are limits and contradictions to this control that provide workers with spaces of resistance. At PartnershipCo, the insecurity created by precarious scheduling encouraged workers to join the union in search of security and assisted the development of a sense of injustice. Though this could evolve into an open challenge to employer control, the union individualized and integrated these tendencies into the workplace regime through the individual grievances procedure and a focus on the enforcement of company policies. In the absence of open resistance, there were, however, examples of hidden resistance within the store.

At ConflictCo, there were few examples of hidden resistance due to the climate of surveillance and fear that marked this workplace regime. For the majority of workers, the same was also true for open resistance. However, a relatively small number of workers had overcome this fear and joined a worker association that used social media networks and the symbolic power of direct action to successfully challenge their employer's control. This demonstrates that, even when only small numbers of workers are able to carve out spaces of resistance within the flexible workplace of the twenty-first century, they may, nevertheless, be able to harness social media in order to successfully raise labor standards through the threat of reputational damage. The centrality of flexible scheduling to the formation of injustices and resistance in the two regimes suggests that while it is a source of control, paradoxically, it also provides fuel for resistance.

CONCLUSIONS
Control in the Twenty-First Century

Beyond Despotism and Hegemony: Extending Flexible Despotism

The findings from ConflictCo and PartnershipCo suggest that a form of flexible despotism is key for understanding workplace control of workers in the twenty-first century. However, this flexible despotism is not one that is based on the use of temporary workers and dual labor markets, as previous accounts have stressed. Instead, ConflictCo and PartnershipCo suggest that control can be simultaneously both secured and obscured through the operation of flexible scheduling and the flexible discipline and schedule gifts it entails. This form of flexible despotism has far greater applicability to a wide range of workplaces than previous accounts of flexible despotism have suggested. However, there are limits to this control, and resistance is possible. In fact, the insecurity that precarious scheduling generates can also heighten feelings of injustice and, in part, has led some workers at ConflictCo to participate in open collective resistance. Moreover, the growth of social media networks suggests that, in the future, even small numbers of workers may be able to leverage symbolic power in order to challenge their employers and raise labor standards through the threat of reputational damage to the organization.

The End of Hegemony

Flexible despotism has emerged from the death of hegemony. The hegemonic workplace regimes of the mid-twentieth century were the outcome of a number

134

of specific social processes. In particular, hegemony was predicated on workers possessing high levels of bargaining power with which they could force concessions from employers. At the same time, employers were inclined to agree to moderate concessions demanded by workers. Markets had become monopolistic, with reduced competition, resulting in higher profits, which in turn enabled employers to offer workers some real compromises and raise labor standards. However, the compromise equilibrium that lay at the heart of hegemony was undermined by the space-time compression that began in the 1970s. Employers faced increasing product market competition, while workers' labor market bargaining power was eroded. The transition to flexible accumulation and the corresponding growth of service sector employment in the United States and the UK further eroded the basis for hegemony, with these jobs tending to provide workers with little structural economic power.

Working-class service sector jobs usually require neither scarce skills nor expertise. Nor do they afford workers with a strategic position within the social division of labor from which it is possible to cause significant economic disruption. In addition, workers' labor market bargaining power in both the UK and the United States has been undermined by high levels of underemployment and increasingly restrictive social security, all of this against the background of a dramatic decline in the associational power granted to workers by unions and collective bargaining in both countries. Therefore, the potential for workplace control to be maintained through hegemonic regimes in the twenty-first century is limited.

The findings from ConflictCo and PartnershipCo confirm the limits of hegemony in the contemporary age. Neither of the workplace regimes made use of truly hegemonic practices, that is, stable compromise equilibriums maintained through the concrete coordination of capital's and labor's interests. Even at PartnershipCo, where a union was recognized and collective bargaining existed, there was little evidence of the union being able to extract significant concessions from the employer or a willingness for the firm to compromise. However, it was expected that workplace regimes in the UK would tend to be further along the continuum from despotism to hegemony than in the United States, a result of there being fewer institutional barriers to labor unions and collective bargaining in the UK, as reflected in higher union membership and greater collective bargaining coverage. In addition, the UK state intervenes to a greater extent directly in the workplace to provide a wider range of employment rights and protections, while social security is also less restricted.

The absence of hegemony can be seen by the fact that ConflictCo was marked by an internal state featuring a high level of worker surveillance, while the unstable and opaque nature of the company policies placed few constraints on managers' arbitrary discipline. Mechanisms that would have protected workers from abusive managers and led to improved working conditions were absent in the organization. Workers were denied a collective voice, with ConflictCo refusing to recognize a union, while individual voices were curtailed by the undeveloped and ineffective grievance procedure. Moreover, workers' "at-will" employment status granted them few legal protections, leading to the unbridled power of managers manifesting in verbal abuse, threats, and bullying. There were therefore few mechanisms by which the interests of workers could be concretely coordinated with those of their employer. The mechanisms that did exist (such as the 401(k) retirement, share, bonus, and health insurance schemes) were of little consequence, for they provided only minimal concessions to the workforce. There was also little sign of hegemony in terms of the work organization at ConflictCo. Employees lacked control over their work and experienced it as both intense and arduous. Pay was low and therefore a cause of outrage, while the pay structure itself was a source of confusion, disappointment, and bitterness, with workers recognizing that they had little opportunity for genuine vertical mobility.

As expected, the workplace regime at PartnershipCo did have more hegemonic features. In particular, the union policed the disciplinary and grievance procedures that rationalized discipline, constrained manager discretion, and provided workers with employment protection. Traditional forms of punishment (e.g., threats of dismissal) were therefore limited at PartnershipCo, where the hegemonic features of the workplace regime rationalized discipline and constrained manager discretion over the formal disciplining of workers. Additionally, PartnershipCo had a loyalty scheme in which workers received a bonus in the form of company shares. It also operated one of the last remaining private sector defined benefit pension schemes. There was also greater contentment with regard to pay, even though this was declining in real terms. This satisfaction derived from workers understanding their situation as being better than that of comparable workers who were less well paid or receiving no pay rise at all. However, contentment with pay does not mean it was a source of consent. Likewise, workers also believed that there was potential for promotion to management. Nevertheless, this contrasted with experiences of mobility within the job structure for hourly paid workers, who had few opportunities for progression unless they managed to become managers.

PartnershipCo's internal state was clearly less despotic than ConflictCo's. Yet, here too, the compromise equilibrium had been actively undermined by management, and the hegemonic mechanisms were in fact structured around extracting concessions from labor. At the heart of PartnershipCo's internal state was a consultation committee process whereby worker representatives could raise issues at the store, regional, or national level. However, this process detached collective issues from the workplace and enabled PartnershipCo to dominate the agenda of these committees. The result of the internal state being structured in this way was that PartnershipCo could extract concessions from the workforce without being challenged effectively by the union. For example, during the time of my fieldwork, PartnershipCo was able to avoid awarding any loyalty bonus shares and claim that it had consulted the union—provoking considerable worker outrage aimed at the union. PartnershipCo was also able to raise the age at which the pension could be claimed, restrict the payment of sick leave, and consistently reduce real pay. Therefore, as predicted by the workplace regime theory outlined in the book's introduction, while PartnershipCo retained some hegemonic features, neither here nor at ConflictCo was control achieved hegemonically. That is to say that control was not based on a stable compromise equilibrium maintained through the concrete coordination of interests between labor and capital.

The Limits of Traditional Despotism

The accounts of work discussed in this book suggest that the hegemonic regimes of the past are unlikely to be restored in the postindustrial working-class workplaces of the twenty-first century. Contemporary workers lack the structural economic power to win concessions from their employers and enforce stable compromise equilibriums.[1] The absence of hegemony should not, however, be mistaken for a return to the despotism of the nineteenth century, as some contemporary accounts have suggested. For even at ConflictCo, the securing of control through despotism was constrained by the ability of the unrecognized union and worker association to leverage symbolic power and utilize state procedures to enforce and raise labor standards. Despite ConflictCo's famed hostility toward organized labor, the worker association and state institutions curbed the ability of managers to blatantly utilize traditional despotic means of control. The limits to despotism at both ConflictCo and PartnershipCo therefore made it imperative that control be achieved by other means than traditional blatant coercion. The findings presented in this book suggest that a workplace regime termed flexible despotism can provide one alternative by which labor control in the twenty-first century is realized.

Temporal Flexible Despotism

Sociologist Jennifer Jihye Chun coined the term "flexible despotism"[2] to refer to the manner in which "flexible firms" achieve control through a dual despotic/

hegemonic regime along the lines of the core/periphery workforce segmentation model. In this form of flexible despotism, contingent workers face a despotic regime and core workers a hegemonic one—albeit with the increased, generalized insecurity created by the presence of contingent workers facing despotic treatment. We can term this workplace regime *numerical flexible despotism*. However, there are two issues with numerical flexible despotism that limit its generalizability. First, the temporary employment on which it is based is fairly unrepresentative of wider labor market experiences in the United States and the UK, and therefore this type of flexible despotism has limited applicability. Second, the distinction between core and periphery workers has become blurred by the increasing insecurity faced by *all* workers.

In numerical flexible despotism it is the use of temporary workers and dual labor markets that both secures and obscures exploitation. However, ConflictCo and PartnershipCo demonstrate that contemporary flexible firms can achieve flexibility temporally via precarious scheduling, with flexibility not being confined to just the temporary workers. In fact, temporal flexibility was experienced across employment statuses at both firms, and its increased use at PartnershipCo had the explicit aim of reducing reliance on temporary and agency workers who were associated with greater recruitment and training costs. This suggests that flexible firms do not need to rely on contingent workers and workforce segmentation strategies, but can instead achieve flexibility through implementing a general flexible regulation of working time across employment statuses. As a consequence, there was little evidence of a dual use of market despotic/hegemonic workplace regimes at either PartnershipCo or ConflictCo. Instead the findings presented in this book enable the identification of what can be termed *temporal flexible despotism*. This new form of flexible despotism secures and obscures exploitation through the flexibility of working time and the flexible discipline and schedule gifts that this enables.

Flexible Discipline

As has been highlighted by a number of researchers, flexible scheduling provides managers with a potent source of power within the workplace in a variety of settings.[3] Indeed, the widespread use of flexible scheduling provides an alternative means of constituting flexible despotism, through "flexible discipline." ConflictCo and PartnershipCo demonstrate the manner in which flexible discipline significantly increases the discretionary power of managers, enabling them to flexibly discipline workers outside of formal procedures by altering their schedules. These alterations force workers to work at times that clash with their home life, as well as reducing their income and ability to plan. A major strength of flexible discipline as a mechanism of workplace control is its subtlety and ambiguity—it is hard for workers to discern whether they are actually being disciplined and, as a result, whether the blame for their suffering lies with their manager or is just the result of shifting demand. This ambiguity reduces the damage of discipline to psychological contracts and makes it easier for managers to rescind punishment. Flexible discipline, therefore, represents a more nuanced means of securing control than traditional disciplinary methods, offering managers the possibility to modulate and adjust the severity of punishment. It is flexible discipline that enables the securing of exploitation under temporal flexible despotism.

Despite the power that flexible discipline provides for securing workplace control, there remain limits to the effectiveness of achieving control purely through coercion—despite advances in digital surveillance technologies. It remains the case, as sociologist Max Weber noted back in 1922, that coercion is costly.[4] This is because surveillance and thus punishment are actually very difficult to undertake when a complex division of labor exists.[5] Therefore, to focus only on punishment represents an overly simplistic one-dimensional view of power. As Michael Burawoy puts it, it is necessary to understand how exploitation is both secured and obscured.[6]

The Absence of Work Games and the Ineffectiveness of Direct Normative Controls

A number of accounts have suggested that, even in the absence of hegemony, control can be aided by work games obscuring the exploitative nature of labor relations. Work games have been identified in some service sector workplaces such as fast-food restaurants, call centers, and casinos, and tend to be based around interactions with customers. Studies in other sectors have found work games involving working time. Given the importance of temporal flexibility to retail firms, it was expected that work games based around flexible working time might play an important role in the workplace regimes of ConflictCo and PartnershipCo. However, there was little evidence of work games, involving time or otherwise, having a significant role in maintaining control at either firm. This was perhaps because workers experienced too much uncertainty due to precarious scheduling for enthralling work games to develop. Without work games to occupy their minds, workers instead turned to escapism and "having a laugh" as coping methods.

This absence of work games raises the question of how control at these firms was aided by the obscuring of labor relations. It was expected that direct normative controls, such as union framing, rituals, and firm propaganda, might provide the answer. Indeed, the union at PartnershipCo had an important symbolic role and did legitimize some elements of the workplace regime. It also avoided framing other contentious issues in ways that would have been detrimental to

PartnershipCo's interests. However, in doing so, it followed its own interests, and these were not always aligned with those of capital. For example, the recruitment activities of union reps involved emphasizing workplace injustices, and, thus, they undermined the creation of consent. Therefore, the union did not always legitimize the workplace regime or increase workers' integration into the firm. Union reps in particular actively increased discontent with regard to some issues.

In contrast to PartnershipCo, the internal state at ConflictCo did not accommodate the union within its structures. Unsurprisingly, the union and the worker association that it supported attempted to frame workplace issues in a manner that was highly hostile to the interests of ConflictCo and undermined workplace control. In the absence of hegemony, therefore, unions are unlikely to be reliable managerial allies for obscuring workplace regimes in the twenty-first century.

The heavy use of propaganda and rituals at ConflictCo also failed to aid control, beyond making clear to workers the rules of the game in terms of what ConflictCo considered to be acceptable behavior (i.e., hostility to unions). In fact, the use of workplace propaganda actually destabilized the workplace regime by reinforcing a sense of injustice through heightening awareness of the disparity between ConflictCo's claims and the obvious reality. It also legitimized opposition to those in control by seeming to imply that this discrepancy was due to a betrayal of the founder's legacy.

Schedule Gifts

With the absence of work games, the unreliability of unions, and the ineffectiveness of rituals, what means of obscuring labor relations exist in the twenty-first-century flexible firm? Ashley Mears, in criticizing the focus on the obscuring effect of work games, argues for the need to go beyond the "situational construction of consent" and instead to place even greater emphasis on the relational nature of control.[7] Experiences of precarious scheduling at ConflictCo and PartnershipCo demonstrate the importance of this relational understanding of control. Precarious scheduling not only enables the securing of control through flexible discipline but also simultaneously obscures workplace relations by enabling the giving and receiving of "schedule gifts." Precarious scheduling necessitates that workers actively and constantly beg managers for schedules to be altered and for more hours to be granted. The acquiescence by managers to a particular worker's needs is often "misrecognized" as an act of kindness that the worker is unable to reciprocate. The inability of workers to reciprocate schedule gifts binds them to the manager through an emotional debt and a sense of moral obligation, while shrouding the manager's act as a gesture of generosity and kindness. Under temporal flexible despotism, then, flexible scheduling not only provides a means for the securing of exploitation, via flexible discipline, but it also enables the obscuring of labor relations through schedule gifts. It is this simultaneous securing and obscuring of exploitation via flexible working time that constitutes the core of this form of the flexible despotic regime.

The Generalizability of Flexible Despotism

Workplace regimes represent the political dynamics, institutional rules, and norms that workers encounter as they go about making their living. While workplace regimes are relatively autonomous to their external contexts, they are, nevertheless, influenced by the wider societal balance of power between capital and labor. For this reason a comparative approach was taken. On the face of it, the two firms shared similar profiles in terms of their domestic market position, yet seemed to have contrasting workplace regimes that were reflective of wider contextual differences between the United States and the UK and thus can help us understand how flexible despotism manifests in different contexts.

Flexible Despotism: Progressive and Reactionary

Comparing the situation of workers in both the UK and United States, we can see that the UK has a more inclusive and extensive welfare system, workers have greater statutory employment protections and rights, and organized labor remains stronger than in the United States. Mirroring this wider context, at the UK case study workers were found to experience greater security due to their employment rights and the policing of a collective agreement by an independent union with significant membership. Workers were thus protected from the extremes of manager tyranny and abuse, while traditional discipline was rationalized by the developed grievance and disciplinary procedures.

The situation found in the UK contrasted with that at the U.S. case study, where workers experienced high levels of employment insecurity and were very fearful of losing their jobs. This was a consequence of the limited rights that at-will employment law granted workers and of the limited protection offered by the welfare state if workers were to lose their job. Moreover, organized labor is significantly weaker in the United States, and employers are drastically more hostile to unions. Reflecting this context, ConflictCo refused to incorporate the union within its internal state and was notorious for its avoidance of unionization and its tradition of ruling through fear on the shop floor. Instead of offering labor concessions, workers experienced poverty pay and poor benefits.

Despite these highly divergent policies and the notable differences in political and economic contexts that they reflected, this book has highlighted how the workplace regime at both firms can best be understood through the lens of flexible despotism, that is, workplace control being achieved via workforce flexibility. At both PartnershipCo and ConflictCo, precarious scheduling was central to control because it enabled flexible discipline and schedule gifts. It was the subtlety of this control that made it such an insidious source of power at both workplaces. However, the greater bargaining power of workers in the UK seemingly gave rise to a more progressive form of flexible despotism than the reactionary form found in the United States, where it complemented more obvious forms of despotism.

That flexible discipline was central to understanding control at ConflictCo, where more traditional forms of discipline were readily available, as well as at the more hegemonic PartnershipCo, is significant. The identification of the role of flexible discipline and schedule gifts at both firms strengthens the case that flexible despotism is a vital feature of workplace regimes in the twenty-first century. Therefore, regardless of industrial relations climates, employment protections, and welfare systems, flexible despotism has the potential to have a wide application given that precarious scheduling is typical of postindustrial working-class jobs and affects between a sixth and a fifth of workers in the United States and Europe— around twenty million and forty million workers in the United States and Europe, respectively.

Workplace Regimes and History

Attempts at the historical periodization of workplace control, such as the one carried out in this book, have been criticized. It is undeniable that variations have existed between workplaces within the same economic sectors and industries and even across nominally similar firms during the decades that this book has identified as "market despotic" and "hegemonic."[8] This fact has led some scholars to object that such periodization constitutes "over-ambitious attempts to create overarching models which explain the sequence or central characteristics of periods of capitalist production." Yet a close reading of these critics finds that, while explicitly opposing such periodization, they implicitly adopt similar ones in their own work. For example, Ackroyd and Thompson speak of the postwar social settlement in which the balance of power between managers and labor ebbed and flowed according to the economic cycle. This period, they argue, collapsed in the 1970s "as employers in Britain launched a major offensive . . . against the informal job controls and formal bargaining mechanisms." They argue that the breakdown of the postwar settlement led to a new pattern of conflict and resistance. Furthermore, they explain how in the 1980s employers "took back control" with the aid of more flexible labor markets and greater state control of labor unions.[9]

These authors go on to argue that the 1990s were marked by greater product market competition, deregulation of internal and external labor markets, and the decline of unions. They then state that this changed the "ground rules" according to which conflict at work takes place, with managers having "greatly increased powers," and that, therefore, "the conditions for the production of responsible autonomy have now gone."[10] In fact, Thompson has gone on to argue in a 2016 article, that there has been a decisive shift in workplace regimes so that "control [now] rests largely on market discipline and performance management." This transformation is argued to be the result of the decline in traditional manufacturing and industrial sectors, where historically worker organizations were strongest, combined with weakened state, corporate employment protections, and the growing financialization of accumulation.[11] While it is no doubt difficult to judge our own position in history from our vantage point of the present, now that the dust has settled on the previous periods, it is quite clear that a unique historical tendency toward hegemony existed for about thirty-five years in the workplaces of the United States and the UK between the Second World War and the end of the 1970s. There was, therefore a generation of researchers who spent their entire career studying hegemonic regimes and believing these to be the norm. However, when we place their work within a wider historical body, it becomes clear that before this hegemonic period there was another era in which a much greater tendency toward coercion existed.

The Future of Control

If this form of flexible despotism has wide applicability to low-end workplaces in the twenty-first century, what does the future hold for workers? Although predictions are a dangerous game, it seems clear that the astronomical growth of personal data has the potential to transform work and employment. More and more of our everyday activities are facilitated by Internet-based platforms and smartphone apps, and the data produced is a highly valuable asset that is captured by the tech giants. We now live in an almost permanent state of connectivity, and the so-called advent of big data and the "datafication" of social life are helping to disrupt long-held business conventions. The growing centrality of data to contemporary economic processes is likely to have two implications for control at work: heightening flexibility and introducing algorithmic control. As technology companies hoover up more and more information on our habits and likes in order to sell this behavioral data to other companies, it has the potential to further heighten the flexible temporality of capitalism. The wealth of data that now exists about our activities, interests, and social groups helps inform ever more sophisticated modeling of demand. And as employers become able to model demand increasingly accurately, an on-demand labor supply will become ever more attractive to them.[12] It seems likely that the on-demand economy, and the precarious working time it entails, will become more common as the century progresses. The flexible despotism identified by this book will, therefore, continue to be a central method of control in low-end workplaces.

Algorithmic Management

As demonstrated by the growth of gig economy platforms, the datafication of economic processes also makes a second form of control possible. Platforms such as Uber make use of what has been termed "algorithmic management,"[13] in which algorithmic control is enabled by platform-based rating and reputation systems. Workers are rated by clients following the completion of tasks and automatically disciplined for not meeting client expectations by work being filtered toward the workers with the highest ratings. In many cases, those with the lowest ratings are even "deactivated"—in other words, dismissed. Algorithmic control is an extension of the "customer management" strategies that first developed in retail in the early 1990s. They entailed positioning customers "as agents in the management circuit" so that "customers, rather than managers, are . . . the ones who must be pleased, whose orders must be followed, whose ideas, whims and desires . . . dictate how work is performed."[14]

Algorithmic control is starting to spread out from the gig economy, with similar rating platforms being used to manage traditional employees.[15] The advantage, in terms of control, of algorithmic-based rating and reputation systems is that they reduce the difficulty and cost of surveillance: customers and coworkers provide the observation of workers and monitoring of performance. The platform's algorithm then automates discipline by putting together these ratings with other relevant information and makes a decision on how the worker should be treated, in other words, whether they should be rewarded or disciplined. The development of algorithmic control reduces barriers to the temporal and spatial fragmentation of work, as a manager does not need to be directly present to monitor workers' activity. Again, this innovation in control suggests that the on-demand nature of work will continue to grow in coming years.

The future of control for low-end workers will likely combine the algorithmic management enabled by platform-based rating and reputation systems with the discipline and misrecognition entailed by flexible despotism. In fact, research suggests that in the gig economy at least one firm may already be combining algorithmic management with flexible despotism. This gig economy platform uses algorithmic management to automatically determine which shifts workers can select, with the best shifts being offered only to those workers with a high rating on the platform.[16] However, the absence of hegemony means that the frontier of control in the future is unlikely to be stable, and the insecurity produced by both the reliance on algorithms and precarious scheduling can be expected to create new forms of resistance and collective organization. Future research is needed to understand the form that resistance to flexible despotism and algorithmic management will take and how this will shape wider conceptions of class conflict in the United States and the UK.

Regardless of the specific workplace regimes that emerge as we progress through the twenty-first century, the task for egalitarians will remain the same. That task, as Elizabeth S. Anderson so eloquently articulates, is not only to highlight those workplace relations that entail domination, subordination, and humiliation, but to challenge them—and, ultimately, to support the oppressed in confronting and transforming those relations that unjustly constrain freedom.[17]

Methodological Appendix

RESEARCH AIM AND QUESTIONS

Employment in the service sector has become increasingly central to the U.S. and UK economies. Yet little is known of how control is achieved in these postindustrial working-class jobs. Given that the aim of this book is to investigate how control is maintained in contemporary low-end service sector workplace regimes, the primary research questions that guide it are:

In what ways is control experienced in low-end service sector workplace regimes?

Are there contradictions or limits to this control, and if there are, what forms of resistance exist?

ANALYTICAL APPROACH

Workers' consciousness is both contradictory and influenced by power. Both the complexity of the social world and the operation of symbolic power can leave people confused and lacking the concepts and categories of meaning to fully grasp their interests. Contradictory consciousness, therefore, represents a number of problems for answering the above research questions, for we cannot simply ask respondents how they are controlled. Lukes explains that when power is operating most effectively, people will be oblivious to its very existence.[1] This means that we also cannot simply add up the sum of individual responses in order to reveal the structures of society, since doing so neglects power relations, and thus data collection needs to be combined with historical analysis and guided by theory.[2]

It is necessary to use theory to extend one's analysis from micro-level practices and perceptions to macro-level power structures, and vice versa, so as to provide an account of how they simultaneously shape one another via "structuration." The need to account for the interplay between micro-level social practices and macro-level social forces is at the heart of Burawoy's "extended case method," detailed below.[3]

However, contradictory consciousness represents another problem for researchers, for it suggests that consciousness is dynamic and multiplex. For example, Fantasia uses three case studies to show that the propensity toward resistance cannot be gleaned from the sum of individual attitudes at one particular time. Hence "cultures of solidarity" emerge only through processes of resistance and conflict, and thus transform dramatically over a short period of time. For example, a 1959 poll of U.S. steelworkers found overwhelming opposition to the strike action proposed by their leaders, but they then supported the strike enthusiastically when it was called, making its 116 days the longest strike in the industry's history.[4] Opinions given by an individual respondent at a given moment in time, Fantasia argues, may therefore be "entirely different from the 'consciousness' expressed by those same 'respondents' in the midst of collective action and interaction."[5] Ethnographic research can help overcome these problems of interpretation, as it is inherently longitudinal in nature while at the same time being embedded within the social context being studied. This enables sensitivity to the contradictory, dynamic, and multiplex nature of worker consciousness, and how it changes in differing conditions.

When challenges to control do take place, James C. Scott highlights that this resistance is more often than not hidden and disguised owing to the fact that it is inevitably carried out by the weak against the powerful. However, ethnographic research provides contextual depth and access to experiential knowledge, as well as closeness to participants, and does not preempt contradictions in consciousness by forcing participants to choose between predetermined responses.[6] Participant observation can also capture the nondiscursive knowledge that underpins social action as the "practical consciousness of everyday life" and, through situational analysis, gives meaning to idioms that otherwise hide informants' true meanings.[7] For these reasons, a broadly ethnographic approach was deemed most appropriate for answering the book's research questions.[8]

THE EXTENDED CASE METHOD

The type of ethnography adopted was that of the extended case method developed by Burawoy. This enables a single ethnographer to "examine the macroworld through the way the latter shapes and in turn is shaped and conditioned by the micro-world, the everyday world of face-to-face interaction." This is achieved through four ethnographic extensions:

1. The extension of the researcher into the lives of participants under study.
2. The extension of observations over time.
3. The extension from microprocesses to macroforces.
4. The extension of theory.

It is in the third and fourth extensions that this approach differs from other forms of ethnography, such as those found in anthropology and grounded theory. These extensions are necessitated by the view that sociological empirical research must encapsulate wider social forces, since what is being studied is always shaped by the wider totality in which it is located—the wider totality being represented by external forces, which are of course also the result of social processes. As social forces lie outside the spatial limits of the participant observation, it is necessary to conceptually substitute forces for processes. However, this substitution introduces a danger of objectifying these forces as natural, everlasting, and unchanging. The avoidance of this objectification requires that we study the "everyday world from the standpoint of structuration, that is, by regarding action as simultaneously shaped and shaping an external field of forces." In this way, the extended case method "bursts the conventional limits of participant observation, which is stereotypically restricted to micro and ahistorical sociology."[9]

Theory makes the extension from microprocesses to macroforces possible by allowing the identification of external forces. Furthermore, it is only through theory that we can understand and make sense of the world around us. All research begins with preconceived theoretical notions acquired from previous research, readings, and personal experiences. It is, therefore, necessary to be conscious of our "theoretical baggage" in order to reduce the influence of bias on results.[10] Moreover, it is through the reconstruction of theory that the extended case method attempts, as its ultimate goal, to make theoretical generalizations, which would be impossible without fully outlining the researcher's preconceived theoretical notions.

Burawoy argues that researchers must first choose a theory, in this case *workplace regime theory*, according to the ability they perceive it has to explain the phenomena in question and to identify the wider social forces that shape it. Then, rather than seeking to confirm the theory, the researcher attempts to find refutations that enable the theory to be elaborated and deepened, and thus reconstructed with reference to existing theories. This process is held to follow the insights provided by Karl Popper and Imre Lakatos in seeking "reconstructions that leave core postulates intact. Therefore, the aim is not to reject bad theories but to improve good ones."[11]

UNIT OF ANALYSIS AND CASES

In the extended case method, then, the "case" is a theoretical construct that represents the unit of analysis, and in this book the theoretically constructed cases are "workplace regimes." This book investigates two workplace regimes that were chosen as they were seen as potentially representing contrasting examples. One appeared closer to a hegemonic regime with a recognized labor union, collective bargaining, and a fairly stable and harmonious industrial relations climate. The other seemed to represent a more despotic regime, being famed for its hostility toward and avoidance of unions, along with its low pay and poor benefits. Moreover, the industrial relations climate at this second case seemed to be marked by conflict, with workers having been widely reported as participating in strikes, protests, and civil disobedience. This selection process necessitated that the research take a cross-national approach—providing two retail cases that appeared to vary with regard to control, yet had similar profiles.

DATA COLLECTION

As the unit of analysis is the workplace regime, it was appropriate to collect data from multiple workplaces operating under the two regimes. The fact that there were no discernible differences in the working conditions across workplaces significantly increases the validity of these case study findings. However, in order to limit the potential for regional labor market differences to affect the findings, the fieldwork was spatially confined. The UK fieldwork was restricted to the London area. The U.S. fieldwork was limited to California—principally the Los Angeles (LA) and San Francisco Bay areas. These regions of California were selected because they seemed particularly marked by a conflictual industrial relations climate.

As is common practice in qualitative research, the sampling of informants was not guided by any attempt to make it representative, but rather to reach "theoretical saturation." This is because the purpose of qualitative data collection is not to attempt to generalize to a population but to generalize to theory.[12] Theoretical saturation is reached when the collection of new data ceases to further elaborate the understanding of a phenomenon. Therefore, the sampling is driven, within practical considerations, by theoretical assumptions as to what data will further elucidate the findings.

Data collection at ConflictCo (a pseudonym) in California took place during two separate and intensive fieldwork trips. The first of these took place from mid-February to mid-March 2013, and the second took place for two weeks at the start of December 2013. The U.S. fieldwork included participation in, and observation of, organizing drives at six stores. As part of this participant observation, I traveled with organizers from the union and worker association to various stores in the LA and San Francisco areas to try to recruit workers to the association. These organizing drives provided an excellent opportunity to speak with workers who were not part of the ConflictCo worker association. The fieldwork also included attendance at two weekly union organizer meetings, two worker activist meetings, two worker activist national video conference calls, and three community ally meetings. Documentary data, such as the staff policy handbook and staff magazine and newspaper articles, was also collected. It was not possible for me to work at ConflictCo due to visa restrictions. This experiential, observational, and documentary data was supported by forty-two semi-structured interviews with thirty-three informants consisting of twenty-four nonmanagerial hourly paid employees (four of whom had recently left ConflictCo); one recently terminated salaried assistant manager who was active in the ConflictCo worker association; seven union organizers; and one senior official (conducted over Skype, as he was based in Washington, D.C.).

The ConflictCo worker informants were drawn from a dozen stores, five in the Los Angeles area and seven in the San Francisco Bay area. The interviews were undertaken at a place chosen by the informant, usually a fast-food restaurant or a café near the worker's store or home; in a few cases interviews were undertaken at the worker's home or inside a car. The interview informants were of mixed gender (approximately 60 percent male, 40 percent female), and represented a range of ages and mixed ethnicities (approximately 30 percent white American, 30 percent black American, 30 percent Latino, and 10 percent Filipino).

A clear source of bias originated from the fact that all the workers who were interviewed were members of the worker association, while only around 1 percent of ConflictCo's California workforce were members (although in the informants' stores membership tended to be around 5 percent to 30 percent). This bias toward members was the result of access to workers requiring the use of a gatekeeper (i.e., the union). However, the impact of this bias was minimized through not only asking the informants about their own experiences but also inviting them to describe the nature of the workplace. For example, rather than only asking, "Why don't you feel loyalty to ConflictCo?," they were also asked, "How do you explain the loyalty of your coworkers? Why haven't more workers joined the worker association?" Additionally, the analysis does not rest on interview data alone, but is also based on observational, experiential, and documentary data. For example, the policy handbook proved particularly useful for outlining the nature of the internal state, while the staff magazine illustrated its symbolic dimension, and the observation of union organizing provided the opportunity to interact with informants who were not members of the worker association. The picture of ConflictCo that emerges in this book should not, therefore, be considered as being painted solely from the interviews; the picture is not in fact a painting at all but rather a jigsaw puzzle whereby the pieces of data gleaned from various sources have been carefully pieced together.

A selective but indicative quantitative analysis of the worker association's performance in the media was also carried out. While far from comprehensive, this provides an indication of the relative success of the worker association in leveraging sources of symbolic power. A search for the company in the online archives of a major U.S. newspaper was undertaken for November of each year between 2009 and 2013.

The UK fieldwork was conducted over a longer period, between June 2012 and June 2013. Interviews were conducted with nineteen workers at four PartnershipCo (a pseudonym) hypermarkets. All but one of these workers were union members, and nine were workplace labor union representatives (union reps). Again, this is a source of bias in the informants chosen, but is less problematic, as participant observation of shop floor work was also possible at PartnershipCo. Observation of union organizing was undertaken at two of these hypermarkets and an additional two stores. Interviews were also undertaken with ten union reps, each from a different store, who were taking part in a short-term secondment to the union to develop their recruitment and organizing skills. Six regional union officials were also interviewed. Five days of union organizing, three union team meetings, and a branch meeting were observed, and the meetings recorded. Notes were also taken from meetings with two senior members of the union leadership. In total, thirty-nine semi-structured interviews with thirty-five informants were undertaken.

Toward the end of the research an opportunity to gain a deeper insight into the lived experience of work at PartnershipCo presented itself. Therefore, two months of participant observation at the Mulling Point hypermarket (a pseudonym) in North London was undertaken. The Mulling Point store had a workforce of approximately 200 employees. This participant observation involved working 8.5 contracted hours per week as a shelf stacker. Work issues were also discussed with colleagues in the canteen before the shifts began and during the train commute to work. The informants who were interviewed included twenty-nine nonmanagerial hourly paid employees (of which nineteen were union reps) and six union officials. These worker informants were also drawn from across ages and were of mixed gender (approximately fifty-fifty). During participant observation at the Mulling Point store I relied on seven key informants, four of whom were part of my shelf-stacking team. Two others worked on the aisle adjacent to mine as a general assistant and a beauty assistant, and another key informant was a worker with whom I had my induction and saw during break times. Only two of these workers were union members. These Mulling Point informants were also of mixed gender (four female and three male) and a range of ages.

The PartnershipCo interviews were conducted at a variety of locations depending on where the informants felt comfortable: store canteens; car parks—usually sitting in their car; meeting rooms; cafés near their store or home; and, in one case, a local pub. The follow-up interviews were carried out over the phone. Two participants were interviewed together, and another five were interviewed during the course of two union rep team meetings (two during one meeting and three during another). This technique was surprisingly useful, as it provided my questions with much greater and more immediate context. Documents such as the staff policy handbook, union collective agreement, union rep scheduling guide, and union rep flexible scheduling guide were collected to complement the interview and observational data.

In total (for both firms), the interview and observational data yielded eighty-one interviews with sixty-eight informants of an approximate average length of forty-five minutes, and two notebooks of observational fieldwork notes. Additionally, twenty-five PartnershipCo and sixteen ConflictCo workers were asked some closed questions at the end of the interviews (there was not sufficient time to do this in all interviews). The purpose of these closed questions was to gather data on some key factors and therefore enable the bulk of the interview to be less structured. The closed questions were not intended to infer meaning in isolation from the interview and/or observational material.

THEORETICAL CODING

Theoretical coding was employed in order to help make sense of the data. Therefore, the data reported in this book was continually reviewed and coded to highlight the components that seemed to be of "potential theoretical significance and/or that appear[ed] to be particularly salient within the social worlds of those being studied," so that indicators of concepts constantly emerged out of the data and guided future data selection.[13]

The interview data in the form of audio files and observational and experiential notes were directly uploaded to Atlas.ti. Traditionally, audio data is transcribed before coding. However, as Wainwright and Russell demonstrate, contemporary computer-assisted qualitative analysis no longer requires this antiquated transformation of the data. The original data itself can now be directly coded, "enabling the researcher to move swiftly between codes and audio excerpts."[14] Not only does this allow closeness to the data that was previously impossible, but it also eliminates a frequent source of errors and saves a considerable amount of time and money on transcribing, which in this case would have been approximately fifty-eight hours of interview data.

Atlas.ti was then used to enable the systematic theoretical coding of the data in line with Vaughan's "theoretical elaboration" coding approach. The initial coding yielded over 4,000 codes. The creation of a large number of initial codes ensures that the analysis has closeness to the data and is truly generated from it. Focused coding was then employed to highlight the most common and revealing initial codes and to merge appropriate initial codes into new codes.[15]

VALIDITY

Qualitative research attains internal validity through production of a coherent and illuminating description of the entity studied. Detailed information about the study needs to be provided so that fellow researchers can judge whether the evidence presented supports the situation depicted and can evaluate how applicable the conclusions are to other research.[16] In regard to external validity, Burawoy argues that an extended case can ultimately only be judged by its product, that is, the quality of the theory it produces—that is to say, whether it pushes a research program forward without violating core postulates, makes a theory more elegant, provides more empirical content, or leads to the discovery of new facts.[17]

REFLEXIVITY

One major potential limit to the validity of the findings is the "positionality" of the researcher in terms of biographical embodiment. It is important to be aware that the observations and interviews were undertaken by a white, male, middle-class doctoral student from the south of England, studying at a prestigious university. These factors are important in how people relate to each other and are likely to have influenced the responses of informants. It is obviously impossible to change such factors, but this must nevertheless be borne in mind when reviewing the findings.

However, these limitations are less problematic for the extended case method than for more positivistic qualitative methods such as grounded theory. First, the researcher's theoretical biases are laid out from the beginning. Second, the altering of the social world by the researcher's intervention is not seen as noise that impairs reliability, and that must, therefore, be reduced. Rather, it creates "perturbations" that can benefit the research.[18] For example, my position as a student at a prestigious university meant that while working at PartnershipCo I was inadvertently a favorite of the managers. Managers would come up to me and ask what it was like to study at Cambridge and would confide in me that they wished that they too had done a PhD. Reflecting on my position as a favorite enabled me to better understand the ways in which managers could reward good behavior, and the workers they liked, through comparing my own experience with that of those who were clearly not favorites. In California my English accent made initiating conversation with ConflictCo workers relatively easy, as the novelty of the way I spoke marked me out as an "exotic" outsider. Workers were thus curious to speak to me, especially once I explained that I had traveled to California because I was interested in their lives. I have attempted to be reflexive about my interventions into the cases in order to render my perturbations a strength of the research.

ETHICS

The main ethical issue concerning this research was to ensure that the participants' relationships with their employer, labor union, worker association, or peers were not negatively affected. Therefore, the data has been anonymized and pseudonyms used.

Ethical concerns unfortunately forced the participant observation of shop floor work at PartnershipCo to be limited to two months. This was because management began laying off workers following the end of the peak Christmas trading period. My manager insisted that I would be kept on, but it was clear that one of my colleagues would lose their job as a consequence. I therefore resigned my position.

It was made clear to all the primary informants that they were under no obligation to participate in the research and could end it at any point. Informed consent was gained from all primary informants, and interview informants signed consent forms. None of the data was gathered covertly, and all primary informants were aware of my research and academic position. When informants were told of the research during the participant observation of union organizing in California, the typical response of the workers was amazement that someone would travel from England to research them, while my coworkers at Mulling Point would either respond with incomprehension as to why their work would be of interest or would joke, "Oh, you'll have a lot to write about here, then."

The decision to access PartnershipCo directly as an employee did present an ethical dilemma and also made abundantly clear how far academia has moved since many classic participant observation studies were carried out. As Glucksmann explains, employers have also become a good deal more closed to external sociological research than they were during the 1960s and 1970s heyday of workplace studies, making open participant observation of workplaces unlikely.[19] A decision was made to attempt to find employment at PartnershipCo so as to make independent contacts but not to collect data while working at the workplace. Fortunately, the manager who hired me suggested that I undertake research at the store and thus nullified these dilemmas, for it meant that no deception was required in order to access the workplace.

Notes

FLEXIBLE DESPOTISM: AN INTRODUCTION

1. For an overview, see Wood, "Flexible Scheduling, Degradation of Job Quality and Barriers to Collective Voice."

2. Although the slightly different wording of questions asked across the surveys means that the findings cannot be directly compared, it is clear that broadly similar levels of precarious scheduling exist across Europe and the United States.

3. Lambert, "Passing the Buck."

4. See, for example, Rubery, Grimshaw, et al., "'It's All about Time.'"

5. McCrate, "Flexibility for Whom?" Precarious scheduling in this study refers to workers who are rarely or never able to change their schedule and only know what their schedule will be one week or less in advance.

6. The General Social Survey is a nationally representative survey. The figures quoted here are the author's own calculation based on T. Smith et al., *General Social Surveys, 1972–2016*.

7. Based on Eurofound's European Working Conditions Survey, which paints a wide-ranging picture of Europe at work across countries, occupations, sectors, and age groups once every five years. The 2015 survey interviewed nearly 44,000 workers in thirty-five countries, including the UK. Analysis by Wood and Burchell, "Precarious Scheduling in the UK."

8. Lee et al., "Working with Machines"; Rosenblat and Stark, "Algorithmic Labor and Information Asymmetries"; Wood et al., "Good Gig, Bad Gig."

9. Pesole et al., *Platform Workers in Europe.*

10. Freelancers Union and Upwork, *Freelancing in America: 2018.*

11. Henly, Shaefer, and Waxman, "Non-standard Work Schedules"; McCrate, "Flexibility for Whom?"; Wood, "Flexible Scheduling, Degradation of Job Quality and Barriers to Collective Voice."

12. J. Hyman, Scholarios, and Baldry, "Getting On or Getting By?," 719–720.

13. Lambert, Haley-Lock, and Henly, "Schedule Flexibility in Hourly Jobs," 304.

14. Author's own calculation based on T. Smith et al., *General Social Surveys, 1972–2016*.

15. Lambert, Fugiel, and Henly, "Precarious Work Schedules among Early-Career Employees in the US."

16. Schneider and Harknett, "Consequences of Routine Work-Schedule Instability for Worker Health and Well-Being."

17. Based on Eurofound's European Working Conditions Survey, which paints a wide-ranging picture of Europe at work across countries, occupations, sectors, and age groups once every five years. The 2015 survey interviewed nearly 44,000 workers in thirty-five countries including the UK. Analysis by Wood and Burchell, "Precarious Scheduling in the UK."

18. Standing, *The Corruption of Capitalism.*

19. Lambert, Haley-Lock, and Henly, "Schedule Flexibility in Hourly Jobs."

20. Webb and Webb, *Industrial Democracy*, 842.

21. Flanders, *Management and Unions.*

22. P. Edwards, "The Employment Relationship and Field of Industrial Relations."

23. P. Edwards, *Conflict at Work*.

24. E. Wright, *Class Counts*, 10.

25. In this book, what is meant by "power" is *social power*: mastery of one's social environment, i.e., power over other people. See Mann, *The Social Sources of Power*, 1–6. Specifically, power is defined as *A's capacity to affect B, so that B's capacity to realize their interests is suboptimal*, a conception that is based on Lukes's definition of power in *Power*, 27.

26. Scott, *Domination and the Arts of Resistance*, xiii.

27. Scott, 20.

28. Hollander and Einwohner, "Conceptualizing Resistance."

29. Ackroyd and Thompson, *Organizational Misbehaviour*.

30. Hochschild, *The Managed Heart*, 126.

31. Gramsci, *Selections from the Prison Notebooks*, 161, 182.

32. Gramsci, 263.

33. Poulantzas, "The Problem of the Capitalist State."

34. Gramsci, *Selections from the Prison Notebooks*, 285, 310.

35. Burawoy, *Manufacturing Consent*; Burawoy, *The Politics of Production*.

36. R. Edwards, *Contested Terrain*, 132.

37. P. Edwards, *Conflict at Work*, 3.

38. Burawoy, *Manufacturing Consent*; Burawoy, "The Roots of Domination."

39. Gramsci argues, in *Selections from the Prison Notebooks*, that, unlike in the United States, hegemony in Europe was born in state and civil society institutions, not in the workplace. However, as European capitalism continued to develop, attempts were made to emulate U.S. workplace hegemony. For example, Gramsci details a failed attempt at Fiat.

40. Burawoy does not conceptualize his typology as a tendency but rather implies that these regimes are the dominant paradigms of each era. Burawoy, in *The Politics of Production*, would later add a third "hegemonic despotic regime"—dominant from the late twentieth century onward. However, as detailed below, this regime is better understood as a transitory phase in which the hegemonic compromise equilibrium is in the process of breaking down.

41. Burawoy, *The Extended Case Method*, 252.

42. P. Edwards, *Conflict at Work*, 52.

43. Harvey, *The Condition of Postmodernity*.

44. Burawoy, *The Politics of Production*.

45. Burawoy, 150.

46. P. Edwards and Scullion, *The Social Organization of Industrial Conflict*.

47. Webster, Lambert, and Bezuidenhout, *Grounding Globalization*.

48. Foucault used Bentham's famous panopticon prison design as a metaphor for modern society. This design enables the guards to view the inside of each inmate's cell from a central viewing station. Of course, it is not possible for the guards to simultaneously observe all cells, but as the prisoners cannot know if they are being monitored, they are forced to act as if they are being watched at all times; see Foucault, *Discipline and Punish*.

49. Foucault, 201.

50. P. Thompson and van den Broek, "Managerial Control and Workplace Regimes."

51. Bain and Taylor, "Entrapped by the 'Electronic Panopticon'?"; Callaghan and Thompson, "Edwards Revisited"; P. Taylor and Bain, "An Assembly Line in the Head"; Woodcock, *Working the Phones*.

52. Bélanger and Edwards, "The Nature of Front-Line Service Work"; Fuller and Smith, "Consumers' Reports"; Sherman, "Beyond Interaction."

53. Fuller and Smith, "Consumers' Reports," 11.

54. Lee et al., "Working with Machines"; Rosenblat and Stark, "Algorithmic Labor and Information Asymmetries"; Wood et al., "Good Gig, Bad Gig."

55. As noted by Sarah O'Conner in a *Financial Times* article, "When Your Boss Is an Algorithm," September 7, 2016.

56. See, for example, Blum, "Degradation without Deskilling"; Chang, "Korean Labour Relations in Transition"; Chun, "Flexible Despotism"; Gottfried, "In the Margins"; Nichols et al., "Factory Regimes and the Dismantling of Established Labour in Asia"; Sallaz, "Manufacturing Concessions."

57. Jennifer Jihye Chun in "Flexible Despotism."

58. Doogan, *New Capitalism?*

59. Geary, "Employment Flexibility and Human Resource Management."

60. Pollert, "The 'Flexible Firm.'"

61. Kalleberg, *Good Jobs, Bad Jobs*, 86.

62. See Wood, "Flexible Scheduling, Degradation of Job Quality and Barriers to Collective Voice."

63. Heyes, "Annualised Hours and the 'Knock.'"

64. Beynon, *Working for Ford*, 146.

65. Chun, "Flexible Despotism"; Gottfried, "In the Margins"; Price, "Controlling Routine Front Line Service Workers."

66. Leidner, *Fast Food, Fast Talk*.

67. Sallaz, "Permanent Pedagogy."

68. Durand and Stewart, "Manufacturing Dissent?"

69. Heyes, "Annualised Hours and the 'Knock'"; Peng, "The Impact of Citizenship on Labour Process"; Sallaz, *Labor of Luck*. Sallaz argues that the workers he studied experienced high levels of job insecurity due to lacking a union and having an "at will employment status," which meant that they could be fired without notice. However, dealers in Las Vegas require a license that takes six weeks of training to obtain at a cost of $800. As Sallaz puts it on page 32, "While dealing is officially classified as semi-skilled labor, mastering even the rudimentary aspects of the job is not easy." Dealers are also expected to have strong interpersonal skills. Sallaz's dealers, therefore, do seem to have a great deal of labor market security. If they lose one job, they can easily get another, and thus they experience a degree of both certainty and labor market bargaining power.

70. Kunda, *Engineering Culture*.

71. Mann, in *The Social Sources of Power*.

72. Lukes, *Power*, 23.

73. Vallas, "The Adventures of Managerial Hegemony," 204–205.

74. Vallas.

75. Fleming and Sturdy, "'Being Yourself' in the Electronic Sweatshop."

76. Burawoy and Lukács, *The Radiant Past*, x.

77. Mears, "Working for Free in the VIP," 1101.

78. Mauss, *The Gift*.

79. Bourdieu, *Outline of a Theory of Practice*; Bourdieu, *The Logic of Practice*.

80. Burawoy, "The Roots of Domination"; Bourdieu, *Pascalian Meditations*.

81. Rubery, Grimshaw, et al., "'It's All about Time.'"

82. Lambert, "Added Benefits."

83. Bozkurt and Grugulis, "Why Retail Work Demands a Closer Look," 2.

84. UK figures based on Rhodes and Brien, "The Retail Industry"; U.S. figures based on BLS, *Industries at a Glance*.

85. Lichtenstein, *The Retail Revolution*; Vidal, "On the Persistence of Labour Market Insecurity and Slow Growth in the US."

86. Giddens, *The Constitution of Society*.

87. Bourdieu, *Outline of a Theory of Practice*.

1. INTERNAL STATES IN THE UK

1. Marx, *Capital*, 549–553.
2. Engels, *The Condition of the Working Class in England*.
3. Burawoy, *The Politics of Production*.
4. Engels, *The Condition of the Working Class in England*, 127, 138.
5. McKendrick, "Josiah Wedgwood and Factory Discipline."
6. Pollard, "Factory Discipline in the Industrial Revolution," 262.
7. Polanyi, *The Great Transformation*.
8. Fraser, *A History of British Trade Unionism, 1700–1998*. According to this author the density among women workers was less than 3 percent.
9. Hobsbawm, *Labouring Men*.
10. Moreover, Hamish Fraser, in *A History of British Trade Unionism, 1700–1998*, acknowledges that these figures do not include many small strikes.
11. Hobsbawm, *Industry and Empire*, 184.
12. Beynon, *Working for Ford*.
13. Burawoy, *The Politics of Production*. See also P. Edwards, *Conflict at Work*.
14. Brown, *Piecework Bargaining*, 24.
15. Flanders, *The Fawley Productivity Agreements*.
16. P. Edwards and Scullion, *The Social Organization of Industrial Conflict*, 198–199, 265.
17. P. Edwards and Scullion, 44.
18. Nichols and Beynon, *Living with Capitalism*, 121, 129 (emphasis in original).
19. Gallie, *In Search of the New Working Class*, 184.
20. Beynon, *Working for Ford*, 140, 158.
21. Pollert, *Girls, Wives, Factory Lives*.
22. See, for example, P. Edwards, *Conflict at Work*.
23. Pollert, *Girls, Wives, Factory Lives*, 53, 61, 131.
24. Glucksmann [a.k.a. Cavendish], *Women on the Line*.
25. Harvey, *The Condition of Postmodernity*. See also Kalleberg, *Good Jobs, Bad Jobs*.
26. BIS, *Statistical Bulletin: Trade Union Membership, 2012*.
27. Brown, Deakin, Hudson, et al., *The Individualisation of the Employment Contract in Britain*; Brown, Deakin, Nash, and Oxenbridge, "The Employment Contract."
28. All informants at PartnershipCo and ConflictCo have been given pseudonyms to protect their identity.
29. Kelly, "Social Partnership Agreements in Britain."
30. See, for example, Woodcock, *Working the Phones*.
31. Fuller and Smith, "Consumers' Reports."
32. Using the Consumer Price Index (CPI), which is not influenced by house prices, reduces this anomalous finding to just 0.3 percent. The CPI was 3.6 percent in 2008; 2.2 percent in 2009; 3.3 percent in 2010; 4.5 percent in 2011; and 2.9 percent in 2012; and averages 3.3 percent over the five years, so it makes no substantive difference to the decline in real wages at PartnershipCo ONS, *2015 Consumer Price Indices*.
33. Gallie, *In Search of the New Working Class*. See also Hyman, "The Politics of Workplace Trade Unionism."
34. Batstone, Boraston, and Frenkel, *Shop Stewards in Action*.
35. Simms, Holgate, and Heery, *Union Voices*.
36. Kelly, *Rethinking Industrial Relations*.

2. INTERNAL STATES IN THE U.S.

1. Burawoy, *The Politics of Production*.
2. Montgomery, *The Fall of the House of Labor*.

3. R. Edwards, *Contested Terrain*.

4. Priestland, *Merchant, Soldier, Sage*.

5. R. Edwards, *Contested Terrain*.

6. Kaufman, *The Global Evolution of Industrial Relations*.

7. Mann, *The Sources of Social Power*.

8. Riga, "Ethnicity, Class and the Social Sources of US Exceptionalism," 200.

9. Gaventa, *Power and Powerlessness*.

10. Mann, *The Sources of Social Power*, vol. 2.

11. Montgomery, *The Fall of the House of Labor*.

12. Montgomery, 115.

13. Beynon, *Working for Ford*, 19.

14. Burawoy, *The Politics of Production*, 142.

15. Burawoy.

16. Silver, *Forces of Labor*.

17. R. Edwards, *Contested Terrain*.

18. Burawoy, *The Politics of Production*.

19. Burawoy.

20. Kaufman, *The Global Evolution of Industrial Relations*.

21. Burawoy, *Manufacturing Consent*, 194.

22. R. Edwards, *Contested Terrain*.

23. Kaufman, "Paradigms in Industrial Relations," 328.

24. Burawoy, *Manufacturing Consent*.

25. Burawoy, *The Politics of Production*.

26. P. Edwards, *Conflict at Work*.

27. Silver, *Forces of Labor*, 152.

28. R. Edwards, *Contested Terrain*, 141.

29. Compa, "An Overview of Collective Bargaining in the United States."

30. More details are provided in the methodological appendix.

31. The "ConflictCo Policy Guide" that informs this analysis was produced by the worker association and brings together all the policies into one handbook, which was then provided to the association's members. However, these members constituted only a very small proportion of ConflictCo's workforce.

32. Kelly, "Social Movement Theory and Union Revitalisation in Britain," 66.

33. Bear, "'This Body Is Our Body.'"

34. Mann, "Response to the Critics."

35. See Burawoy and Lukács, *The Radiant Past*; Fleming and Sturdy, "'Being Yourself' in the Electronic Sweatshop"; Vallas, "The Adventures of Managerial Hegemony."

II. THE DESPOTISM OF TIME

1. In a personal correspondence Burawoy has pointed out that he paid little attention to working time, as he took it for granted as being fixed both in its duration and its location in the day. He could not imagine the scheduling nightmare the workers in this study experience.

3. DESPOTIC TIME IN THE UK

1. Burawoy, "Ethnographic Fallacies."

2. E. Thompson, "Time, Work-Discipline, and Industrial Capitalism," 93–94.

3. Brown, Deakin, Hudson, et al., *The Individualisation of the Employment Contract in Britain*; Brown, Deakin, Nash, and Oxenbridge, "The Employment Contract"; Kalleberg, *Good Jobs, Bad Jobs*.

4. See also Henly, Shaefer, and Waxman, "Non-standard Work Schedules"; J. Hyman, Scholarios, and Baldry, "Getting On or Getting By?"; Lambert, "Passing the Buck"; Lambert, Haley-Lock, and Henly, "Schedule Flexibility in Hourly Jobs."

5. Wood, "Flexible Scheduling, Degradation of Job Quality and Barriers to Collective Voice."

6. This excludes online-only "stores" that customers do not visit. This is because it was not possible to access these stores. However, new flexible contracts were also introduced for these stores. In these workplaces, the rationale stated in the guide to flexible contracts was that they enabled the daily matching of changes in orders and thus eliminated the previous need for agency workers and the associated agency fees. Consequently, these flexible contracts differed from those used in traditional stores, as the workers were contracted to work 3.75 core hours three to five days a week, which could be increased by up to 3.75 hours with two hours' notice.

7. Burchell, "The Prevalence and Redistribution of Job Security and Work Intensification"; De Witte et al., "Associations between Quantitative and Qualitative Job Insecurity and Well-Being"; Standing, *Global Labour Flexibility*; Wood, "Powerful Times"; Wood and Burchell, "Unemployment and Well-Being."

8. For similar accounts see, Beynon, *Working for Ford*; Chun, "Flexible Despotism"; Gottfried, "In the Margins"; Heyes, "Annualised Hours and the 'Knock'"; Price, "Controlling Routine Front Line Service Workers."

4. DESPOTIC TIME IN THE U.S.

1. The research took place before the Affordable Care Act came into force. However, the prevalence of low hours and the intensity of the unpredictability at ConflictCo were claimed to have been exacerbated, though not caused, by ConflictCo reducing the number of workers who received thirty hours of work a week and who would, therefore, be eligible for employer provided insurance when the act's employer mandate came into force in 2015.

2. Giddens, *The Constitution of Society*.

III. THE DYNAMICS OF WORK AND SPACES OF RESISTANCE

1. Burawoy, *Manufacturing Consent*; Burawoy, "The Roots of Domination."

2. Bourdieu, *Outline of a Theory of Practice*; Mauss, *The Gift*; Mears, "Working for Free in the VIP."

3. Scott, *Domination and the Arts of Resistance*.

5. THE DYNAMICS OF WORK AND SCHEDULING GIFTS

1. See Bélanger and Edwards, "The Nature of Front-Line Service Work"; Fuller and Smith, "Consumers' Reports."

2. Burawoy, *Manufacturing Consent*; Burawoy, "The Roots of Domination."

3. Friedman, "Responsible Autonomy versus Direct Control over the Labour Process."

4. Burawoy, *Manufacturing Consent*; Burawoy, "The Roots of Domination."

5. Burawoy, *Manufacturing Consent*, 86.

6. Burawoy, "The Roots of Domination," 7–8.

7. Roy cited in Burawoy, *Manufacturing Consent*, 84.

8. Burawoy, 89.

9. Roy, "Work Satisfaction and Social Reward in Quota Achievement."

10. Roy, "Banana Time."

11. Beynon, *Working for Ford*, 118. I am grateful to Huw Beynon for pointing out this finding of his research to me.

12. Pollert, *Girls, Wives, Factory Lives*, 141, 144.

13. Leidner, *Fast Food, Fast Talk*.

14. Sallaz, "Permanent Pedagogy."

15. Durand and Stewart, "Manufacturing Dissent?"; Sallaz, *Labor of Luck*.

16. Heyes, "Annualised Hours and the 'Knock'"; Peng, "The Impact of Citizenship on Labour Process."

17. Leidner, in *Fast Food, Fast Talk*, shows how work games in the fast-food sector were incentivized through symbolic prizes such as music albums, etc.

18. P. Edwards, *Conflict at Work*.

19. Sallaz, "Permanent Pedagogy."

20. Beynon, *Working for Ford*.

21. Roy, "Banana Time."

22. Burawoy, *Manufacturing Consent*; Burawoy, "The Roots of Domination."

23. Ackroyd and Thompson, *Organizational Misbehaviour*.

24. Pollert, *Girls, Wives, Factory Lives*.

25. Rachel also provided an exemplary illustration of "contradictory consciousness," for, despite stating that this abuse had been going on for fifty years, twelve minutes later she extolled the virtues of the founder and said that if he were alive "he'd be saying 'wow, I can't believe my kids are doing this.'"

26. Mears, "Working for Free in the VIP," 1101.

27. Bourdieu, *Outline of a Theory of Practice*, 192.

28. I am indebted to Michael Burawoy for pointing this out to me.

29. Burawoy, "The Roots of Domination," 193–194.

30. The account of a retail manager provided by Andrew Smith and Fiona Elliot in "The Demands and Challenges of Being a Retail Store Manager" suggests that schedule gifts are the result of genuine attempts by managers to try to help workers reconcile life-work conflict and that they are oblivious to their control function. This account supports Bourdieu's assertion in *Outline of a Theory of Practice* that misrecognition leaves the dominator just as deceived as the dominated.

6. LIMITS OF CONTROL AND SPACES OF RESISTANCE

1. As predicted by R. Hyman, "Strategy or Structure?"

2. Kelly, *Rethinking Industrial Relations*.

3. Blackburn and Mann, "Ideology in the Non-skilled Working Class," 155; Fantasia, *Cultures of Solidarity*; Mann, "The Social Cohesion of Liberal Democracy"; Mann, *Consciousness and Action among the Western Working Class*.

4. Beynon, *Working for Ford*.

5. See Scott, *Domination and the Arts of Resistance*.

6. Ackroyd and Thompson, *Organizational Misbehaviour*.

7. Coulter, *Revolutionizing Retail*; Lichtenstein, *The Retail Revolution*.

8. See, for example, R. Hyman, *Strikes*.

9. Arquilla and Ronfeldt, *Swarming and the Future of Conflict*; Heckscher and Carré, "Strength in Networks."

10. Chun, *Organizing at the Margins*.

CONCLUSIONS: CONTROL IN THE TWENTY-FIRST CENTURY

1. Although social media may provide workers with an alternative source of power, at present workers' experiments with leveraging symbolic power remain embryonic.

2. Chun, "Flexible Despotism."

3. Beynon, *Working for Ford*; Chun, "Flexible Despotism"; Gottfried, "In the Margins"; Heyes, "Annualised Hours and the 'Knock'"; Price, "Controlling Routine Front Line Service Workers."

4. Weber, *Economy and Society*.

5. Granovetter, "The Impact of Social Structure on Economic Outcomes."

6. Burawoy, *Manufacturing Consent*.

7. Mears, "Working for Free in the VIP."

8. P. Edwards, *Conflict at Work*.

9. Ackroyd and Thompson, *Organizational Misbehaviour*, 23, 60, 101.

10. Ackroyd and Thompson, 61, 101.

11. Thompson, "Dissent at work and the resistance debate: departures, directions, and dead ends," 7.

12. See Rosenblat and Stark, "Algorithmic Labor and Information Asymmetries," for a discussion of how workers with formal autonomy over working time can be "nudged" to work at certain times in the gig economy. Lehdonvirta, "Flexibility in the Gig Economy," and Wood et al., "Good Gig, Bad Gig," provide evidence of the structural constraints inherent to the gig economy, such as lack of work, competition, and high levels of dependence, which limit genuine worker choice over working time.

13. Lee et al., "Working with Machines"; Rosenblat and Stark, "Algorithmic Labor and Information Asymmetries"; Wood et al., "Good Gig, Bad Gig"; Wood, "The Taylor Review."

14. Fuller and Smith, "Consumers' Reports," 11.

15. O'Conner, "When Your Boss Is an Algorithm"; Owen, "Customer Satisfaction at the Push of a Button"; Buckingham and Goodall, "Reinventing Performance Management"; Kesslar, "The Influence of Uber Ratings Is About to Be Felt in the Hallways of One of the World's Largest Banks."

16. Ivanova et al., "The App as a Boss?"

17. Anderson, "Where Despots Rule."

METHOLOGICAL APPENDIX

1. Lukes, *Power*.

2. Mann, "In Praise of Macro-Sociology."

3. Burawoy, *The Extended Case Method*.

4. Fantasia, *Cultures of Solidarity*.

5. Fantasia, 6.

6. Scott, *Domination and the Arts of Resistance*.

7. Burawoy, introduction to *Ethnography Unbound*, 5.

8. Similar to the approach taken in Fantasia, *Cultures of Solidarity*.

9. Burawoy, introduction to *Ethnography Unbound*, 6; Burawoy, *The Extended Case Method*, xv.

10. Vaughan, "Theory Elaboration."

11. Burawoy, "Introduction: Reaching for the Global," 7.

12. Bryman, *Social Research Methods*.

13. Bryman, 542.

14. Wainwright and Russell, "Using NVivo Audio-Coding," 3.

15. As suggested by Charmaz, *Constructing Grounded Theory*.

16. Schofield, "Increasing the Generalisability of Qualitative Research."

17. Burawoy, *The Extended Case Method*.

18. Burawoy.

19. Glucksmann [a.k.a. Cavendish], *Women on the Line*.

Bibliography

Ackroyd, Stephen, and Paul Thompson. *Organizational Misbehaviour*. London: Sage, 1999.

Anderson, Elizabeth S. "Where Despots Rule: Interview." *Jacobin*, June 29, 2017. https:// jacobinmag.com/2017/06/private-government-interview-elizabeth-anderson.

Arquilla, John, and David Ronfeldt. *Swarming and the Future of Conflict*. Santa Monica, CA: RAND Corporation, 2000.

Bain, Peter, and Phil Taylor. "Entrapped by the 'Electronic Panopticon'? Worker Resistance in the Call Centre." *New Technology, Work and Employment* 15, no. 1 (2002): 2–18.

Batstone, Eric, Ian Boraston, and Stephen Frenkel. *Shop Stewards in Action: The Organization of Workplace Conflict and Accommodation*. Oxford: Wiley-Blackwell, 1977.

Bear, Laura. "'This Body Is Our Body': Vishwakarma Puja, the Social Debts of Kinship and Theologies of Materiality in a Neo-liberal Shipyard." In *Vital Relations: Kinship as a Critique of Modernity*, edited by Susan McKinnon, 155–179. Santa Fe, NM: School for Advanced Research Press, 2013.

Bélanger, Jacques, and Paul Edwards. "The Nature of Front-Line Service Work: Distinctive Features and Continuity in the Employment Relationship." *Work, Employment and Society* 2, no. 3 (2013): 433–450.

Beynon, Huw. *Working for Ford*. London: Allen Lane, 1973.

BIS [Department for Business, Innovation and Skills]. *Statistical Bulletin: Trade Union Membership, 2012*. London: UK Government, Department for Business, Innovation and Skills, 2013.

———. *Statistical Bulletin: Trade Union Membership, 2013*. London: UK Government, Department for Business, Innovation and Skills, 2014.

Blackburn, Robert M., and Michael Mann. "Ideology in the Non-skilled Working Class." In *Working-Class Images of Society*, edited by Bulmer Martin, 131–160. London: Routledge.

BLS [Bureau of Labor Statistics]. *Industries at a Glance: Retail Trade*. Washington, DC: United States Department of Labor, 2015. http://www.bls.gov/iag/tgs/iag44–45.htm.

Blum, Joseph A. "Degradation without Deskilling: Twenty-Five Years in the San Francisco Shipyards." In *Global Ethnography: Forces, Connections, and Imaginations in a Postmodern World*, edited by Michael Burawoy, Joseph A. Blum, Sheba George, Zsuzsa Gille, and Millie Thayer, 106–136. Berkeley: University of California Press, 2000.

Bourdieu, Pierre. *The Logic of Practice*. Stanford, CA: Stanford University Press, 1990.

———. *Outline of a Theory of Practice*. Cambridge: Cambridge University Press, 1977.

———. *Pascalian Meditations*. Stanford, CA: Stanford University Press, 2000.

Bozkurt, Odul, and Irena Grugulis. "Why Retail Work Demands a Closer Look." In *Retail Work*, edited by Irena Grugulis and O. Bozkurt, 1–21. Basingstoke: Palgrave Macmillan, 2011.

Brown, William. *Piecework Bargaining*. London: Heinemann, 1973.

Brown, William, Alex Bryson, John Forth, and Keith Whitfield, eds. *The Evolution of the Modern Workplace*. Cambridge: Cambridge University Press, 2009.

Brown, William, Simon Deakin, Maria Hudson, Cliff Pratten, and Paul Ryan. *The Individualisation of the Employment Contract in Britain*. Research Series. London: Department of Trade and Industry, 1998.

Brown, William, Simon Deakin, David Nash, and Sarah Oxenbridge. "The Employment Contract: From Collective Procedures to Individual Rights." *British Journal of Industrial Relations* 38, no. 4 (2000): 611–629.

Bryman, Alan. *Social Research Methods*. Oxford: Oxford University Press, 2008.

Buckingham, Marcus, and Ashley Goodall. "Reinventing Performance Management." *Harvard Business Review*, April 2015, 40–50.

Burawoy, Michael. "Ethnographic Fallacies: Reflections on Labour Studies in the Era of Market Fundamentalism." *Work, Employment and Society* 27, no. 3 (2013): 526–536.

———. *The Extended Case Method: Four Countries, Four Decades, Four Great Transformations, and One Theoretical Tradition*. Berkeley: University of California Press, 2009.

———. "Introduction: Reaching for the Global." In *Global Ethnography: Forces, Connections, and Imaginations in a Postmodern World*, edited by Michael Burawoy, Joseph A. Blum, Sheba George, Zsuzsa Gille, and Millie Thayer, 1–40. Berkeley: University of California Press, 2000.

———. Introduction to *Ethnography Unbound: Power and Resistance in the Modern Metropolis*, edited by Michael Burawoy, Alice Burton, Ann Arnett Ferguson, Kathryn J. Fox, Joshua Gamson, Leslie Hurst, Nadine G. Julius, Charles Kurzman, Leslie Salzinger, Josepha Schiffman, and Shiori Ui, 1–8. Berkeley: University of California Press, 1991.

———. *Manufacturing Consent: Changes in the Labor Process under Monopoly Capitalism*. Chicago: University of Chicago Press, 1979.

———. *The Politics of Production: Factory Regimes under Capitalism and Socialism*. London: Verso Books, 1985.

———. "The Roots of Domination: Beyond Bourdieu and Gramsci." *Sociology* 46, no. 2 (2012): 187–206.

Burawoy, Michael, and Janos Lukács. *The Radiant Past: Ideology and Reality in Hungary's Road to Capitalism*. Chicago: University of Chicago Press, 1992.

Burchell, Brendan J. "The Prevalence and Redistribution of Job Security and Work Intensification." In *Job Insecurity and Work Intensification*, edited by Brendan J. Burchell, David Ladipo, and Frank Wilkinson, 61–76. London: Routledge, 2002.

Callaghan, George, and Paul Thompson. "Edwards Revisited: Technical Control in Call Centres." *Economic and Industrial Democracy* 22, no. 1 (2001): 13–37.

Chang, Dae-oup. "Korean Labour Relations in Transition: Authoritarian Flexibility?" *Labour, Capital and Society* 35, no. 1 (2002): 10–40.

Charmaz, Kathy. *Constructing Grounded Theory: A Practical Guide through Qualitative Analysis*. London: Sage, 2006.

Compa, Lance. "An Overview of Collective Bargaining in the United States." In *El derecho a la negociación colectiva: Monografías de temas laborales*, edited by J. G. Hernández, 91–98. Seville: Consejo Andaluz de Relaciones Laborales, 2014.

Chun, Jennifer Jihye. "Flexible Despotism: The Intensification of Insecurity and Uncertainty in the Lives of Silicon Valley's High-Tech Assembly Workers." In *The Critical Study of Work: Labor, Technology, and Global Production*, edited by R. Baldoz, C. Koeber, and P. Kraft, 127–154. Philadelphia: Temple University Press.

———. *Organizing at the Margins: The Symbolic Politics of Labor in South Korea and the United States*. Ithaca, NY: ILR Press, 2009.

Coulter, Kendra. *Revolutionizing Retail: Workers, Political Action, and Social Change*. London: Palgrave Macmillan, 2014.

De Witte, Hans, Nel De Cuyper, Yasmin Handaja, Magnus Sverke, Katharina Näswall, and Johnny Hellgren. "Associations between Quantitative and Qualitative Job Insecurity and Well-Being." *International Studies of Management and Organization* 40, no. 1 (2010): 40–56.

Doogan, Kevin. *New Capitalism? The Transformation of Work*. Cambridge: Polity Press, 2009.

Durand, Jean-Pierre, and Paul Stewart. "Manufacturing Dissent? Burawoy in a Franco-Japanese Workshop." *Work, Employment and Society* 12, no. 1 (1998): 145–159.

Edwards, Paul K. *Conflict at Work: A Materialist Analysis of Workplace Relations*. Oxford: Blackwell, 1986.

——. "The Employment Relationship and Field of Industrial Relations." In *Industrial Relations: Theory and Practice*. 2nd ed. Edited by Paul K. Edwards, 1–36. Oxford: Blackwell, 2003.

Edwards, Paul K., and Hugh Scullion. *The Social Organization of Industrial Conflict*. Oxford: Blackwell, 1982.

Edwards, Richard. *Contested Terrain: The Transformation of the Workplace in the Twentieth Century*. New York: Basic Books, 1979.

Engels, Frederick. *The Condition of the Working Class in England*. Oxford: Oxford University Press, 1993 [1845].

Fantasia, Rick. *Cultures of Solidarity: Consciousness, Action, and Contemporary American Workers*. Berkeley: University of California Press, 1988.

Flanders, Alan. *The Fawley Productivity Agreements: A Case Study of Management and Collective Bargaining*. London: Faber and Faber, 1964.

——. *Management and Unions: The Theory and Reform of Industrial Relations*. London: Faber and Faber, 1970.

Fleming, Peter, and Andrew Sturdy. "'Being Yourself' in the Electronic Sweatshop: New Forms of Normative Control." *Human Relations* 64, no. 2 (2011): 177–200.

Foucault, Michel. *Discipline and Punish: The Birth of the Prison*. New York: Vintage Books, 1977.

Fraser, Hamish W. *A History of British Trade Unionism, 1700–1998*. London: Macmillan, 1999.

Freelancers Union and Upwork. *Freelancing in America: 2018*. https://www.slideshare.net/upwork/freelancing-in-america-2018-120288770/1.

Friedman, Andy. "Responsible Autonomy versus Direct Control over the Labour Process." *Capital and Class* 1, no. 1 (1977): 43–57.

Fuller, Linda, and Vicki Smith. "Consumers' Reports: Management by Customers in a Changing Economy." *Work, Employment and Society* 5, no. 1 (1991): 1–16.

Gallie, Duncan. *In Search of the New Working Class*. Cambridge: Cambridge University Press, 1978.

Gaventa, John. *Power and Powerlessness: Quiescence and Rebellion in an Appalachian Valley*. Chicago: University of Illinois Press, 1982.

Geary, John F. "Employment Flexibility and Human Resource Management: The Case of Three American Electronics Plants." *Work, Employment and Society* 6, no. 2 (1992): 251–270.

Giddens, Anthony. *The Constitution of Society*. Cambridge: Polity Press, 1981.

Glucksmann, Miriam [a.k.a. Ruth Cavendish]. *Women on the Line*. London: Routledge, 2009 [1982].

Gottfried, Heidi. "In the Margins: Flexibility as a Mode of Regulation in the Temporary Help Service Industry." *Work, Employment and Society* 6, no. 3 (1992): 443–460.

Gramsci, Antonio. *Selections from the Prison Notebooks*. New York: International Publishers, 1971.

Granovetter, Mark. "The Impact of Social Structure on Economic Outcomes." *Journal of Economic Perspectives* 19, no. 1 (2005): 33–50.

Harvey, David. *The Condition of Postmodernity: An Enquiry into the Origins of Cultural Change*. Oxford: Blackwell, 1989.

Heckscher, Charles, and Françoise Carré. "Strength in Networks: Employment Rights Organisation and the Problem of Co-ordination." *British Journal of Industrial Relations* 44, no. 4 (2006): 605–628.

Henly, Julia R., H. Luke Shaefer, and Elaine Waxman. "Non-standard Work Schedules: Employer- and Employee-Driven Flexibility in Retail Jobs." *Social Service Review* 80, no. 4 (2006): 609–634.

Heyes, Jason. "Annualised Hours and the 'Knock': The Organisation of Working Time in a Chemicals Plant." *Work, Employment and Society* 11, no. 1 (1997): 65–81.

Hirsch, Barry T., and David Macpherson. *2015 Union Membership and Coverage Database from the CPS.* http://www.unionstats.com/.

Hobsbawm, Eric. *Industry and Empire: New Edition.* London: Penguin, 1999.

———. *Labouring Men: Studies in the History of Labour.* London: Weidenfeld and Nicolson, 1964.

Hochschild, Arlie R. *The Managed Heart: Commercialization of Human Feeling.* Berkeley: University of California Press, 2003.

Hollander, Jocelyn A., and Rachel L. Einwohner. "Conceptualizing Resistance." *Sociological Forum* 19, no. 4 (2004): 533–554.

Hyman, Jeff, Dora Scholarios, and Chris Baldry. "Getting On or Getting By? Employee Flexibility and Coping Strategies for Home and Work." *Work, Employment and Society* 19, no. 4 (2005): 705–725.

Hyman, Richard. "The Politics of Workplace Trade Unionism: Recent Tendencies and Some Problems for Theory." *Capital and Class* 3, no. 2 (1979): 54–67.

———. "Strategy or Structure? Capital, Labour and Control." *Work, Employment and Society* 1, no. 1 (1987): 25–55.

———. *Strikes.* London: Macmillan, 1989.

Ivanova, Mirela, Joanna Bronowicka, Eva Kocher, and Anne Degner. "The App as a Boss? Control and Autonomy in Application-Based Management." Europa Universität Viadrina. https://cihr.eu/wp-content/uploads/2015/07/The-App-as-the-Boss.pdf.

Kalleberg, Arne L. *Good Jobs, Bad Jobs: The Rise of Polarized and Precarious Employment Systems in the United States, 1970s–2000s.* New York: Russell Sage, 2011.

Kaufman, Bruce E. *The Global Evolution of Industrial Relations: Events, Ideas and the IIRA.* Geneva: International Labour Office, 2004.

———. "Paradigms in Industrial Relations: Original, Modern and Versions In-Between." *British Journal of Industrial Relations* 46, no. 2 (2008): 314–339.

Kelly, John. *Rethinking Industrial Relations: Mobilisation, Collectivism and Long Waves.* London: Routledge, 1998.

———. "Social Movement Theory and Union Revitalisation in Britain." In *Trade Unions: Resurgence or Demise?*, edited by Sue Fernie and David Metcalf, 62–82. London: Routledge, 2005.

———. "Social Partnership Agreements in Britain: Labour Co-operation and Compliance." *Industrial Relations* 43, no. 1 (2004): 267–292.

Kesslar, Sarah. "The Influence of Uber Ratings Is About to Be Felt in the Hallways of One of the World's Largest Banks." *Quartz*, March 13, 2017. https://qz.com/930080/jp-morgan-chase-is-developing-a-tool-for-constant-performance-reviews/.

Kunda, Gideon. *Engineering Culture: Control and Commitment in a High-Tech Corporation.* Philadelphia: Temple University Press, 1992.

Lambert, Susan J. "Added Benefits: The Link between Work-Life Benefits and Organizational Citizenship Behavior." *Academy of Management Journal* 43, no. 5 (2000): 801–815.

———. "Passing the Buck: Labor Flexibility Practices That Transfer Risk onto Hourly Workers." *Human Relations* 61, no. 9 (2008): 1203–1227.

Lambert, Susan J., Anna Haley-Lock, and Julia R. Henly. "Schedule Flexibility in Hourly Jobs: Unanticipated Consequences and Promising Directions." *Community, Work and Family* 15, no. 3 (2012): 293–315.

Lambert, Susan J., Peter J. Fugiel, and Julia R Henly. "Precarious Work Schedules among Early-Career Employees in the US: A National Snapshot." University of Chicago, 2014. https://ssa.uchicago.edu/sites/default/files/uploads/lambert.fugiel.henly_.precarious_work_schedules.august2014_0.pdf.

Lee, Min K., Daniel Kusbit, Evan Metsky, and Laura Dabbish. "Working with Machines: The Impact of Algorithmic, Data-Driven Management on Human Workers." In *Proceedings of the 33rd Annual ACM SIGCHI Conference, Seoul, South Korea*, 1603–1612. New York: ACM Press, 2015.

Lehdonvirta, Vili. "Flexibility in the gig economy: managing time on three online piecework platforms." *New Technology, Work and Employment* 33, no. 1 (2018): 13–29.

Leidner, Robin. *Fast Food, Fast Talk: Service Work and the Routinization of Everyday Life.* Berkeley: University of California Press, 1993.

Lichtenstein, Nelson. *The Retail Revolution: How Wal-Mart Created a Brave New World of Business.* New York: Picador, 2009.

Lukes, Steven. *Power: A Radical View.* Basingstoke: Palgrave Macmillan, 1974.

Mann, Michael. *Consciousness and Action among the Western Working Class.* Cambridge: Cambridge University Press, 1973.

———. "In Praise of Macro-Sociology: A Reply to Goldthorpe." *British Journal of Sociology* 45, no. 1 (1994): 37–54.

———. "The Social Cohesion of Liberal Democracy." *American Sociological Review* 35, no. 3 (1970): 423–441.

———. *The Social Sources of Power: A History of Power from the Beginning to A.D. 1760.* Cambridge: Cambridge University Press, 1986.

———. *The Sources of Social Power: Volume 2. The Rise of Classes and Nation-States, 1760–1914.* Cambridge: Cambridge University Press, 1993.

Marx, Karl. *Capital: A Critique of Political Economy.* London: Penguin UK, 1976 [1867].

Mauss, Marcel. *The Gift: The Form and Reason for Exchange in Archaic Societies.* London: Routledge, 2002 [1954].

McCrate, Elaine. "Flexibility for Whom? Control over Work Schedule Variability in the US." *Feminist Economics* 18, no. 1 (2012): 39–72.

McKendrick, Neil. "Josiah Wedgwood and Factory Discipline." *Historical Journal* 4, no. 1 (1961): 30–55.

Mears, Ashley. "Working for Free in the VIP: Relational Work and the Production of Consent." *American Sociological Review* 80, no. 6 (2015): 1099–1122.

Montgomery, D. *The Fall of the House of Labor.* Cambridge: Cambridge University Press, 1987.

Nichols, Theo, and Huw Beynon. *Living with Capitalism.* London: Routledge and Kegan Paul, 1977.

Nichols, Theo, Surhan Cam, Wen-chi Grace Chou, Soonok Chunm, Wei Zhao, and Tongqing Feng. "Factory Regimes and the Dismantling of Established Labour in Asia: A Review of Cases from Large Manufacturing Plants in China, South Korea and Taiwan." *Work, Employment and Society* 18, no. 4 (2004): 663–685.

O'Conner, Sarah. "When Your Boss Is an Algorithm." *Financial Times*, September 8, 2016.

ONS [Office for National Statistics]. *2015 Consumer Price Indices—CPI Annual Percentage Change: 1989 to 2015.* London: United Kingdom Government Office for National Statistics. http://www.ons.gov.uk/ons/datasets-and-tables/data-selector.html?cdid=D7G7&dataset=mm23&table-id=1.2.

Owen, David. "Customer Satisfaction at the Push of a Button." *New Yorker*, February 5, 2018.

Peng, Thomas. "The Impact of Citizenship on Labour Process: State, Capital and Labour Control in South China." *Work, Employment and Society* 25, no. 4 (2011): 726–741.

Pesole, Annarosa, Cesira Urzi Brancati, Enrique Fernández Macías, Federico Biagi, Ignacio González Vázquez. *Platform Workers in Europe.* Luxembourg: Publications Office of the European Union,

Polanyi, Karl. *The Great Transformation: The Political and Economic Origins of Our Time.* Boston: Beacon Press, 2001 [1944].

Pollard, Sidney. "Factory Discipline in the Industrial Revolution." *Economic History Review* 16, no. 2 (1963): 254–271.

Pollert, Anna. "The 'Flexible Firm': Fixation or Fact?" *Work, Employment and Society* 2, no. 3 (1988): 281–316.

———. *Girls, Wives, Factory Lives.* London: Palgrave Macmillan.

Poulantzas, Nico. "The Problem of the Capitalist State." *New Left Review* 1, no. 58 (1969): 67–78.

Price, Robin. "Controlling Routine Front Line Service Workers: An Australian Retail Supermarket Case." *Work, Employment and Society* 30, no. 6 (2016): 915–931.

Priestland, David. *Merchant, Soldier, Sage: A New History of Power.* London: Penguin, 2012.

Rhodes, Chris, and Philip Brien. "The Retail Industry: Statistics and Policy." House of Commons Library Briefing Paper. London: House of Commons Library, 2015. http://researchbriefings.files.parliament.uk/documents/SN06186/SN06186.pdf.

Riga, Liliana. "Ethnicity, Class and the Social Sources of US Exceptionalism." In *Global Powers: Michael Mann's Anatomy of the Twentieth Century and Beyond*, edited by Ralph Schroeder, 185–208. Cambridge: Cambridge University Press, 2016.

Rosenblat, Alex, and Luke Stark. "Algorithmic Labor and Information Asymmetries: A Case Study of Uber's Drivers." *International Journal of Communication* 10 (2016): 3758–3784.

Roy, Donald F. "Banana Time: Job Satisfaction and Informal Interaction." *Human Organization* 18, no. 4 (1959): 158–168.

———. "Work Satisfaction and Social Reward in Quota Achievement: An Analysis of Piecework Incentive." *American Sociological Review* 18, no. 5 (1953): 507–514.

Rubery, Jill, Damian Grimshaw, Gail Hebson, and Sebastian M. Ugarte. "'It's All about Time': Time as Contested Terrain in the Management and Experience of Domiciliary Care Work in England." *Human Resource Management* 54, no. 5 (2015): 753–772.

Rubery, Jill, Kevin Ward, Damian Grimshaw, and Huw Beynon. "Working Time, Industrial Relations and the Employment Relationship." *Time and Society* 14, no. 1 (2005): 89–110.

Sallaz, Jeffery J. *Labor of Luck: Casino Capitalism in the United States and South Africa.* Berkeley: University of California Press, 2009.

———. "Manufacturing Concessions: Attritionary Outsourcing at General Motor's [*sic*] Lordstown, USA Assembly Plant." *Work, Employment and Society* 18, no. 4 (2004): 687–708.

———. "Permanent Pedagogy: How Post-Fordist Firms Generate Effort but Not Consent." *Work and Occupations* 42, no. 1 (2015): 3–34.

Schneider, Daniel, and Kristen Harknett. "Consequences of Routine Work-Schedule Instability for Worker Health and Well-Being." *American Sociological Review* 84, no. 1 (2019): 82–114.

Schofield, Janet W. "Increasing the Generalisability of Qualitative Research." In *Social Research: Philosophy, Politics and Practice*, edited by Martyn Hammersley, 200–225. London: Sage, 1993.

Scott, James C. *Domination and the Arts of Resistance: Hidden Transcripts*. New Haven, CT: Yale University Press, 1992.

Sherman, Rachel. "Beyond Interaction: Customer Influence on Housekeeping and Room Service Work in Hotels." *Work, Employment and Society* 25, no. 1 (2011): 19–33.

Silver, Beverly. *Forces of Labor: Workers' Movements and Globalisation since 1870*. Cambridge: Cambridge University Press, 2003.

Simms, Melanie, Jane Holgate, and Edmond Heery. *Union Voices: Tactics and Tensions in UK Organising*. Ithaca, NY: ILR Press, 2012.

Smith, Andrew, and Fiona Elliot. "The Demands and Challenges of Being a Retail Store Manager: 'Handcuffed to the Front Doors.'" *Work, Employment and Society* 26, no. 4 (2012): 676–684.

Smith, Tom W., Peter Marsden, Michael Hout, and Jibum Kim. *General Social Surveys, 1972–2016*, 2016.

Standing, Guy. *The Corruption of Capitalism: Why Rentiers Thrive and Work Does Not Pay*. London: Biteback Publishing, 2016.

———. *Global Labour Flexibility: Seeking Distributive Justice*. Basingstoke: Palgrave Macmillan, 1999.

Taylor, Ciaren, Andrew Jowett, and Michael Hardie. *An Examination of Falling Real Wages, 2010–2013*. London: Office for National Statistics, 2014. http://www.ons.gov.uk/ons/dcp171766_351467.pdf.

Taylor, Phil, and Peter Bain. "An Assembly Line in the Head: Work and Employee Relations in the Call Centre." *Industrial Relations Journal* 30, no. 2 (1999): 101–117.

Thompson, Edward P. "Time, Work-Discipline, and Industrial Capitalism." *Past and Present* 38 (1967): 56–97.

Thompson, Paul. "Dissent at work and the resistance debate: departures, directions, and dead ends." *Studies in Political Economy A Socialist Review* 97, no. 2 (2016): 106–123.

Thompson, Paul, and Diane van den Broek. "Managerial Control and Workplace Regimes: An Introduction." *Work, Employment and Society* 24, no. 3 (2010): 1–12.

Vallas, Steven P. "The Adventures of Managerial Hegemony: Teamwork, Ideology, and Worker Resistance." *Social Problems* 50, no. 2 (2003): 204–225.

Vaughan, Diane. "Theory Elaboration: The Heuristics of Case Analysis." In *What Is a Case? Exploring the Foundations of Social Inquiry*, edited by Charles Ragin and Howard S. Becker, 173–202. Cambridge: Cambridge University Press, 1992.

Vidal, Matt. "On the Persistence of Labour Market Insecurity and Slow Growth in the US: Reckoning with the Waltonist Growth Regime." *New Political Economy* 17, no. 5 (2012): 543–564.

Wainwright, Megan, and Andrew Russell. "Using NVivo Audio-Coding: Practical, Sensorial and Epistemological Considerations." *Social Research Update* 60 (2010): 1–4.

Webb, Sidney, and Beatrice Webb. *Industrial Democracy*. London: Longmans, Greens, 1897.

Weber, Max. *Economy and Society: An Outline of Interpretive Sociology*. Berkeley: University of California Press, 1978 [1922].

Webster, Edward, Rob Lambert, and Andries Bezuidenhout. *Grounding Globalization: Labour in the Age of Insecurity*. Oxford: Blackwell, 2008.

Wood, Alex J. "Flexible Scheduling, Degradation of Job Quality and Barriers to Collective Voice." *Human Relations* 69, no. 10 (2016): 1989–2010.

———. "Networks of Injustice: Worker Mobilisation at Walmart." *Industrial Relations Journal* 46, no. 4 (2015): 259–274.

———. "Powerful Times: Flexible Discipline and Schedule Gifts at Work." *Work, Employment and Society* 32, no. 6 (2018): 1061–1077.

———. "The Taylor Review: understanding the gig economy, dependency and the complexities of control." *New Technology, Work and Employment* 34, no. 2 (2019): 111–115

Wood, Alex J., and Brendan J. Burchell. "Precarious Scheduling in the UK." Last modified August 17, 2017. https://www.sociology.cam.ac.uk/news/precarious-scheduling-in-the-uk.

———. "Unemployment and Well-Being." In *The Cambridge Handbook of Psychological and Economic Behaviour*, 2nd ed., edited by Alan Lewis, 234–259. Cambridge: Cambridge University Press.

Wood, Alex J., Mark Graham, Vili Lehdonvirta, and Isis Hjorth. "Good Gig, Bad Gig: Autonomy and Algorithmic Control in the Global Gig Economy." *Work, Employment and Society* 33, no. 1 (2019): 56–75.

Woodcock, Jamie. *Working the Phones: Control and Resistance in Call Centres.* London: Pluto Press, 2017.

Wright, Chris, and William Brown. "The Effectiveness of Socially Sustainable Sourcing Mechanisms: Assessing the Prospects of a New Form of Joint Regulation." *Industrial Relations Journal* 44, no. 1 (2013): 20–37.

Wright, Erik O. *Class Counts.* Student ed. Cambridge: Cambridge University Press, 2000.

Index

Page numbers in *italics* indicate tables and charts.

Ackroyd, Stephen, 7–8, 125, 142–143
Affordable Care Act (U.S.), 162n1
Airtasker, 3
algorithmic management, 3, 14, 144–145
analytical approach, 147–148
Anderson, Elizabeth S., vi
Arkwright, Richard, 29, 52
Arquilla, John, 132
ASDA, 20
Atlas.ti, 153
"at-will" employment status, 1, 26–27, 30, 57–58, 62, 63, 92–93, 136, 141, 159n69
Australia, workplace regimes in, 13, 15

Batstone, Eric, 47
Bear, Laura, 68
benefits. *See* pay, bonuses, benefits, and profit-sharing
Bentham, Jeremy, 158n48
Beynon, Huw, 15, 33, 54, 107, 109, 110
Bezuidenhout, Andries, 13
bonuses. *See* pay, bonuses, benefits, and profit-sharing
Boraston, Ian, 47
Bourdieu, Pierre, 18, 21, 23, 100, 113, 117, 163n30
Brazil, workplace regimes in, 12
Brown, William, 32
Burawoy, Michael: Chicago machine shop ethnography, 10, 11, 106–107; on extended case method, 148, 149, 154; on securing and obscuring of exploitation, 139; on work games, 106–107, 110, 117, 118; on working time, 161n1; workplace regime theory of, 10–12, 14–18, 29, 30, 34, 53, 55, 73, 75, 158n40

call centers, 4, 13, 16, 17, 107–108, 109, 139
Carré, Françoise, 132
cashiers and checkouts, 103–104
casino dealers, 16, 139, 159n69

Cavendish, Ruth (Miriam Glucksmann), 34–35, 155
chemical plant ethnography, 15, 16, 33, 108
Chicago machine shop ethnography, 10, 11, 106–107
childcare issues, 49, 83, 85–86, 87, 94
China, work games in, 16, 108
Chun, Jennifer Jihye, 14, 132, 137–138
"coaching for improvement" as disciplinary procedure at ConflictCo (U.S.), 62–63
collective bargaining. *See* unions and collective bargaining
Colorado miners' strike (1914), 53
compensation. *See* pay, bonuses, benefits, and profit-sharing
competitive capitalism, 55, 135
ConflictCo case study (U.S.), 19–24; escapism, 100, 109–110, 111; internal labor market, 90–93; methodological approach, 150–155; pay, bonuses, benefits, and profit-sharing, 60, 61, 64–66, 90–92; reputational damage, threat of, 23, 132–133; resistance, 101, 120–121, 126–133; schedule gifts, 100, 114, 117, 118–119, 141; work dynamics in low-end retail, 102–105, 118; work games, absence of, 99–100, 108–109, 111–112, 118, 139–140. *See also* internal state at ConflictCo; temporal despotism at ConflictCo; worker association at ConflictCo
"ConflictCo cheer," 27–28, 68, 70–71, 126
Consumer Price Index (CPI), 160n32
contradictory consciousness, 148, 163n25
customer management strategies, 14, 40, 144

data collection techniques, 150–153
Deliveroo, 3
Denmark, precarious scheduling in, 4
despotic time. *See specific entries at* temporal despotism
despotism in the flexible workplace. *See* flexible despotism

disciplinary procedures: "coaching for improvement" at ConflictCo (U.S.), 62–63; at PartnershipCo (UK), 41–42, 51. *See also* flexible discipline

domestic abuse dynamic and worker acceptance of exploitation, 112–113

Edwards, Paul, 11, 32–33, 109
Edwards, Richard, 10
egalitarians, vi
electronic surveillance and panopticon, 13, 19, 158n48. *See also* surveillance
Elliot, Fiona, 163n30
employment insecurity at ConflictCo (U.S.), 26–27, 57–58, 90, 110, 127, 141
employment security: in hegemonic regimes, 11, 107; at PartnershipCo (UK), 38, 47, 76, 90, 107; work games and, 16, 105, 107
Engels, Friedrich, 30
escapism, 100, 107, 109–111, 139
ethical research issues, 155
Europe: precarious scheduling in, 4–5, 142; workplace hegemony in, 9. *See also specific countries*
European Working Conditions Survey, 157n7, 157n17
exploitation, 7–8, 102–119; escapism and, 100, 107, 109–111, 139; explaining worker acceptance of, 112–113; obscuring, 10–11, 16, 22, 102, 120; through normative control, 16–17, 19; work dynamics in low-end retail and, 103–106, 119; by workplace regimes and workplace hegemony, 8–13. *See also* flexible despotism; resistance; schedule gifts; work games
extended case method, 148–150, 154

Facebook, 61, 129–132
"facing up," 103
family life. *See* work-life balance and temporal despotism
Fantasia, Rick, 148
fast-food workers, 16, 107, 108, 128, 139, 163n17
Financial Times, 2
Fiverr, 3
flexibility, functional, 103–104
flexible contracts at PartnershipCo (UK), 81–82, 162n6
flexible despotism, 1–24, 134–145; decline of hegemony and rise of, 134–37; disciplining and controlling effects of, 15; dual core/peripheral labor market theories and, 14–15;

electronic surveillance and panopticon, 13, 19, 158n48 (*See also* surveillance); exploitation and resistance in workplace and, 7–8 (*See also* exploitation; resistance); future of, 143–145; generalizability of, 141–142; historical development of workplace regimes and, 8–13, 29–35, 52–56, 142–144; internal state and internal labor market, interaction of, 10–12, 75 (*See also* internal labor market, *and specific entries at* internal state); limits of market despotism in contemporary workplace and, 137; methodological approach to studying, 147–155; normative controls, 16–17; normative controls and, 16–17, 19, 139–140 (*See also* normative controls); on-demand economy driving, 1–2, 5, 14, 15, 19, 24, 102, 119, 144; power relationship, work viewed as, 6–7; precarious scheduling practices, 2–6, 15, 21, 157n5; retail sector, focus on, 20; schedule gifts and, 112–119, 140 (*See also* schedule gifts); service sector and customer service management, 14; temporal *versus* numerical flexibility, focus on, 2–3, 19, 20–21, 137–138 (*See also* numerical flexible despotism; *specific entries at* temporal despotism); types of jobs affected by, 5; in U.S. *versus* UK, 5–6, 19–24, *20*, 141 (*See also* United Kingdom; United States); work games and, 16, 105–112 (*See also* work games); worker-controlled *versus* employer-controlled flexibility, 3–6, 78; workplace regimes and workplace hegemony, 8–13, 158nn39–40 (*See also* workplace regimes)
flexible discipline, 100, 102, 113, 134, 138–139; at ConflictCo (U.S.), 74, 90, 95–98; control of workers via, 28, 74, 140, 141, 142; defined, 15; at ParternshipCo (UK), 74, 76, 87–89; precarious scheduling enabling, 5, 142; schedule gifts obscuring, 18, 21, 140, 141; subtlety and ambiguity of, 22
flight attendants ethnography, 8
flirting, having a laugh, horseplay, and messing around, 100, 107, 110–111, 139
Ford, Henry, 33, 54
Ford Motor Company and Fordism, 12, 15, 17, 20, 33–34, 54, 107, 110, 111, 122, 128
Foucault, Michel, 13, 40, 60, 62, 158n48
founder personality cult at ConflictCo (U.S.), 27–28, 66–68, 69–70, 130–131, 163n25
Fourier, Charles, 30
France: precarious scheduling in, 4; work games in, 16

Fraser, Hamish, 160n8, 160n10
Frenkel, Stephen, 47
Friedman, Andrew, 106
functional flexibility, 103–104

Gallie, Duncan, 47
General Motors, 20, 128
General Social Survey, 157n6
Germany, precarious scheduling in, 4
gifts and gift theory. *See* schedule gifts
gig economy labor platforms, 1, 3, 14, 144–145,
    164n12
Glucksmann, Miriam (Ruth Cavendish),
    34–35, 155
Gramsci, Antonio, 8–10, 13, 158n39
Great Depression, 54–56
Great Recession/global economic crisis, 2,
    4–5, 36
grievance procedures: open-door policy at
    ConflictCo (U.S.), 27, 63–64, 67, 72; at
    PartnershipCo (UK), 43–45, 51

Handy, 3
Harvey, David, 12
having a laugh, horseplay, messing around, and
    flirting, 100, 107, 110–111, 139
Heckscher, Charles, 132
hegemonic workplace regimes: ConflictCo
    (U.S.) never fully embracing, 64, 135–136;
    decline of, 12–13, 35, 56, 134–137; historical
    development of, 8–9, 31–35, 53–56; internal
    state and internal labor market, 10–11,
    158nn39–40; PartnershipCo (UK) resem-
    bling, 26, 39, 44, 50–51, 136–137; in UK,
    31–35; in U.S., 53–56; work games in,
    105–106, 107, 118
historical development of workplace regimes,
    8–13, 29–35, 52–56, 142–143
Hochschild, Arlie, 8
horseplay, messing around, flirting, and having
    a laugh, 100, 107, 110–111, 139

identity, appropriation of, 8
Imperial Tobacco Factory study, 34, 107, 111
Indian shipbuilders' study, 68
injustice, workplace framing of, 60–61,
    122–123, 130–131
Instagram, 131
intensity of work, 91, 99, 104–105, 162n1
internal labor market: at ConflictCo (U.S.),
    90–93; defined, 75, 76; internal state,
    interaction with, 10–12; at PartnershipCo
    (UK), 76–77

internal state at ConflictCo (U.S.), 26–28,
    52–72; "at-will" employment status at,
    26–27, 57–58, 62, 63; "coaching for
    improvement" as disciplinary procedure at,
    62–63; compared to PartnershipCo (UK), 28,
    39, 44, 52, 60, 62, 71, 72, 90; "ConflictCo
    cheer," 27–28, 68, 70–71; employment
    insecurity, 26–27, 57–58, 90, 110, 127, 141;
    hegemonic practices never fully embraced at,
    64, 135–136; historical background to
    workplace regimes in UK and, 52–56;
    injustice, framing of, 60–61, 130–131; market
    despotism at, 27–28, 71–72, 137; normative
    controls, destabilizing effects of, 27–28, 68–71,
    139–140; open-door grievance policy, 27,
    63–64, 67, 72; pay, bonuses, benefits, and
    profit-sharing, 60, 61, 64–66; Policy Guide,
    58–59, 161n31; precarious scheduling, 57,
    73–74; propaganda, ritual, and founder
    personality cult at, 27–28, 66–68, 69–70,
    130–131, 140, 163n25; research and observa-
    tions, 56–57; surveillance, 61–62; unions,
    hostility to, 27, 28, 58–59, 67, 68–69, 127, 141;
    worker association at, 27, 28, 59–61, 68, 72
internal state at PartnershipCo (UK), 25–26,
    29–51; collective agreement with union at,
    25–26, 37–39, 47–50; compared to
    ConflictCo (U.S.), 28, 39, 44, 52, 60, 62, 71,
    72, 90; disciplinary procedures, 41–42, 51;
    employment contracts, 25, 36–37; employ-
    ment security, 38, 47, 107; escapism at, 100;
    grievance procedures, 43–45, 51; hegemonic
    workplace regime, resembling, 26, 39, 44,
    50–51, 136–137; historical background to
    workplace regimes in UK and, 29–35;
    Mulling Point hypermarket study, 36, 37,
    44–45; normative control at, 26, 47–50,
    139–140; pay, bonuses, benefits, and
    profit-sharing, 45–46, *46, 47,* 51; precarious
    scheduling, 26, 39, 43, 44, 47, 48, 49;
    precarious scheduling, use of, 26, 39, 43, 44,
    47, 48, 49; research and observations, 35–36;
    surveillance at, 40–41; workers' power and
    rights at, 36–38
Iran, workplace regimes in, 12
Ireland, precarious scheduling in, 4

Japan, flexible despotism in, 12

Kabyle peasants (Algeria), gift-giving among,
    18, 23, 113, 117
Kalleberg, Arne, 15
Kelly, John, 38, 60, 122

labor matching reviews at PartnershipCo (UK), 79–80, 123
labor unions. *See* unions and collective bargaining
Lakatos, Imre, 149
Lambert, Rob, 13
Lambert, Susan, 2
Las Vegas casino dealers, 16, 139, 159n69
learning games, 16, 108, 109
Leidner, Robin, 163n17
Ludlow Massacre, 53, 55
Lukács, Janos, 17
Lukes, Steven, 147, 158n25

"making out" work games, 106–107
Mann, Michael, 69
market despotism: at ConflictCo (U.S.), 27–28, 71–72, 137; limits of, in contemporary workplace, 137; before Second World War, 8; in UK, 29–31; in U.S., 52–54; work games and, 106
Marx, Karl, 11, 29–30
Mauss, Marcel, 18, 100, 113
Mears, Ashley, 18, 100, 113
messing around, flirting, having a laugh, and horseplay, 100, 107, 110–111, 139
mobility issues within pay and job structures, 22, 73, 78, 91, 136
monopoly capitalism, 54–55, 135
Montgomery, David, 54
Mulling Point hypermarket (UK) study: "facing up," 103; internal state at PartnershipCo and, 36, 37, 44–45; methodological approach to, 152, 155; schedule gifts at, 115; temporal despotism at PartnershipCo and, 78, 83, 84, 88
My-Guide (software), 61

National Labor Relations Board, 59
Nichols, Theo, 33
normative controls, 16–17, 19, 139–140; at ConflictCo (U.S.), 27–28, 68–71, 139–140; PartnershipCo (UK), union at, 26, 47–50, 139–140
numerical flexible despotism: defined, 139; temporal *versus* numerical flexibility, focus on, 2–3, 19, 20–21, 137–138; temporary contract workers and, 80–81

on-demand economy, 1–2, 5, 14, 15, 19, 24, 102, 119, 144
open-door policy at ConflictCo (U.S.), 27, 63–64, 67, 72

panopticon, electronic, 13, 19, 158n48. *See also* surveillance
paper mill study, 17
PartnershipCo case study (UK), 19–24; employment security, 38, 47, 76, 90, 107; internal labor market at, 76–77; methodological approach, 150–155; pay, bonuses, benefits, and profit-sharing, 45–46, *46*, *47*, 51, 77–78; resistance, 101, 120, 121–126; schedule gifts, 100, 114, 115–117, 118–119, 140; work dynamics in low-end retail, 102–105, 118, 119; work games, absence of, 99–100, 110–112, 118, 139–140. *See also* internal state at PartnershipCo; Mulling Point hypermarket (UK) study; temporal despotism at PartnershipCo
part-time workers, 37, 79, 81–84, 92, 93, 97
paternalism in the workplace, 54, 55
pay, bonuses, benefits, and profit-sharing: at ConflictCo (U.S.), 60, 61, 64–66, 90–92; at PartnershipCo (UK), 45–46, *46*, *47*, 51, 77–78
Polanyi, Karl, 31
Pollard, Sidney, 31
Pollert, Anna, 34, 107, 111
Popper, Karl, 149
positionality of researcher, 154–155
Poulantzas, Nico, 9
power: defined as social power, 158n25; work viewed as power relationship, 6–7
precariat class, 5
precarious scheduling: concept of, 2–6, 15, 21, 157n5; at ConflictCo (U.S.), 57, 73–74, 90, 93–95, 98, 162n1; flexible discipline, enabling, 142; insecurity generated by, 134, 139; at PartnershipCo (UK), 26, 39, 43, 44, 47, 48, 49, 73–74, 78–87, 88, 89; resistance and, 101, 120–123, 126, 130, 131, 133; schedule gifts and, 112–114, 116, 118, 140, 142; similar levels, in U.S. *versus* Europe, 157n2; temporal flexiblity achieved by, 138, 142; ubiquity of, 4–5, 142
product, appropriation of, 8
profit-sharing. *See* pay, bonuses, benefits, and profit-sharing
propaganda and ritual at ConflictCo (U.S.), 27–28, 66–68, 69–70, 130–131, 140, 163n25

reflexivity issues, 154–155
reputational damage, threat of, 23, 132–134
resistance, 7–8, 23, 101, 120–133; at ConflictCo (U.S.), 101, 120–121, 126–133; hidden resistance, 8, 101, 123, 133; injustice, workplace framing of, 122–123, 130–131;

at PartnershipCo (UK), 101, 120, 121–126; precarious scheduling and, 57, 73–74, 90, 93–95, 98, 162n1; propensity toward, analyzing, 148; reputational damage, through threat of, 23, 132–134; respect, ConflictCo workers' emphasis on, 130–131; sabotage, 125–126; social media and, 23, 61, 101, 121, 128–134, 163n1; surveillance and, 124, 126; swarming, 131–132; team systems generating, 17; union, open resistance through, at PartnershipCo, 121–122; work to rule/go slow tactics, 124–125; worker association at ConflictCo and, 101, 127–133

respect, ConflictCo workers' emphasis on, 130–131

restocking shelves, 103–104, 105

retail sector, focus on, 20

ritual and propaganda at ConflictCo (U.S.), 27–28, 66–68, 69–70, 130–131, 140, 163n25

Rockefeller, John, Jr., 53, 55

Ronfeldt, John, 132

Roy, Donald, 11, 107, 110, 111

Russell, Andrew, 153

sabotage, as resistance, 125–126

Sallaz, Jeffery J., 159n69

schedule gifts, 112–119, 140–141; concept of, 18–19; at ConflictCo (U.S.), 100, 114, 117, 118–119, 140; flexible discipline obscured by, 18, 21, 140, 141; gift theory and, 18, 23, 100, 113; managerial intentions regarding, 117, 163n30; misrecognition of, 18, 21, 100, 113, 114–115, 117, 163n30; at PartnershipCo (UK), 100, 114, 115–117, 118–119, 140; precarious scheduling and, 112–114, 116, 118, 140, 142; work games replaced by, 23

schedule insecurity and temporal despotism: at ConflictCo (U.S.), 94–95; injustice, workplace framing of, 122–123; at PartnershipCo (UK), 86–87

Scott, James C., 7, 101, 148

Scullion, Hugh, 32–33

seniority rules, 10, 54, 73, 75, 76

service sector economy, 14

shelf stacking, 103–104, 105

short hour contracts, 3, 82–84

Slater, Samuel, 52

Smith, Andrew, 163n30

social media, 23, 61, 101, 121, 128–134, 163n1

social power, 158n25

Social Security, US introduction of, 55–56

socialist workplaces, 17

South Africa, workplace regimes in, 12, 13

South Korea, workplace regimes in, 13

spaces of resistance. See resistance

speedometer factory, female workers at, 34–35

Standard Oil of New Jersey strikes, 53, 55

Standing, Guy, 5

Stockholm syndrome, 112–113

surveillance: at ConflictCo (U.S.), 61–62; electronic surveillance and panopticon, 13, 19, 158n48; at PartnershipCo (UK), 40–41; resistance and, 124, 126

swarming, 131–132

Sweden, precarious scheduling in, 4

TaskRabbit, 3

team systems, 17

temporal despotism at ConflictCo (U.S.), 73–74, 90–98; at-will employment and, 92–93; flexible discipline, 74, 90, 95–98; internal labor market and, 90–93; pay and mobility issues related to, 90–92; precarious scheduling, 73–74, 90, 93–95, 98, 162n1; schedule insecurity, 94–95; work-life balance, impairment of, 93–94

temporal despotism at PartnershipCo (UK), 73–74, 75–89; flexible contract workers, 81–82, 162n6; flexible discipline, 74, 76, 87–89; internal labor market and, 76–77; labor matching reviews for standard contract workers, 79–80, 123; part-time workers, 37, 79, 81–84, 92, 93, 97; pay and mobility issues related to, 77–78; precarious scheduling, 73–74, 78–87, 88, 89; schedule insecurity, 86–87; short hours contracts, 82–84; temporary contract workers and numerical flexibility, 80–81; work-life balance, impairment of, 84–86

temporal versus numerical flexibility, focus on, 2–3, 19, 20–21, 137–138

temporary workers, 14, 15, 36–38, 80–81

textile factory, work games in, 16, 108

theoretical coding, 153–154

Thompson, E. P., 75–76

Thompson, Paul, 7–8, 125, 142–143

turnover rates and rise of paternalism, 54

Twitter, 129, 130

Uber, 3

unions and collective bargaining: ConflictCo (U.S.) hostility to, 27, 28, 58–59, 67, 68–69, 127, 141; hegemonic workplace regimes and, 31–35; historical development of, 31, 53, 55; injustice, workplace framing of, 60–61, 122–123; Mulling Point hypermarket study,

unions and collective bargaining (*continued*)
36, 37, 44–45, 78, 83, 84, 88, 103, 115, 152,
155; normative control, unions contributing
to, 26, 47–50, 139–140; open resistance
through, 121–122; partnership agreements,
38; PartnershipCo (UK), collective
agreement with union at, 25–26, 37–39,
47–50; recruitment techniques, 49–50.
See also worker association at ConflictCo
United Kingdom: algorithmic management in,
3; compared to U.S., 5–6, 19–24, *20*, 141;
hegemonic workplace regimes in, 31–35;
market despotism in, 29–31; precarious
scheduling in, 4. *See also* Mulling Point
hypermarket study; PartnershipCo
United States: algorithmic management in, 3;
compared to UK, 5–6, 19–24, *20*, 141;
hegemonic workplace regimes in, 53–56;
market despotism in, 52–54; precarious
scheduling in, 4; Social Security, state
introduction of, 55–56; workplace hegemony
in, 9. *See also* ConflictCo
Upwork, 3

validity, internal and external, 154
Vallas, Steven, 17
Vaughan, Diane, 153
VIP nightclubs, 18
Vishwakarma (Indian shipbuilders' patron
deity), 68

wages. *See* pay, bonuses, benefits, and
profit-sharing
Wainright, Megan, 153

Walmart, 20
Webb, Sidney and Beatrice, 6
Weber, Max, 139
Webster, Edward, 13
work, appropriation of, 8
work games, 16, 105–112; absence of, at
PartnershipCo (UK) and ConflictCo (U.S.),
99–100, 108–112, 118, 139–140; escapism
replacing, 100, 107, 109–111, 139; exploitation obscured by, 10–11; in hegemonic *versus*
market despotic regimes, 105–106, 107, 118;
importance of, in contemporary workplace,
19; schedule gifts replacing, 23; situational
construction of consent in, 18
work intensity, 91, 99, 104–105, 162n1
work to rule/go slow tactics, 124–125
worker association at ConflictCo (U.S.):
internal state at ConflictCo and, 27, 28,
59–61, 68, 72; methodological bias and,
151–152; Policy Guide, availability of,
161n31; resistance to exploitation and, 101,
127–133; temporal despotism and, 96
work-life balance and temporal despotism: at
ConflictCo (U.S.), 93–94; at PartnershipCo
(UK), 84–86
workplace regimes: concept of, 8–9; historical
development of, 8–13, 29–35, 52–56,
142–145; methodological approach to
studying, 149, 150. *See also* flexible
despotism; hegemonic workplace regimes;
market despotism
Wright, Erik Olin, 7

zero hour contracts, 1, 3, 93

CPSIA information can be obtained
at www.ICGtesting.com
Printed in the USA
LVHW110002240720
661391LV00003B/277